"LICENTIOUS LIBERTY"
IN A
BRAZILIAN GOLD-MINING REGION

D1418045

Kathleen J. Higgins

"LICENTIOUS LIBERTY"
IN A
BRAZILIAN GOLD-MINING REGION

Slavery, Gender, and Social Control
in
Eighteenth-Century Sabará, Minas Gerais

The Pennsylvania State University Press
University Park, Pennsylvania

Library of Congress Cataloging-in-Publication Data

Higgins, Kathleen J., 1956–
    "Licentious liberty" in a Brazilian gold-mining region : slavery,
gender, and social control in eighteenth-century Sabará, Minas
Gerais / Kathleen J. Higgins.
        p.   cm.
    Includes bibliographical references and index.
    ISBN 0-271-01910-7 (cloth : alk. paper)
    ISBN 0-271-01911-5 (pbk. : alk. paper)
    1. Slavery — Brazil — Sabará — History — 18th century.   2. Gold mines
and mining — Brazil — Sabará — History — 18th century.   3. Sex role
— Brazil — Sabará — History — 18th century.   4. Women slaves — Brazil
— Sabará — History — 18th century.   I. Title.
HT1129.S2H53   1999
306.3'62'098151 — dc21
                                                                98-43338
                                                                    CIP

Copyright © 1999 The Pennsylvania State University
All rights reserved
Printed in the United States of America
Published by The Pennsylvania State University Press,
University Park, PA 16802–1003

It is the policy of The Pennsylvania State University Press to use acid-free
paper for the first printing of all clothbound books. Publications on
uncoated stock satisfy the minimum requirements of American National
Standard for Information Sciences — Permanence of Paper for Printed
Library Materials, ANSI Z39.48–1992.

To My Children
Helen, Isaac, and Leo

Contents

Figures, Tables, Illustrations, and Maps

Figures

Tables

Illustrations

Maps

Acknowledgments

This project could not have been completed without the encouragement and assistance of many individuals and organizations. I am deeply grateful to institutions, colleagues, friends, and family who made it possible for me to write a history of slavery in colonial Sabará, Minas Gerais.

First, I wish to acknowledge the institutions that funded my research. A grant from the Tinker Foundation permitted me to make a preliminary trip to Brazil in the summer of 1981 to locate archives and documentary sources. Research in Minas Gerais during 1982–83 was supported by a Fulbright-Hays fellowship from the U.S. Department of Education. A fellowship from the American Council of Learned Societies supported new research and writing in 1993–94.

At Yale University, where this book first began as a dissertation, I am most grateful to Emilia Viotti da Costa, my adviser. Her excellent, insightful critiques had an enduring positive influence on this project. I also wish to thank the Department of History at Yale University for providing timely financial assistance critical to the completion of the dissertation.

The University of Iowa has supported this project in a number of important ways. An Old Gold Fellowship in the summer of 1991 and a Semester Assignment in 1993–94 provided both time and funding for research and writing. Graduate student research assistants have provided invaluable help at various stages of my work. I thank David Gilbert, Juan Manuel Casal, Anne-Marie Gill, Minta Perez, and Craig Klein for all their labors.

My colleagues at the University of Iowa have demonstrated continuous support and enthusiasm for my research. Leslie Schwalm and Charles Hale both read early drafts of chapters, and Malcolm Rohrbough read a final draft of the entire manuscript. I am grateful for their insights and suggestions for revisions.

The University of Iowa Library also deserves thanks for the support services it has offered, especially those of Inter-Library Loan, Map Collections, and the Information Arcade. I thank Mary McInroy, the map librarian, for her help in producing two of the maps used in this book.

Beyond the borders of Iowa City, many others have provided valuable advice and assistance along the way. Alida Metcalf and Muriel Nazzari both read and commented on draft chapters and conference papers. They, with Joan Meznar, periodically fielded my questions and continually shared their enthusiasm for my topic as only fellow historians of Brazil can. In the final stages of my project, Linda Lewin fielded my questions and enthusiastically shared her valuable expertise on Brazilian inheritance laws. I also wish to thank Richard Graham who directed my master's thesis, served on my dissertation committee, and first provoked my interest in research in Brazilian history.

I deeply appreciate the generosity and helpfulness of the Brazilians who assisted me in the course of my research. The Director of the Arquivo Público Mineiro, Francisco de Assis Andrade, graciously allowed me to have documents held in that archive reproduced with the assistance of staff member Cida Gorgulho. My principal supporter and friend while I was staying in Minas Gerais, the Director of the Museu do Ouro, Maria Luisa Querini, also allowed me to have documents in that archive reproduced. The entire staff of the Museu do Ouro was unfailing in its encouragement of my investigations and extremely tolerant of the presence of another body in its small quarters.

I wish to thank Robert Conrad and Mary Karasch who reviewed the manuscript for the Pennsylvania State University Press; their excellent suggestions, incorporated into the final revision, greatly improved the book. I also thank Sanford Thatcher, my editor, for both his advice and his answers to the innumerable questions that I have posed about the production of this book.

Some of my ideas in this book, especially those in Chapter 5, were first presented in two articles published in *Slavery and Abolition, A Journal of Comparative Studies*. I wish to thank the editor of that journal, Gad Heuman, and Stuart Schwartz, a member of its Editorial Advisory Board, for their assistance in shepherding those articles to publication.

In my own family, I thank my husband, Daniel Goldstein, without whose support this book would never have been finished. My children, Helen, Isaac, and Leo, did not help me finish (quite the opposite is true); but as their lives so enrich my own, they have certainly made my journey to a finished manuscript a joyful experience. It is therefore with great pleasure that I dedicate this book to them.

Introduction

In this book, I write about the slaves, freed slaves, and free colonists who lived and worked in the *vila* (town) of Nossa Senhora de Conceição de Sabará and in the surrounding *comarca* (judicial district) of Sabará, Minas Gerais, during the eighteenth century. Beginning at the end of the seventeenth century, a gold rush had brought slavery to this frontier region of colonial Brazil, along with new relationships for slaves, their owners, non-slaveholders, and crown administrators. Confirmation of major strikes in the rugged hills of the interior in 1695 brought thousands of new immigrants across the Atlantic Ocean to Brazil and drew colonizers farther from the established and largely coastal settlements than they had ever ventured before.[1] Indeed, the discovery of gold in Brazil forever redefined Portugal's empire in the New World by shifting the productive forces in the colony away from a declining agricultural economy toward mineral extraction, which was to fire an economic boom lasting for much of the eighteenth century.

1. On migration into Minas Gerais, see Charles R. Boxer, *The Golden Age of Brazil, 1695–1750: Growing Pains of a Colonial Society* (Berkeley and Los Angeles: University of California Press, 1962), 49; Donald Ramos, "From Minho to Minas: The Portuguese Roots of the Mineiro Family," *HAHR* 73 (November 1993), 639–62.

The arrival of new immigrants to the interior hills of Minas Gerais[2] represented a profound shift in the settlement patterns of Brazil. At the time of the major gold strikes, most of the colonial population lived along the littoral, with the largest towns situated on the eastern and northeastern coasts. The city of Salvador in the northeastern captaincy of Bahia served as Portugal's administrative center in Brazil.[3] To the south, Rio de Janeiro was a smaller town that did not become Brazil's colonial capital until 1763. Although Portuguese immigrants and their descendants also inhabited the captaincy of São Paulo, which lay to the south of Rio de Janeiro, that region was still sparsely populated on the eve of the gold rush compared with Bahia or even Pernambuco and was much more loosely integrated into metropolitan rule than were other Brazilian settlements. The goldfields, lying to the north of the captaincy of São Paulo and to the north and west of the captaincy of Rio de Janeiro, were located in a region previously uninhabited by European colonizers or their descendants. (See Map 1.) In addition, no large established Indian settlements existed in these gold-bearing lands where new and permanent colonial settlements took root and developed into prosperous mining towns.[4]

---

2. The location of the principal gold deposits was referred to by colonial officials as the land of the general mines, and the appellation has remained the same, even today.

3. In the Portuguese colonies of Brazil and elsewhere, the regional political subdivisions were called *captaincies*.

4. The sources consulted indicate that there were few Indians living in proximity to mining sites and their related settlements. In addition, there were only scarce references to Indian servants or slaves who lived among the free colonists. In the records of colonial officials that I have seen, there is virtually no discussion about contacts between miners and Indians in Minas Gerais proper. Kenneth R. Maxwell mentions hostile Indians in the region between the Rio coast and the mines in *Conflicts and Conspiracies: Brazil and Portugal, 1750–1808* (Cambridge: Cambridge University, 1973), 85, but Indian-European conflicts of the variety that characterized the *sertão* of Bahia and essentially closed it to permanent European settlement in the seventeenth century were not notable in the mining region during the eighteenth century. See Stuart B. Schwartz, *Sovereignty and Society in Colonial Brazil: The High Court of Bahia and Its Judges, 1609–1751* (Berkeley and Los Angeles: University of California Press, 1973), 128. For a thorough discussion of Portuguese contacts with Indians in the São Paulo region of Brazil, see John Monteiro, *Negros da terra: Indios e bandeirantes nas origens de São Paulo, Brasil* (Companhia das Letras, 1994). Monteiro reassesses the historical contributions on this subject made by renowned Brazilian historians, including Afonso de Escragnole Taunay's *História geral das bandeiras paulistas*, 11 vols. (São Paulo: H. L. Canton, 1924–50). In his dissertation, "São Paulo in the Seventeenth Century: Economy and Society" (University of Chicago, 1985), Monteiro asserted that the mining areas were thoroughly depopulated at the time of the gold rush as a consequence of *paulista* incursions into the region for purposes of slave hunting. Without further documentation, it is difficult to confirm this

I have limited my research to just one of these prosperous mining towns — Sabará — and its surrounding judicial district (*comarca*). The town was the political seat of the *comarca* and the heart of the commercial life of this subregion. The town council that met there addressed issues affecting all smaller communities in the region. The notarial documentation for the entire *comarca* was kept in records in the town center. The town and its surrounding judicial district are therefore the logical unit of analysis for a subregional study of this kind. Moreover, in the second half of the eighteenth century, demographic records indicate that close to one-third (31.6 percent) of the captaincy's total slave population resided in the town and *comarca* of Sabará.⁵ Thus, my analysis of slave lives and experiences in Sabará holds true for much (if not all) of Minas Gerais. By the end of the eighteenth century, Minas Gerais had four hundred thousand inhabitants (54 percent of whom were slaves) and rivaled the slave-based sugar plantation society of Brazil's northeastern coast, in terms of both total population and economic significance.⁶ Compared with other non-Brazilian slave societies, Minas Gerais was of great importance and represented a major destination for African slaves arriving in the New World in the 1700s. This study of slavery in Sabará, Minas Gerais, thus focuses attention on one of the principal slave societies in the New World.⁷

In the following chapters, I explore a number of topics: the origins of the gold economy and settlements, the development of gold mining and urban marketing, patterns of slaveholding and working conditions for slaves, the influence and relative weakness of the Catholic Church in Sabará, the patterns of manumission decisions and crown-colonist interactions. In exploring these topics, I hope to emphasize several inter-related

---

point or to assess the impact that early gold-seeking expeditions had on the original inhabitants of Minas Gerais. See pages 222 and 248. On Indians in colonial Brazil, see also John Hemming, *Red Gold: The Conquest of the Brazilian Indians, 1500–1760* (Cambridge, Mass.: Harvard University Press, 1978).

5. Jose Joaquim Rocha, "Memória histórica da capitania de Minas Gerais," *RAPM* 2 (1897): 511.

6. "População da provincia de Minas Gerais," *RAPM* 4 (1899): 294–95.

7. The Portuguese trade transported 1.4 million slaves from Angola to Brazil between 1701 and 1800. The Angola trade accounted for 70 percent of the Brazilian-bound slaves. Philip Curtin, *The Atlantic Slave Trade: A Census* (Madison: University of Wisconsin Press, 1969), 211. In the 1720s, Minas Gerais was receiving five to six thousand African slaves annually, but this figure would have continued to rise steadily throughout the 1740s. James Lockhart and Stuart B. Schwartz, eds., *Early Latin America: A History of Colonial Spanish America and Brazil* (New York: Cambridge University Press, 1983), 372.

Map 1. Modern boundaries of Minas Gerais. (Courtesy World Countries, 1995, ESRI)

arguments: the conditions of slave life, which included opportunities for autonomous behavior, were not static in this slave society; slave autonomy in Sabará diminished as the eighteenth century came to a close; slave autonomy was, at least in this historical context, a gender-related phenomenon. Indeed, one effective way to understand the history of eighteenth-century Sabará may be to consider it in terms of the evolving status, autonomy, and influence of non-White women. The changing experiences of these women reflected the economic, demographic, and cultural evolution of the slave society as a whole.

The dynamic interactions among slaves, freed slaves, free colonists, and crown officials in Sabará were profoundly shaped by the following factors: the accessibility and widespread dispersal of gold deposits, the emergence of small urban centers in which commercial activities thrived, the sexual division of labor among slaves working in mining and commerce, and the changing sex ratio in the population of free White colonists settling in the region. The last two factors ensured that enslaved women's experiences (sexual, reproductive, and economic) were pivotal in the definition of the slave regime. One result of the conflicts and alliances among masters, slaves, and royal officials in the context of these influential factors was that opportunities for slaves' autonomy were greater or more widely available than were those in large-scale plantation societies elsewhere in Brazil or in other nonurban regions of the New World. Moreover, the defining features of slave autonomy in Minas Gerais were gender related; it is nearly impossible to explain adequately for whom and why slave autonomy in the gold mines was most extensive or most limited without reference to the sex of the enslaved. Gender was, in fact, a critical determinant of the likelihood of a slave's access to unregulated income, unsupervised free time, masters' and mistresses' personal patronage, and manumission.

Throughout this book, I tell numerous stories about individual people. The sources that I have relied on have naturally led me to relate many partial stories. I wish I knew more about each and every one of them. I have also endeavored to link these anecdotes to the larger framework of a gold economy that thrived and then declined. My intent has been to depict both free and enslaved individuals as historical actors and to connect the experiences of both to a larger ongoing process of social and economic development.

The sources used in this study of an eighteenth-century frontier region reflect a number of important characteristics of colonial Brazilian society. The first of these is that from the top of the social order to the bottom, the vast majority of Sabará's inhabitants were illiterate. The slaveholders therefore did not, as a rule, produce written accounts of their lives in the form of diaries or correspondence to relatives, business associates, or government officials. Men and women slaveholders in Sabará were almost as unlikely to know how to read and write as were their own slaves.[8] It was a very rare inventory or will of an individual slaveholder that listed among his or her assets even a single book. It was common for testators to place their mark at the end of a scribe-written testament as these individuals often could not even sign their own names. Only particularly wealthy individuals made references to keeping financial records in account books, and no such personal business records were encountered in my search for sources.

The largely illiterate colonial society of Brazil did not read or even produce newspapers. Indeed, the printing press did not arrive in Brazil until King John VI arrived with the Portuguese court in Rio de Janeiro as they fled Napoleonic invasion in 1808. There were therefore no printed sources originating in Brazil during the entire colonial era. Colonial officials were literate as were district and local judges and clergy. Government correspondence, notarial documents, municipal council records, and ecclesiastical records of one kind or another are, by default, *the* sources on which historians of the colonial period must rely, and such sources are in and of themselves fragile, fragmentary, and scattered about in different locations throughout what is now modern Brazil. Fortuitously, official colonial records, whether produced by administrative authorities or in Church documents, provide rich (albeit brief) details about the lives of both enslaved and free individuals.

The colonists I have chosen to write about lived, for at least some portion of their lives, in the *vila* (town) of Nossa Senhora de Conceição de Sabará and in the surrounding *comarca* (judicial district) also named Sabará. The *comarca* was one of four subsectors of the captaincy of Minas Gerais. The *vila* of Sabará was the working residence of appointed crown officials charged with taxing the district's mining production and the location for meetings and deliberations of the (indirectly elected as well as appointed members of the) municipal council. The notarial office served not only those individuals who lived in the town boundaries, but also those who resided in outlying parishes of the *comarca*. Notaries docu-

8. To provide some sense of comparative perspective on illiteracy in Brazil, it should be noted that in Brazil in 1872, only 19.8 percent of the total female population was literate. At that time, literacy was higher in major coastal cities such as Rio de Janeiro (41.2 percent for men, 29.3 percent for women) and much lower in interior regions of Brazil such as Minas Gerais. Brazil, Diretoria Geral de Estatística, *Recenseamento da população do Império do Brasil a que se procedeu no dia 10. de agosto de 1872* (Rio de Janeiro: Leuzinger, 1973–76), 22: 1–2.

Line drawing of the living and working quarters of the Intendant of the Mines, Sabará, Minas Gerais, by Ivan. F. (1983)

mented a wide variety of events and personal decisions including business transactions such as sales and contracts for individuals and partnerships, wills and inventories of estates, interpersonal disputes, and letters of manumissions for slaves. These documents along with other ecclesiastical and administrative records (local, regional, and supraregional) are the sources from which I have gleaned the often partial, but nonetheless intriguing glimpses into past lives.

Although the geographical framework of this book is fixed and narrowed to examine only one portion of a large colonial mining region, the chronological boundaries of the work are extensive. The *vila* of Sabará was officially established in 1711, and the sources I use begin roughly at that time and continue until 1808, the year in which King John VI and his court fled Napoleon's army, established a new imperial center in Rio de Janeiro, and permanently altered colonial relations between Brazil and Portugal. In this time span, a small population of perhaps four to five thousand slaves and just over two hundred masters grew to over sixty thousand slaves and more than fifty thousand free colonists (see Table 2.1). In the course of this century, the experiences of the first generations of enslaved and free people naturally varied considerably from those of the succeeding generations. I repeatedly emphasize the social, economic, and demographic changes that, over time, shaped and reshaped the lives of

Sabará's colonists. At various points, I make explicit comparisons between the economic, social, and demographic circumstances for slaves, free people, men, and women during the height of the gold boom (pre-1760) and the substantially different circumstances of the postboom period (post-1760).

Although it should hardly be necessary to say so, the slave-based economies and societies of colonial Brazil were fundamentally characterized by inequality, exploitation, and violence directed against men, women, and even newborn children. New World slavery was a coercive, unjust, and cruel institution, and among the experiences of slaves in eighteenth-century Sabará, Minas Gerais, inequality, exploitation, and violence also prevailed. Without negating the truth of slavery's multiple inequities, I can still state that opportunities for slave autonomy, slave resistance, and escape from slavery through the mechanism of manumission existed in eighteenth-century Sabará. In exploring these opportunities, I remain highly conscious of their limits, both in identifying those among slaves who were most *and* least likely to have been able to seize opportunities for autonomous behavior and also by suggesting how opportunities for autonomous behavior changed or diminished over the course of the century studied.

In the field of Brazilian slavery, some scholars have expressed concern that studies drawing attention to the evidence of slave autonomy and slave resistance have the potential (although unintended) effect of detracting from an overall understanding of master-slave relationships as oppressive, cruel, and inhumane. Although I am sympathetic to such concerns and have no scholarly interest whatsoever in "rehabilitating" the historical image of Brazilian slavery,[9] I nonetheless find merit in the depiction of slaves as historical actors who were sometimes able to limit and even redirect their masters' actions. Strategies employed to control slaves were not simply inventions of the masters, but also represented informed, contextualized responses to the ceaseless as well as intermittent efforts of captives to subvert their owners' goals. The oppression of slaves and their resistance (as expressed in autonomous behavior) were therefore fundamentally related phenomena both of which deserve the attention of historians. In my own understanding of the lives of slaves and ex-slaves in Sabará, Minas Gerais, the oppressive and arbitrary circumstances of their enslavement informed, defined, and limited expressions of autonomous behavior.

---

9. Jacob Gorender, *A escravidão reabilitada* (São Paulo: Editora Atica, 1990).

In Brazilian historiography, apologetic depictions of slavery are encapsulated in Gilberto Freyre's profoundly influential 1933 epic *Casa grande e senzala*.[10] Freyre's sympathetic portrait of Brazil's seignorial traditions has been dubbed "patriarchalist" by its numerous critics as it is based on the metaphor that characterizes slave society and master-slave relationships as an extensive "family" system governed by a benign (even affectionate) patriarch. The revisionist scholarship on Brazilian slavery, which emerged in force in the 1960s, is, by way of reference to Freyre, "antipatriarchalist" in its depictions of slavery as a harsh and oppressive social system.[11] In this study of slavery in colonial Minas Gerais, I position myself within the "antipatriarchalist" historiography and particularly so in reference to the history of women slaves. The oppression of slave women was pivotal in the construction of relationships between the enslaved and the free in Sabará. In focusing attention on the role of women's enslavement in the mining region and on their particular opportunities for autonomous behavior, I am especially cognizant of the need to confront persistent myths about affectionate relationships between free men and enslaved women in colonial Brazil and the purported influence that enslaved women derived from such liaisons. In Minas Gerais, the most famous story emblemizing such affectionate relationships is that of Xica da Silva, a *mulata* ex-slave and concubine to an eighteenth-century diamond contractor. According to legend, the White lover's passion for Xica led him to build for her an artificial lake, complete with manned sailing ships, because she had never seen the open sea.[12] The unproved legend of Xica da Silva has been used uncritically by (otherwise quite skeptical) historians of slavery and race relations in Brazil as evidence of a universally existent sexual attraction for non-White women in Portuguese men.[13] The overt promotion of "passion"

---

10. *Casa grande e senzala* (Rio de Janeiro: Maia e Schmidt, 1933). *Casa grande e senzala* was translated as *The Master and the Slaves: A Study in the Development of Brazilian Civilization*, trans. Samuel Putnam (New York: Knopf, 1946).

11. Challenges to the benign patriarchalist interpretation emerged in the 1960s with the works of *paulista* scholars: Fernando Henrique Cardoso, *Capitalismo e escravidão no Brasil meridional* (1962); Octávio Ianni, *As metamorfoses de escravo: Apogeu e crise no Brasil meridional* (1962); Emilia Viotti da Costa, *Da senzala á colônia* (1966); Florestan Fernandes, *O negro no mundo dos brancos* (1972). For a review of antipatriarchalist Brazilian scholarship in the 1970s and 1980s, see Stuart B. Schwartz, "Recent Trends in the Study of Brazilian Slavery," in Stuart B. Schwartz, ed., *Slaves, Peasants, and Rebels: Reconsidering Brazilian Slavery* (Champaign/Urbana: University of Illinois Press, 1992).

12. Boxer, *The Golden Age*, 219–20.

13. "The sexual attraction which coloured women exercised for many Portuguese is too well known to need additional emphasis here," wrote Boxer in *The Golden Age*. Boxer nev-

(as opposed to the possibility of rape or coercion) in explanations of the physical liaisons sought by White male colonists with slave women has served to support a resiliently benign view of racial and sexual relationships in Brazil's past.[14] Even in recent revisionist accounts that call attention to the vulnerability of slave women to sexual exploitation, the legend of Xica lives on in such statements as "a female slave could have more to gain from being a White man's concubine than a Black man's wife."[15]

In my research on the lives of slave women in colonial Sabará, I examine the phenomenon of being a White man's concubine without extolling the purported benefits of the experience. Enslavement denied to non-White women all the (albeit) limited protections and individual control that a patriarchal society offered to free White women. Sexual relationships between free men and enslaved women were, for example, not marital relationships, and they denied to slave women whatever legal protections marriage offered in Portuguese society. Although recent demographic studies have clearly demonstrated that in colonial Brazil legal marriages were not universal in the free population, such marriages remained the idealized social and economic state of virtually all honorable, and especially White, women.[16] In contrast, legal marriage between an enslaved woman (or ex-slave) and a free White man was an anathema. Slavery in Sabará, as elsewhere in colonial Brazil, denied to enslaved women both honor and protection and commonly placed them in the especially odious role of unprotected sexual servants.

In their doubly exploited positions as laborers and vulnerable sexual

---

ertheless went on to describe "the enduring passion felt by many White men for Black or mulata women, best exemplified in the career of Xica da Silva," 15–17.

14. The partial social acceptance (or contingent social mobility), under certain circumstances, of the mixed-race children of these sexual relationships is the underpinning feature of many traditional discussions of racial tolerance and racial "democracy" in Latin American historical and sociological literatures. See Frank Tannenbaum, *Slave and Citizen: The Negro in the Americas* (New York: Knopf, 1947); Carl Degler, *Neither Black nor White: Slavery and Race Relations in Brazil and the United States* (New York: Macmillan, 1971). On the persistence of ideas about benign race relations in Brazil, see Emilia Viotti da Costa, "The Myth of Racial Democracy," in *Myths and Histories* (Chicago; University of Chicago Press, 1985).

15. A. J. R. Russell-Wood, *The Black Man in Slavery and Freedom in Colonial Brazil* (New York: St. Martin's Press, 1982), 181.

16. For a review of illegitimacy statistics in colonial Brazil demonstrating the relative absence of marriage there, see Muriel Nazzari, "Concubinage in Colonial Brazil: The Inequalities of Race, Class, and Gender," *Journal of Family History* 21 (April 1996): 110; for a review of Brazilian scholarship on the significance of marriage versus concubinage, see Elizabeth Anne Kuznesof, "Sexuality, Gender, and the Family in Colonial Brazil," *Luso-Brazilian Review* 30:1 (1993): 119–31.

servants, enslaved women in Sabará nonetheless also experienced opportunities for autonomy and resistance. Colonial authorities were often just
as concerned with the "licentious liberty" that women slaves expressed as
they were with that of enslaved men. The governors of Minas Gerais
voiced continual frustration with their inability to contain undesirable actions and strategies of enslaved women as these women sought to achieve
some degree of autonomy in their lives. In contrast to what is suggested in
older "patriarchalist" interpretations of the lives of enslaved women, the
documentary evidence consulted in my research suggests that whatever influence slave women could exercise over their own experiences was far less
likely to have been derived from amorous relationships with free White
men than from their income-earning roles in an urban market economy.
Slave women were also far fewer than were slave men and did not pose as
significant a physical threat to the White male colonists who were almost
always outnumbered by their enslaved men. In addition, ex-slave women
did not compete (as freedmen could) with White men for gold-bearing
lands. The opportunities for autonomous actions or decision making that
these particular factors facilitated were, as with all other conditions of
slaves' lives in Sabará, subject to change over time. In the course of the
eighteenth century, slave women experienced increasingly difficult economic and social circumstances and fewer opportunities to shape their
own experiences or thwart their owners' goals. The autonomy of slave
women diminished as one generation of slaves and slaveholders gave rise
to another and as the supply of gold in the mining lands dwindled from
one decade to the next.

What it meant "to be a slave" in colonial Sabará, Minas Gerais, therefore depended on many different and changing variables.[17] In the pages
that follow, I hope to demonstrate that sex, race, migration, economy, ge-
ography, and colonial politics all could and did shape both individuals'
experiences and those of their generation. My purpose in telling both individual and collective stories is to argue that master-slave relationships in
the eighteenth-century gold-mining region of eighteenth-century Sabará
were simultaneously oppressive and disorderly, contractual as well as per-

17. The phrase "to be a slave" refers to the book of that title, *Ser escravo no Brazil* (São
Paulo: Editora Brasiliense, 1982), written by Katia M. de Queirós Mattoso, published in
English as *To Be a Slave in Brazil, 1550–1888* (New Brunswick: Rutgers University Press,
1986). Lauded by some scholars and pointedly criticized by others, the author addresses and
describes many features of slave life across a broad span of time, but limited to the city of
Salvador, Bahia, in northeastern Brazil. See Gorender, *A escravidão reabilitada*.

sonal, an enduring set of social and economic relationships that nonetheless evolved from one generation to the next. To make this argument, I call attention to the "disorders" caused by enslaved men and women, to the negotiated ends to enslavement that are explicit in purchased manumissions, to the fact that adult slaves exchanged their labor for goods, arms, influence, or freedom, and to the changing opportunities for autonomy that slaves of different sexes experienced across generations. In other words, I observe and explore the limits of what contemporary critics referred to as the slaves' "licentious liberty."

My intention here is to further complications of the original "antipatriarchalist" revisionist historiography by contributing to an increasingly complex consideration of slavery as it existed throughout Brazil. In its time, the original "antipatriarchalist" historiography had the much narrower (and thoroughly justifiable) purpose of revealing and emphasizing the cruelty and inhumanity of slavery in order to debunk the peculiarly Brazilian myths of benign patriarchalism and racial democracy.[18] I do not dispute the "antipatriarchalist" conclusion; rather I, like other younger scholars of Brazilian history,[19] add complexity to the story of how cruelty toward and control of slaves could take different forms, and to the story of how inhumane practices could be continually reproduced under changing social, economic, demographic, and environmental circumstances.

For Brazilians, complicating the history of eighteenth-century Minas Gerais in any manner at all is a significant act in and of itself, in part because so much *mineiro* history remains to be written and in part because the colonial past of this region is as important to Brazilians as the colonial pasts of Massachusetts, Virginia, or South Carolina are to North Americans. Historians of Brazil, Africa, and New World slavery also know, however, that the vast majority of the (at least ten million) Africans who came as slaves to the Americas lived and died in Brazil, and in the eighteenth century (described in Brazilian periodization as the *siglo do ouro* — the century of gold) the vast majority of Brazil's new slaves were sold to the colonists in Minas Gerais.[20] I have thus located my own complications to

18. See note 11 above.
19. I am not the first or only historian working to complicate this historiography in Brazil. See Schwartz, "Recent Trends."
20. This information has been widely available since the 1969 publication of Philip Curtin's *The Atlantic Slave Trade: A Census* (Madison: University of Wisconsin Press, 1969). On the eighteenth-century trade to Brazil, see also Joseph Miller, *Way of Death: Merchant Capitalism and the Angolan Slave Trade, 1730–1830* (Madison: University of Wisconsin Press, 1988).

the "antipatriarchalist" metanarrative in an examination of master-slave relationships that were enacted in the most significant economic region of eighteenth-century Brazil, which was also one of the largest, richest, and most significant slave societies in the western hemisphere in this period. It is worth repeating here that by the end of the eighteenth century, Minas Gerais had close to four hundred thousand inhabitants (54 percent enslaved).[21] My examination of evidence from Sabará, Minas Gerais (representing one of four subdistricts of the captaincy), thus focuses on issues of slave control and slave autonomy in one of the New World's principal, yet least studied, slave societies.

The particular complications that I bring to bear on our understanding of what should remain a profoundly antipatriarchalist view of master-slave relationships in colonial Minas Gerais (as well as in colonial Brazil as a whole) are often rooted in questions of gender. As we see in the discussions of how the early mining economy and society developed (Chapters 1 and especially 2), prevailing ideas about gender roles were very powerful in shaping and reshaping slavery and colonial *mineiro* society. The colonizers' commitment to a sexual division of labor in which the work of miners was defined as the work of men may have been the single most important determinant of the evolutionary path of the colonial slave society of Minas Gerais. Male colonizers preferred to buy only male slaves as miners. This ideological commitment to male-defined work has no parallel in areas of agriculturally based slavery elsewhere in the New World. We do not see elsewhere in Brazil (or Jamaica, or South Carolina, or Virginia, or Louisiana, or Cuba) colonizers who owned twenty-eight men and one woman as did *mineiro* colonists such as Bras de Barro Soares in 1719.[22] The demographic consequences of his choice, and others like it, strongly affected the relationships between masters and slaves and those among the slaves themselves and informed the actions and decrees of colonial authorities, particularly in regard to issues of slave control.

Ideas about gender roles also powerfully shaped the colonizers' behavior as migrants in that Portuguese men were the explorers of the frontier; they were the adventurers who sought the gold in the interior; they monopolized the riches of the region; and, in the absence of legal marital relationships, they did not share those riches with the women with whom they had the sexual relationships that produced an obvious proportion of the earliest generation of locally born children and heirs. Portuguese law did pro-

---

21. "População da provincia de Minas Gerais," *RAPM* 4 (1899): 294–95.
22. See below Chapter 1, note 72.

vide for the right of natural (illegitimate) children to inherit from their parents, but Portuguese law did not provide women in sexual partnerships with community property rights unless these partnerships took place in legal marriages. Portuguese colonizers denied to women of color the legal marriages they *would* enter into with White women.

Ideas about gender and racial hierarchies combined to shape and reshape the experiences of enslaved women and freed slave women in the course of the eighteenth century. As I argue in Chapters 3 and 4, the values the colonizers evinced in the commitments to racial hierarchy and gender subordination help to explain important social practices in colonial Minas Gerais such as concubinage, and despite organized opposition and policing of the flock from the Catholic Church, these values superseded commitments of obedience to, or of faith in, Church tenets. The colonial population saw itself as Catholic, embraced much of Catholic ritual and practice, but when the racial, social, class, and gender interests of male colonists conflicted with Church precepts, noncompliance prevailed. The individual provisions of testators, the records of *Visita Inquisitors,* and the baptismal records (with godparent data) all demonstrate the colonizers' deep commitments to gender and racial inequalities. As we see in these two chapters, for male colonists, these commitments led to persistent rejection of legal marriages, preferences for the lightest-skinned concubines, and preferences in godparentage roles that would enhance (not diminish) their existing authority. For both male and female slaveholders, commitments to Christian precepts of spiritual equality and beliefs in individual salvation competed with expressions of commitment to a racially stratified, culturally Catholic world (as expressed in organizations of brotherhoods and godparent choices) and to a class-based society based on enslavement of the bodies (although not the souls) of Africans and their descendants.

As discussed in the framework of an analysis of manumission practices (Chapter 5), for male and female slaves in Sabará, both the gold-mining cycle itself and the changing demography of the frontier region wrought powerful changes and defined the circumstances in which men and women experienced their enslavement. The early wealth of the mining cycle gave way to increasing impoverishment, and with this economic decline, certain opportunities for personal expressions of autonomy diminished for all. It remained true, however, that men and women experienced enslavement differently and that the measures of the slave experience varied in important ways for both sexes. One measure was the availability of the opportunity for the purchasing of freedom; another was the sexual exploitation that one was likely to endure; yet another the likelihood of control over working conditions on a daily basis. In the latter half of the eighteenth century, slaves also experienced a generationally defined shift in slaveholding patterns in which women emerged as a significant proportion of the owners of slaves, either in their own right or as joint owners of community property. Women owners exercised control of men and women slaves in ways that differed from men owners, and women employed very different manumission choices, especially in regard to mixed-race progeny of enslaved women.

The experiences of Sabará's enslaved men and women were both regionally and generationally defined, and their stories add to our understanding that, even at a given moment in history, there was not just one kind of slave or one kind of slavery in Brazil. On the other hand, as we see in Chapter 6, the dramas of relentless slave resistance and persistent intracolonial conflicts, and the effects of both on official efforts to achieve social control, speak to certain continuities in master-slave relationships, which were replicated, however uneasily, from one generation to the next. The story of powerful slave owners who could and did thwart colonial authority also has its parallels in numerous New World settings. Slavery in Sabará, Minas Gerais, had both its unique features and those it shared with other colonial slave regimes.

Numerous topics have remained outside the scope of this work on slavery in colonial Sabará, Minas Gerais. Much remains to be written on the social and economic history of Sabará and on eighteenth-century Minas Gerais more generally. Slave families, the internal workings of both Black and White brotherhoods, non-Catholic religious experiences and practices, and the free population of color in Minas Gerais with its growing role in supporting a changing *mineiro* economy are only a few subjects that merit further investigation. I am hopeful that those who address these challenging subjects in the future will bear in mind the multiple and evolving impacts of race and gender hierarchies, demography, environment, and economy, as I have tried to do in the analyses that I have addressed in this book.

Rushing for Gold in Minas Gerais

Brazil had been a colony of Portugal for two hundred years when gold mining became a profitable enterprise and a full-time occupation for large numbers of colonists. Although the discovery of the coastal shores of Brazil took place in 1500, not until 1711 was the *vila* (town) of Nossa Senhora de Conceição de Sabará officially established. In contrast to the early discovery of mineral wealth in Spanish America, the great gold strikes in Brazil occurred long after the colony had developed important agricultural products both for export and for internal consumption and long after the Portuguese had, to one degree or another, started searching for deposits. The presence of agricultural settlements in Brazil meant that the measures taken by the crown to encourage gold explorations and mining initially could not directly compete with or threaten existing economic or political interests in the already developed colonial centers or in Lisbon.

Gold was, of course, an invaluable commodity, and Portuguese crown policies changed over time as more ore became available in the interior lands of colonial Brazil. It is not really possible to know exactly how much gold was mined in the captaincy of Minas Gerais, but estimates of total production in the eighteenth century indicate that at least 640,000 kilograms (1,408,000 pounds) of what was produced in that time came to the attention of fiscal authorities. From 1735 to 1750, the years of highest production, fiscal records suggest that close to ten metric tons of gold were produced annually.[1] In those years, more than ninety thousand slaves were laboring in the captaincy, and close to one-fourth of these were located in the *comarca* of Sabará.[2] (See Fig. 1.1.)

In the nearly two centuries before Brazil's bounty in gold had finally come to light, the Spanish discoveries of gold and silver in Peru and Mexico had been both an obvious source of envy for the Portuguese crown and a principal source of information or expectation about mining economies. Initial expectations about processes of mineral extraction in Minas Gerais were, not surprisingly, strongly influenced by perceptions of the Spanish experience in the New World.[3] In keeping with the contemporary depictions of colonial Peru, Portuguese administrators conceived of a mine as a hole dug deep in the ground, perhaps into the side of an enormous mountain — just like the silver mines of Potosí in the Andes.[4] Brazil's impressively large deposits of gold were not, however, located in the Andes or in an analogous site.

The gold-bearing lands formed part of an ancient watershed for several major drainage systems: the São Francisco river flowing to the north, the Dôce river flowing north and east, the Rio Grande and (its tributary) the Rio das Mortes flowing west to the basin of the River Plate. Over time, the waters of these systems had cut deep into the earth's surface and created a landscape noted for high, rugged peaks, long chains of hogback mountains, and deep canyons, as well as high plateaus and open valleys. Although the maximum elevation in the region is only 2,100 meters, the total relief is approximately 1,400 meters. Erosion by wind and water had exposed ore-bearing rocks at the earth's surface, usually in or near the water

1. Virgílio Noya Pinto, *O ouro brasileiro e o comércio anglo-português*, 2d ed. (São Paulo: Companhia Editora Nacional, 1979), 114.

2. Boxer, *The Golden Age*, 341–46.

3. Despite serious economic crises in the sugar industry in the second half of the seventeenth century, on the eve of the gold rush, sugar remained the economic foundation of colonial Brazil. André João Antonil, *Cultura e opulência do Brasil, por suas drogas e minas* (Lisbon, 1711; rpt. São Paulo: Companhia Melhoramentos, 1976); Schwartz, *Sovereignty and Society in Colonial Brazil*, 139; Schwartz, *Sugar Plantations in the Formation of Brazilian Society, 1550–1835* (New York: Cambridge University Press, 1985).

4. Alvará, 15 August 1618, reproduced in Manoel José Pires da Silva Pontes, "Revisão dos regimentos das minas do imperio do Brasil, com notas e observações do guarda mor geral das minas na provincia de Minas Geraes," *RAPM* 7 (1902): 834–48, articles 7, 8, 13, 18, 19, etc. A specific reference to mines of Peru and New Spain is made in article 36.

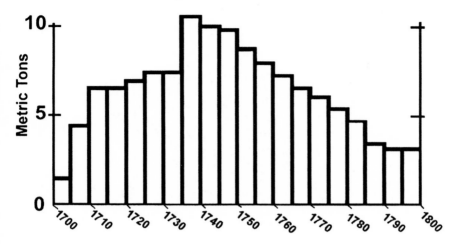

Fig. 1.1.   Gold production, captaincy of Minas Gerais. (Virgílio Noya Pinto, *O ouro brasileiro o comércio anglo-português,* 2d ed. [São Paulo: Companhia Editora Nacional, 1979], 115.)

sources.[5] With ore deposits located at the surface in innumerable locations throughout an ancient watershed, alluvial, not deep-shaft mining was characteristic throughout the colonial period.[6] (See Maps 2 and 3.)

The social, economic, and political consequences of alluvial ore deposits in colonial Brazil were legion. Unlike those of Spanish America, the mining lands of Brazil spanned an immense geographical area characterized by steep hills and dense vegetation where days, even weeks, of walking were

5. Rocks of this age are highly mineralized, and this area of Brazil is known today for its deposits of iron and manganese. John Van N. Dorr II, "Physiographic, Stratigraphic, and Structural Development of the Quadrilátero Ferrífero, Minas Gerais, Brazil," *U.S. Geological Service Professional Paper* 641–a, 1A.

6. Although gold did exist in veins of ore running deep beneath the earth's surface in Minas Gerais, mines to exploit such veins were most successfully developed in Brazil in the nineteenth century. There was some nonalluvial mining in the eighteenth century, although it did not in any way predominate. Luis Gomes Ferreyra, *Erario mineral* (Lisbon: Impressor do Senhor Patriarca, 1735), 2. The Morro Velho mine (in Nova Lima, Minas Gerais) developed by the Saint John del Rey Mining Company in the nineteenth and twentieth centuries became renowned in 1931 as the deepest gold mine in the entire world. Dorr, "Physiographic, Stratographic, and Structural Development of the Quadrilátero Ferrífero, Minas Gerais, Brazil," 1A; Marshall Eakin, "Nova Lima: Life, Labor, and Technology in an Anglo-Brazilian Mining Community" (Ph.D. diss., University of California, 1981); Douglas Cole Libby, *Transformação do trabalho em uma economia escravista Minas Gerais no seculo XIX* (São Paulo: Editora Brasiliense, 1988).

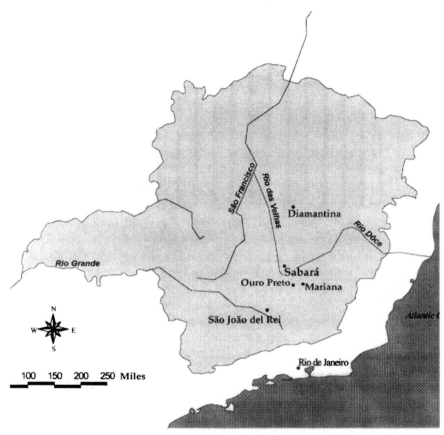

Map 2. Urban centers of colonial Minas Gerais. (Courtesy World Countries, 1995, ESRI)

required to travel from one settlement to another.[7] In contrast to Peruvian deep-shaft mines, which were fewer in number and more readily monitored, the more diffuse nature of ore deposits in Minas Gerais led to a widespread dispersal of the miners and made the collection of taxes in gold for the royal treasury exceedingly difficult. Adding to the difficulty was the fact that the techniques of production required for alluvial mining did not

7. W. L. von Eschwege, *Pluto brasiliensis*, trans. Domício de Figueiredo Murta (Berlin, 1833; rpt. São Paulo: Livraria Itatiaia Editora, 1979), 1, p. 30. Eschwege writes, for example, that the distance between Ouro Preto and Marianna, which in his time took two hours on a rough road (he was in Brazil during the years 1810–21), had required three days to travel early in the eighteenth century.

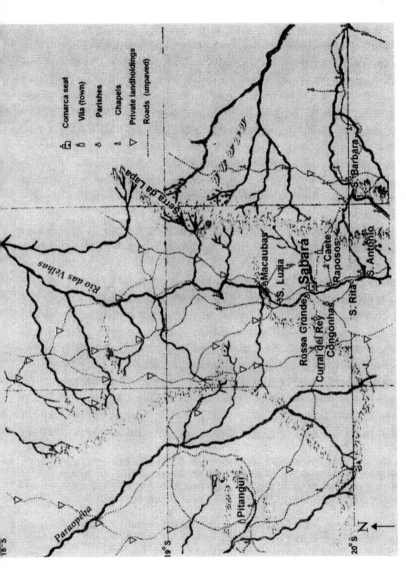

Map 3. Populated centers of *comarca* of Sabará, Minas Gerais. The *comarca* extended from approximately 20 degrees south northward to 13 degrees south. The most populated areas lay within the eastern half of the *comarca* between 20 degrees south and 18 degrees south as shown here. (Courtesy Arquivo Público Mineiro, José Joaquim da Rocha, Mapa da Comarca de Sabará, 1778.)

allow crown officials to monopolize or supervise any one necessary aspect of ore extraction.[8] Traffic in contraband gold and the emergence of a thriving clandestine economy unregulated by royal tax collectors therefore plagued Portuguese authorities throughout the eighteenth century.

It took considerable time, even after gold was found in Brazil, for local and metropolitan officials to realize that their expectations did not mesh with the location of ore deposits in Brazil. The location of these deposits determined, in great measure, how they were to be mined. The gold was initially easily accessible, even by hand, in the streams and river beds of the region. The larger lumps were called *faisqueiras*, which meant that they glittered or gleamed in the sunlight and thus were readily sighted by prospectors. Weights of the largest of these were considerable, ranging from three-fourths of a pound to three pounds or even more.[9] Some of these nuggets were described as the size of pears or even ox tongues.[10] According to Boxer, the quality of the gold in Minas Gerais varied between 21 1/2 and 22 1/2 carats.[11]

Individual miners normally panned for gold by using a *bateia*, a large, shallow, funnel-shaped pan most often made of wood. These pans were almost two feet across and five or six inches deep at the center. Standing in water, miners filled their *bateias* with five to six pounds of gravelly, quartz-laden subsoil called *cascalho,* which typically lay beneath a surface layer of sand or clay. Enough water was added to just cover the contents of the pan, which the miner then gently rotated in a circular fashion. Because of their higher specific density, the gold particles sank to the bottom of the funnel-shaped basin, and the miner tipped out lighter-weight extraneous particles with the water. This first washing in the *bateia* could take from five to ten minutes, but repeated washings with clean water were often necessary to separate the gold from the surrounding subsoil.[12] Exactly how much gold a miner found in any given spot was, of course, highly variable

8. In Spanish America, for example, production of silver depended on the delivery of mercury used in the amalgamation process. In 1559, the Spanish crown assumed control of all exports of mercury from Spain to America. Peter Bakewell, *Silver Mining and Society in Colonial Mexico, Zacatecas, 1546–1700* (Cambridge: Cambridge University Press, 1971), 151.

9. Augusto de Lima Júnior, *A capitania das Minas Gerais* (1943; rpt. Belo Horizonte: Livraria Itatiaia Editora, 1978), 45.

10. John Mawe, *Viagens ao interior do Brasil,* trans. Selena Benevides (1812; rpt. Belo Horizonte: Livraria Itatiaia Editora, 1978), 70; Lima Júnior, *A capitania das Minas Gerais,* 45.

11. Boxer, *The Golden Age,* 38.

12. Mawe, *Viagens ao interior do Brasil,* 70.

and largely a matter of luck. Contemporary observers did report, however, that in one small waterway five *arrobas* (i.e., 165 pounds) of gold were extracted from a section only twelve meters in length.[13] Such stories naturally brought thousands of fortune hunters into the region.

If rivers and streams were too deep or in flood, miners also searched for *cascalho* by digging on or near the banks of water courses or adjacent hillsides where erosion had created clefts or ravines. When the *cascalho* was deeper in the subsoil, miners dug large pits called *catas* into banks and hillsides, and water was sometimes diverted to these sites by wooden aqueducts. Larger enterprises that employed numerous slaves and created extensive diggings were called *lavras* or *lavras de mineração;* these made use of some simple hydraulic machinery and sometimes extensive series of graded canals and wooden troughs. An early nineteenth-century traveler, John Mawe, described such graded canals as twenty or thirty feet long, two to three feet wide, and one foot deep. A series of these descending channels would end in a deeper trench. Six to seven slaves would be assigned to the task of panning in each level of the graded canals, with the use of the wooden *bateia*.[14]

How the mines were discovered, who the principal discoverers were, and how the discoverers and later settlers conceived of and organized a labor force to extract gold deposits are factors as central to understanding crown-colonist relationships in the mining region as are the pre-existing conditions of alluvial ore scattered across thousands of square miles. One important fact about the discoverers was that they were private entrepreneurs, not agents of the Portuguese crown. Portuguese law as defined in the Philipine Code had decreed that the possession of mineral rights was vested in the crown.[15] The subsoil of the empire belonged to the king. In practice, however, because the king could not command the labor necessary to develop mines, the crown authorized private exploitation of mineral lands in exchange for a fifth part of the ore extracted. Consequently, control over the labor force working in the mines lay with private individuals, not the royal government. The relationships between owners and slaves in Sabará and elsewhere in the mining region were also largely privately defined.

13. Antonil, *Cultura*, 166.

14. Mawe, *Viagens ao interior do Brasil*, 69.

15. *Ordenações filipinas, ordenações e leis do reino de Portugal recopiladas por mandato d'el Rei D. Felipe, o primeiro*, ed. Fernando H. Mendes de Almeida (rpt. São Paulo: Edição Saraiva, 1960), L. II Título XXXIV.

In the popular histories of Sabará and in the stories told to visiting tourists today, the first settler and official discoverer of the mines of the Rio das Velhas region was a *paulista* (from São Paulo) named Manuel de Borba Gato, who first had come into the area in the company of his father-in-law Fernão Dias Pais.[16] Pais was a legendary *bandeirante* (explorer) who in 1674 went north from São Paulo in an unsuccessful search for emeralds.[17] Although he had once been a successful planter of wheat and owner of hundreds of Indian slaves, Pais apparently no longer saw his or his family's future as rooted in an Indian-supported agricultural economy.[18] He therefore gambled (and lost) his fortune on the decades-old belief that emeralds lay somewhere in the country's interior. Some years later, Borba Gato continued the search for precious minerals and stones in the unexplored lands near the Rio das Velhas and is credited with locating the first significant quantities of alluvial gold. He was also accused of hiding his discoveries from the crown's tax collectors.[19]

The Portuguese king, his various ministers, and the Overseas Council

16. Diogo de Vasconcellos, *História antiga das Minas Gerais* (rpt. of 1904 publication), 4th ed. (Belo Horizonte: Livraria Itatiaia Editora, 1974), 247; Lucia Machado de Almeida, *Passeio a Sabará* (São Paulo: Livraria Martins, 1956), 13.

17. In the captaincy of São Paulo, the colonists, known as *paulistas*, were less oriented to an export-based colonial trade and made their living cultivating foodstuffs with the help of Indians whom they had captured and enslaved. Throughout the sixteenth and seventeenth centuries, the *paulistas* organized expeditions exploring the noncolonized areas of Brazil to hunt down Indians and bring them back to their colonial settlements. These *paulistas* often traveled with their own Indian slaves in expeditionary groups called *bandeiras*. Participants in the *bandeiras* were known as *bandeirantes*. Frequently spending months exploring the interior known as the *sertão*, they searched for the new sources of labor necessary to the growth and development of the agricultural economy emerging in and around the town of São Paulo. Boxer, *The Golden Age*, 31–35; Myriam Ellis, "As bandeiras na expansão geográfico do Brasil," in *História geral da civilização brasileira*, ed. Sérgio Buarque de Holanda, tomo 1, vol. 1 (São Paulo: Difel, 1981), 273–96; Richard Morse, ed., *The Bandeirantes: The Historical Role of the Brazilian Pathfinders* (New York: Knopf, 1965); the works of Alfredo Ellis Júnior, including *Meio século de bandeirismo (1590–1640)* (São Paulo: Revistas dos Tribunais, 1939) and *O bandeirismo paulista e o recuo meridiano* (São Paulo: Companhia Editora Nacional, 1936), as well as the works of Taunay, especially *História geral*, have informed much of the study of *bandeiras* in the twentieth century. For a re-evaluation of the course and process of *bandeirismo* in seventeenth-century São Paulo, see Monteiro, "São Paulo in the Seventeenth Century: Economy and Society" (Ph.D. diss., University of Chicago, 1985).

18. Monteiro, "São Paulo in the Seventeenth Century," 248.

19. According to Boxer, Borba Gato was implicated in the assassination of one Dom Rodrigo Castel-Blanco, administrator of the mines in São Paulo, and his stay in the Rio das Velhas stemmed from efforts to evade royal authorities. *The Golden Age*, 35.

from time to time had encouraged *paulistas* like Pais and Borba Gato and other Portuguese colonists in Brazil to take up the search for deposits of gold and silver. Their support for individual expeditions did not necessarily extend to finances.[20] Because the risks were so often theirs alone, the early colonists of São Paulo much preferred to hunt for Indians *rather than* to look for gold. Writing in the early seventeenth century, the Jesuit priest André João Antonil noted this preference and observed that colonists were "content with the fruits which the surface of the abundant lands provided, and with the fishes of the large and agreeable rivers," and they therefore "did not try to divert the natural courses of these rivers to examine their depths, nor did they attempt to open the bowels of the earth, as an insatiable ambition had persuaded those of many other nations to do." The "disposition to hunt Indians in the forests" also "diverted [colonists] from this effort" to discover gold.[21]

If the *bandeirantes'* primary objective—the search for Indians—remained constant throughout most of the seventeenth century, their primary hunting grounds did not. These shifted from the Spanish colonial and Guarani Indian borderlands lying west of the captaincy to the north, toward what eventually became the site of Brazil's eighteenth-century mining boom. The Portuguese crown could not have directed this change any more than it could have controlled the slave-hunting objectives of the *bandeirantes* themselves. The shift in the hunting grounds occurred sometime around 1640 and was due mainly to the depletion of the Indian population in the region where *bandeiras* (slaving expeditions) had once been most common.[22] In response to the scarcity of labor necessary to support local agriculture, *paulistas* looked north for a viable substitute for the once plentiful Guarani Indians. Their search met with only partial success, and in the later part of the seventeenth century, the *paulistas* discovered that the "harvests" of the *sertão* no longer supported the expansion or even

20. Manoel da Silveira Cardoso, "The History of Mining in Colonial Brazil, 1500–1750" (Ph.D. diss., Stanford University, 1940), 60–61.

21. "Foi sempre fama constante que no Brasil havia minas de ferro, ouro e prata. Mas, também, houve sempre bastante descuido de as descobrir e de aproveitar-se delas, ou porque, contentando-se os moradores com os frutos que dá a terra abundantemente na sua superfície, e com os peixes que se pescam nos rios grandes e aprazíveis, não trataram de divertir o curso natural destes, para lhes examinarem o fundo, nem de abrir áquela as entranhas, como persuadiu a ambição insaciável a outras muitas nações, ou porque o gênio de buscar índios nos matos os desviou desta diligência menos escrupulosa e mais útil." Antonil, *Cultura*, 163.

22. Monteiro, "São Paulo in the Seventeenth Century," 175, 216.

maintenance of São Paulo's once thriving agricultural economy.[23] It was in this context that colonists like Fernão Dias Pais and his son-in-law Manuel de Borba Gato had taken up the search for mineral wealth in earnest.

When Fernão Dias Pais set out on his quest in 1674, the king demonstrated his support for the adventure by conferring on him the title of "governor of all soldiers, and of other people who may have gone to discover silver mines and emeralds, who may go now, or who may later be sent." Along with the title and the authority behind it, the colonial government in Bahia promised Pais one thousand *cruzados* to help finance his trip, but only a smaller sum actually reached him.[24] His expedition was, in fact, financed nearly entirely by Pais himself, at a cost of more than six thousand *cruzados,* a considerable sum for the period.[25] Moreover, Pais borrowed additional sums of money to finance his trip, and when he died still searching for emeralds, he owed more than one thousand *cruzados* to his creditors.[26]

Despite his failure, Pais's expedition to find the legendary emeralds looms large in the popular histories of *bandeirantes,* in which the courage, daring, and financial entrepreneurship of the Brazilian explorers are lauded. The success of his son-in-law is also a famous story that emphasizes Borba Gato's early efforts to elude crown authority.[27] The fact that their efforts were privately financed and carried out without direct participation of royal authorities was both an essential aspect of their actions and a central part of their characterizations as historical figures. They have been inscribed in Brazilian histories as either heroic pursuers of private and individualistic goals or roguish opponents to crown authority.[28] Their admirable efforts as entrepreneurs and courageous, daring explorers are countered by a view of the crown as overbearing and over-regulatory. Despite this view of colonial authorities as powerful and effective, the discovery of gold by Borba Gato and so many other individuals who rushed into

23. Monteiro, "São Paulo in the Seventeenth Century," 217, 248.

24. The *cruzado* was worth between 400 and 480 *réis,* the basic unit of Portuguese currency. One hundred *réis* was worth eight pence in English currency in 1705. Cardoso, "The History of Mining in Colonial Brazil," 104–5.

25. Cardoso, "The History of Mining in Colonial Brazil," 103.

26. Cardoso, "The History of Mining in Colonial Brazil," 104.

27. Boxer summarized much of the story of Manuel de Borba Gato in *The Golden Age,* chap. 3. He regarded many of the secondary accounts as untrustworthy or fanciful, particularly that of Vasconcellos, *História antiga.*

28. It seems to me that even Pais's failure is regarded as a good thing, because it led to Borba Gato's success. His failure also avoided an immediate or earlier crown presence in the mining region.

the region meant that the Portuguese crown had a difficult time regulating *privately controlled* gold production.[29]

The Portuguese authorities had anticipated the need for regulations controlling private production of gold in Brazil. The 1618 mining code promulgated in response to the discovery of small quantities of gold in the captaincy of São Paulo addressed the issues of claim registration, measurements of awarded mining grants, and responsibilities of miners and royal officials in the mining areas. In this and all subsequent codes addressing the working of mines in Brazil, the discoverer or co-discoverers of gold became entitled to specific allotments of land, which they then had to register with a colonial official. The crown also took an allotment from the discovered site for itself, and subsequently arriving miners could ask for land grants if they had the capital and labor to work their allotments. From these privately exploited mining lands, the crown expected payment of one-fifth of all revenues.[30]

With no knowledge of the terrain in which ore deposits were later found in Minas Gerais, the designers of the 1618 mining code called for the establishment of a foundry house in a location convenient to the mines, to which miners would bring nuggets and dust to be rendered into gold bars. The foundry officials would take all the miners' gold and return four-fifths of it as bars.[31] In this manner, the crown would receive its *quinto,* the fifth portion of all gold mined in the region. Because of the actual conditions in the mining region, virtually no foundry location would have been convenient to all the miners. In view of the actual simplicity of production techniques, colonial officials could exercise little control over mining activities. The crown therefore had few means at its disposal to guarantee that miners bothered to bring their gold to the foundry.

Although the provisions of the 1618 mining code were ill-suited to alluvial mining, they nonetheless provided lasting precedence for crown policies throughout the remainder of the colonial period. In confronting the problems of tax collection in the gold-mining regions of São Paulo and later in Minas Gerais, the crown reconsidered its policies and indicated its flexibility and willingness to seek alternative solutions to pressing colonial

29. Borba Gato himself is transformed into a loyal citizen of the crown in the later conflict between *paulistas* and *emboabas* (gold miners from Bahia) and a deliverer of some of the earliest taxed gold to the king. Boxer, *The Golden Age,* 53.

30. Alvará, 15 August 1618, reproduced in Pontes, "Revisão dos regimentos," *RAPM* 7 (1902): 834–48. See in particular articles 1, 2, 3, 4.

31. Alvará, 15 August 1618, in Pontes, "Revisão dos regimentos," 834–48; see articles 53–57.

problems. Despite several reconsiderations, however, the policy calling for the establishment of foundry houses remained in force, and the town of Sabará acquired its own as did the principal towns of all other *comarcas*.[32]

Royal officials understood that voluntary compliance with tax regulations was an unreasonable expectation to have of ordinary citizens. As the royal adviser Alexandre de Gusmão asked in 1750: "Is it possible that anyone should voluntarily surrender a fifth part of his wealth when it was possible to save it with little risk and trouble?"[33] As circumstances demonstrated, there was very little risk and trouble for miners to save their wealth "because of the various roads and paths known to the miners by which they are able to reach their destination without passing by the smelting houses."[34] With the mining fields spanning such large areas in Minas Gerais, evading payment of the fifths was much more convenient than was compliance with the law.

More effective enforcement of tax collection from mines than that provided by the system of foundry houses was hampered by defenders of metropolitan interests in Lisbon. In 1695, the solicitor to the Royal Treasury opposed measures to be taken against contrabandists discovered in the port of Lisbon on the grounds that at least this gold would enter the kingdom of Portugal. If it did not enrich the king himself, such smuggling did indeed benefit the king's subjects, "who, as much and even more than the Treasury itself, made Kings rich."[35] The solicitor argued that a system of rigorous enforcement against contrabandists in Portugal might encourage miners to seek alternative destinations for their gold, with the most likely result that even more gold than ever wound up in foreign ports to the detriment of the Portuguese empire as a whole. The difficulty of policing contrabandists while they were still in Brazil was understood, but rigorous enforcement of contraband laws in the metropolitan port had more powerful opponents and entailed greater political costs.

---

32. After 1750, when capitation for the fifths ended, miners were required to bring all gold extracted to the foundry houses located in the capital of each *comarca*. Alvará de 3 de dezembro de 1750, *RAPM* 7 (1901): 917–20.

33. Alexandre de Gusmão to Friar Gaspar da Encarnação, 19 December 1750, cited in Cardoso, "A History of Mining in Colonial Brazil," 432.

34. Artur de Sá e Menezes to the king, 12 June 1697, in A. H. C. Doc. of Rio, no. 2080, cited in Cardoso, "The Collection of the Fifths in Brazil, 1695–1709," *HAHR* 20 (August 1940):362.

35. Acta of the Overseas Council, 4 November 1695, cited in Cardoso, "The Collection of the Fifths," 372. These measures included searching arriving ships from Rio and Bahia and seizing any untaxed cargo, including nuggets, gold dust, and fraudulently produced gold bars.

In 1702, partly to protect metropolitan contrabandists and partly to prevent diversion of gold from Portuguese to foreign ports, the Overseas
Council reiterated that the fiscalization of gold shipments should take
place in Brazil and not in Portugal.[36] Consequently, a royal mint was established in Rio de Janeiro to augment the system of foundry houses as the
means to collect the fifths in Brazil. Although colonial officials offered
substantial incentives to encourage miners to make use of the mint,[37] the
results were a substantial disappointment. It was estimated that only one
in twenty persons brought their gold to the mint; others disposed of it
elsewhere.[38] Smuggling gold out of Brazil continued, and the total receipts
of fifths declined even as the production of gold in the region of Minas
Gerais was known to be growing rapidly.

The crown's desire to regulate the region's gold output mounted as the
mining economy of Minas Gerais began to experience increased production. Increasingly, the crown chose to ignore the interests of those who had
stood to gain from the uninterrupted flow of contraband into the mother
country. Still, until the true potential of the mining region was understood
in Lisbon, the king remained attentive to the demands of sugar planters in
the northeast. For the first decade of the eighteenth century, colonial policies continued to favor the interests of these Brazilian colonists over those
of the *paulistas* who first advocated promotion of the gold-mining economy. The principal concern of northeastern planters was that the new
mines would deprive them of labor for their sugar plantations.

As both the export-oriented production of sugar cane in the northeast
and internally oriented agricultural economy of São Paulo depended on the
availability and exploitation of slave labor, the colonists of Brazil expected
that whoever discovered substantial quantities of gold in the backlands of
crown territory would use slave laborers to mine it. The Portuguese crown
also shared the expectation that someone other than Portuguese colonists
would do the actual digging for precious minerals. The 1618 mining code
defined a worked mine (*mina povoada*) as one having at least two *slaves*

36. Acta of the Overseas Council, 6 March 1702, cited in Cardoso, "The Collection of the
Fifths," 372.
37. One incentive was that the mint was to make gold coins equal in value to those in
Portugal; these could then be easily shipped home. A second advantage was to pay 20 percent
more at the mint for the gold than the fixed (i.e., government-declared) value of gold in the
mining region. These measures were thought to encourage the flow of gold to the mint in
Rio.
38. Arquivo Histórico Colonial, documents of Rio, no. 3121, cited in Cardoso, "The Collection of the Fifths," 371.

or four other laborers present. Lacking such a force, the miner had to demonstrate that he himself actually labored in the mine or forfeit his claim.[39] Provisions of the code protected miners from imprisonment for their debts and from seizure of assets as payment for debts. Among the protected assets were mining equipment and *slaves*.[40]

Later legislation envisioned the slaves used in mining as Indians. When Salvador Correia de Sá e Benevides was named Administrator of the Mines in 1644, his authority in the region of São Paulo was detailed in a new decree. This new *regimento* specifically mentioned Indians as potential workers in the mines and also as explorers for deposit sites. If Benevides required *indios não domesticados* (Indians living in the interior) for use as laborers, he was to consult the Captain-General of São Paulo for instructions about how to capture such Indians. If Benevides came on deposits of large quantities of gold, the crown was prepared to authorize the further capture of Indians to mine the deposits.[41]

As the population of available Indians had declined toward the end of the seventeenth century, the slave-labor force in eighteenth-century Minas Gerais came to be almost totally African slaves and their descendants. Issued after the verification of major gold deposits and after the first miners had begun work in the region, the *Regimento das minas do ouro de 1702* codified the essential character of the Brazilian mines as being a place of free mine owners and unfree mine workers. In this code, the measurement and distribution of mining lands related directly to the labor force available to the miner. According to its provisions, the laborers in gold mines were mostly African slaves.[42]

The 1702 *regimento* called for the discoverer of a gold deposit to register the claim to the deposit site with an official known as the Superintendent of the Mines. In a move to gain the compliance of *paulista* settlers in the region, Manuel de Borba Gato (rehabilitated by a new governor as a founder father of the mining lands) was appointed to this position for the *comarca* of Rio das Velhas (later renamed Sabará).[43] Once the claim was

39. Alvará, 15 August 1618, *RAPM* 7 (1902): 841.

40. Alvará, 15 August 1618, *RAPM* 7 (1902): 845.

41. "Regimento de sua majestade para as minas do sul, 7 June 1644," in *RIHGB* 56: 1a, 111. This further confirms the connection between the crown's desire to find and exploit gold deposits and its unwillingness to condemn the virtual enslavement of Indians in Brazil.

42. "Regimento das minas do ouro de 1702," in Ministerio da educação e saude, Biblioteca Nacional, *Documentos históricos* 80 (1948): 329–44.

43. Boxer, *The Golden Age*, 64.

registered, another official, the *Guarda-Mor* of the Mines, awarded the discoverer two land grants, known as *datas*, for the discovered area. An additional *data* was allotted to the Royal Treasury. Others wishing to work the discovered gold deposit could, on request, receive a *data* based on the number of slaves they owned: thirty *braças*[44] to those who owned twelve slaves or more, or two and one-half *braças* for each slave owned, should there be fewer than twelve. One stated purpose of this system of distribution was to provide equal treatment of miners, both rich and poor, but clearly it also served to maximize the productivity of mining grants.[45]

The 1702 *regimento* reflected the changing conception of Brazil's labor force as in this document the term *slave* was linked with Africans. Article 5 awarded two and one-half *braças* per slave, whereas Article 7 described the award as two and one-half *braças* per Black.[46] The *regimento* did not mention Indians as slaves (which indeed it could not, for Indian slavery was illegal at this date) but rather as paid workers of the crown who would work the *data* allotted to the Royal Treasury. The 1702 code thus indicated both that the labor force under the control of private individuals was composed of enslaved Africans and that the use of African slaves in mining was, from the crown's point of view, desirable. The *regimento* specifically limited the role of the at least nominally free Indians to that of laborers for the crown.[47]

Although the mining legislation demonstrated support for the use of African slaves, for the first decade of the eighteenth century the Portuguese crown prohibited an unrestricted flow of African labor to the mines to assure the supply of slave labor for sugar planters from the northeast.[48]

44. The calculation of thirty *braças* in modern terms is somewhat problematic as the term *braça* has multiple definitions. My opinion is that the reference here is to *braças quadradas*, squared *braças*, in which case thirty *braças* equals a little over nine hectares, or 22.6 acres.

45. "Regimento das minas do ouro de 1702," article 5, 330–32. The degree to which all the provisions of this mining code were enacted and the levels of compliance with these provisions are not completely understood. A brief look at the *datas* registered with the Guarda-Mor of the *comarca* of Sabará indicated that at least some claims were awarded based on the number of slaves owned, but a detailed analysis of *datas* in Minas Gerais still awaits further research. One obvious flaw in the 1702 code that suggests that it was largely inadequate for its objectives was that it does not deal with the issue of water rights. See Robert Southey, *History of Brazil* (London, 1817–19), 3, p. 251.

46. "Regimento das minas do ouro de 1702," article 5; see in particular 332.

47. "Regimento das minas do ouro de 1702," article 22, 339–40.

48. Alvará régio, 20 January 1701, in Arquivo do Estado de São Paulo, *DI* 51 (1930);12–14.

The crown's attempt, during this decade, to accommodate the interests of both miners and planters satisfied neither group and in fact served only to place colonists and crown officials at considerable odds with one another.

Crown policies in support of sugar planters in the northeast dated from the last quarter of the seventeenth century when the sugar economy began to suffer from the competition of cane plantations in the West Indies.[49] As prices for their sugar fell increasingly lower, many Brazilian planters became heavily indebted and sought the crown's help in protecting their economic assets. The crown responded to their petitions by issuing decrees that prevented seizures of working assets as payments for debts. Among the protected assets were the land, the sugar mill, and the slaves of the planters. First extended to those planters in the principal areas of sugar cultivation, such protection was eventually extended to other areas in Brazil. Toward the end of the seventeenth century, no planters in any state in Brazil could suffer a foreclosure of their estates for debts incurred.[50] In this way, the king ensured that colonists could continue to grow sugar in Brazil.

The sugar planters were quick to take advantage of the broad nature of the protections offered to them by the crown, and soon there were complaints that the planters abused their lenders by always increasing their debt without risk of overextending their capital. In the face of these abuses, the crown put an end to the incurring of large debts by the planters when it announced in 1694 that planters could be foreclosed on all assets except their *engenhos* (sugar mills) and the slaves that worked there.[51]

In the initial years of the eighteenth century, when the gold rush was first gathering momentum, the problems facing the northeastern sugar economy had not diminished. A contemporary observer and author of the famous treatise *Cultura e opulência do Brasil*, the Jesuit priest André João Antonil, saw the gold boom as the death knell of the sugar plantation as

49. Frederic Mauro, *Nova história e novo mundo* (São Paulo: Editôra Perspectiva, 1969),112; Schwartz, *Sugar Plantations in the Formation of Brazilian Society*, 183–84.

50. See, for example, "Provisão—Concede aos moradores da capitania de Parahiba não poderem ser executados nas fábricas de seus engenhos," 4 December 1694, in José Justino de Andrade e Silva, *Colleção chronológica da legislação portuguesa compilada e annotada* (Lisbon: Imprensa Nacional, 1859), 10, 360.

51. "Provisão—Declara a de 12 de janeiro deste anno, sobre as execuções nas propiedades dos engenhos e lavouras de assucar do Rio de Janeiro," in Silva, *Colleção*, 10, 359. On the question of debt moratoria in an earlier period in Bahia, see Schwartz, *Sugar Plantations in the Formation of Brazilian Society*, 195.

prices of all commodities rose rapidly in response to the demand created by miners.[52] This rise was especially true for the prices of African slaves. Indebted planters were sorely tempted by, and many succumbed to, the allure of high prices for slaves and sold them to entrepreneurs heading for the mines. Other planters who wished to continue cane cultivation could not compete with the prices that miners offered for slaves, and thus a labor shortage in the northeast was one result of the gold rush. The crown faced a considerable dilemma because, on the one hand, it did not want to stifle gold production in the now bustling mining region. On the other hand, it was not yet prepared at this early juncture to abandon the cultivation of sugar cane on which, in the king's words, "the common commerce of all my vassals" still depended.[53] Unable to resolve the contradictions of this situation, the crown nonetheless acted to control the supply and distribution of slave labor in Brazil.

The crown's 1694 withdrawal of absolute protection for planters from foreclosures unintentionally served to increase the attractiveness of selling slaves to miners for exorbitant prices in the first years of the gold boom. This policy worked against the interests of the Royal Treasury, which apparently agreed with Antonil's assessment that the sugar economy in the northeast represented the "true mines of Brazil and Portugal."[54] The crown wanted to maintain an ample supply of slaves for the northeast, and to help achieve this goal, in an *alvará régio* issued on 20 January 1701, the king prohibited the planters from selling their laborers to miners.[55]

At the same time, the crown decreed that only a portion of new African slaves arriving in Brazil could be sold by the slave traders to the *paulistas*.[56] "So that the paulistas do not lack for slaves for the working of their mines, nor that the other inhabitants of the whole state of Brazil should not lack those slaves needed for their cultivations and the operation of engenhos," the king declared that of all the Africans arriving in Rio de Janeiro from Angola, only two hundred could be sold to the *paulistas* for use in the mines.[57] The offer of so limited a number of Africans was a poor compromise for the *paulistas*, and the decree prohibited the sale of any other

52. Antonil, *Cultura*, 171.
53. Alvará régio, 20 January 1701, Arquivo do Estado de São Paulo, *DI* 51 (1930):12–14.
54. Antonil, *Cultura*, 194.
55. Alvará régio, 20 January 1701, *DI* 51 (1930): 12–14.
56. In this early period of the gold rush, most who entered into the newly discovered mining lands were *paulistas*, and for this reason the language of the royal decrees regulating miners refers specifically to them.
57. Alvará régio, 20 January 1701, *DI* 51 (1930): 12–14.

slaves to the mines from elsewhere in Brazil. Thus, the crown protected
northeastern sugar planters at the expense of the *paulistas*.[58]

At the same time that the flow of African slaves to the mines was being
restricted, the crown asserted that Indians from the *aldeias*, Indian villages
run by religious orders, could be used to work in the mines to a very
limited degree. When, in January 1701, the crown first proposed to work
the royal *datas* with these Indians, the king stated that only five Indians
from each *aldeia* could be removed for mine work and that each year the
workers were to be allowed to return home so that they would not lose
"the love of their villages."[59] That any *aldeia* Indians actually spent time
working royal *datas* remains in doubt; shortly after the king's decree outlining this new system of Indian-labor exploitation, Governor Artur de Sá
e Menezes ordered all Indians who might be in the mines to return to their
aldeias in São Paulo to defend them and the city of Santos from the threat
of Spanish attack.[60] Both these decrees suggest that Indians were not available to miners in numbers sufficient to make up for the restriction placed
on the sale of African slaves to *paulista* miners.[61]

The governor of Brazil, Dom Alvaro da Silveira e Albuquerque, argued
that restricting sales of Africans to miners was not in the king's best interests. Residing in the capital of Salvador in August 1702, the governor
wrote to the king to advise him that two hundred slaves were too few to
satisfy the *paulistas*. He pointed out that if the *paulistas* could not acquire
additional slaves by buying them in Bahia, all business in the mining region would collapse. Such a consequence would mean that the royal revenues generated by both the mining and the levels of commerce in Bahia
that such mining had fostered would be diminished.[62] In a later letter dated

58. The crown, in fact, took special care to ensure that no one who bought slaves in Rio
would then resell them to the *paulistas*. The *alvará* called for the registration of the names of
buyers and sellers of slaves in Rio and the names and markings of the slaves destined for the
mines. The penalty for selling additional slaves to the *paulistas* was a fine, double the value of
the slave — one-half of this sum going to the informant and one-half going to the Royal
Treasury. Of course, if the crown was the informant, the entire fine reverted to the treasury.
Alvará régio, 20 January 1701, *DI* 51 (1930): 13.

59. Carta régia, 30 January 1701, *DI* 51 (1930): 16.

60. Bando — De Arthur de Sá e Menezes mandando que se recolhessem ás suas aldeias os
indios das minas, 26 November 1701, in *DI* 51 (1930): 50.

61. The Brazilian mining region thus was distinct from those in Spanish America in yet
another way — there were no large populations of Indians with considerable expertise in met-
alworking and refining ore in Minas Gerais as there were in the highlands of colonial Peru
and in colonial Mexico. Introduction of an outside labor force was therefore necessary.

62. Dom Alvaro da Silveira e Albuquerque to the king, 2 August 1702, in *DI* 51 (1930):
122–24.

10 March 1703, Dom Alvaro reaffirmed the connection between the free flow of slaves to the mining region and the enrichment of the Royal Treasury. He put it succinctly: *"[N]ão hindo escravos, não haverá quintos"* — no slaves, no fifth — to his mind it was that simple.[63]

Dom Alvaro recommended to the king that 20 percent of the arriving African slaves be reserved for planters in the northeast to be sold to them at reasonable prices. The crown should allow the rest of the arriving slaves to be sold freely to miners or anyone who wanted to buy them. Such a change would remedy *paulistas'* claims that no further mines would be discovered without laborers to work them. It would also allow the crown to protect the sugar planters without creating consequences prejudicial to its own treasury.[64]

Although the governor was advancing the miners' point of view, sugar planters also had outspoken defenders. The Jesuit Antonil argued that agriculture was a more natural and profitable enterprise for colonists to be engaged in. He also attacked the gold mines by criticizing the scandalous and ruthless behavior that miners evinced.[65] Observing the disturbances that the mining boom brought to what he viewed as the traditional and proper ways of life in Brazil and condemning the fruits of avarice that the mining life bore in the colony, Antonil wrote: "There is no judicious person who would not admit that God permitted the discovery of so much gold in these mines so as to punish Brazil with it, just as in this time of so many wars, he punishes the Europeans with [the discovery of] iron."[66]

The policy of restricting the numbers of slaves sold to the *paulistas* might have been entirely avoided had the crown been able to finance or otherwise promote a massive increase in the slave trade to Brazil. Like the restriction on sales to miners, the expansion of sales to all Brazilians might also have kept prices low enough for northeastern planters to maintain their access to the slave market. For whatever reasons, this situation did not develop.[67] In July 1706, the king again instructed the new governor of

63. Dom Alvaro da Silveira e Albuquerque to Dom Rodrigo da Costa, 10 March 1703, in *DI* 51 (1930):155.

64. Dom Alvaro da Silveira e Albuquerque to the king, 2 August 1702, in *DI* 51 (1930):122–24.

65. Antonil, *Cultura*, 194.

66. "Nem ha pessoa prudente que não confesse haver Deus permitido que se descubra nas minas tanto ouro para castigar com ele ao Brasil, assim como está castigando no mesmo tempo tão abundante de guerras, aos europeus com o ferro," Antonil, *Cultura*, 195.

67. An in-depth analysis of the slave trade to Minas Gerais in the first decade of the eighteenth century is not currently available in secondary sources. For a recent discussion of

Rio de Janeiro, Dom Fernando Martins Mascarenhas de Lancastro, to
strictly enforce the annual quota of two hundred slaves to the mines.[68] In
view of the number of false starts for mining in Brazil, it is no wonder that
the crown was slow to react to the new potential of Brazilian mines. In the
end, however, the crown's analysis of the situation changed as it became
clearer that the mines as well as the sugar plantations could enrich Portugal. With this new assessment of the situation, on 24 March 1709, the
king revoked the limitation on the number of slaves going to the mines.
The *paulistas* were now free to buy and sell slaves as they wished. They
could bring to the mines all the Africans that they saw fit "for experience
having demonstrated that from this freedom everyone will have the greater
conveniences, and much increase to my fifths."[69]

By amending its policy controlling the distribution of slave sales in Brazil, the Portuguese crown had finally equated its interests with that of the
miners. The estimated production of the gold mines in Brazil during the
first decade of the eighteenth century exceeded one thousand *arrobas* or
thirty-two thousand pounds of gold.[70] Improved methods of collecting the
fifths of this gold depended on the colonial government's ability to monitor the free trade and commerce of the mining region. The crown could
not easily monitor what was not legal, including the traffic in slaves. The
lifting of restrictions on slave sales to Minas Gerais restored these transactions to the arena of legalized commerce and thereby transformed them
into a potential source of taxable revenue for the crown. Indeed for a
significant part of the eighteenth century, the slaves themselves became the
principal source of royal revenues in the mining region.[71]

The slaves in Sabará and throughout the mining region became an early
target of royal taxation in part because they so quickly became the vast
majority of the population. With the lifting of restrictions on sales of

---

the slave trade to Minas Gerais, see Laird W. Bergad, "After the Mining Boom: Demographic
and Economic Aspects of Slavery in Mariana, Minas Gerais, 1750–1808," *LARR* 31:1
(1996): 67–97.

68. Carta régia to D. Fernando Martins Mascarenhas de Lancastro, 17 July 1706, in *DI*
52: 34.

69. "[P]or ter mostrado a experiencia desta liberdade poderão todos ter as mayores con-
veniencias, e muito ascressimo aos meus quintos," Ordem régia, dirigida ao governador do
Rio de Janeiro, March 24, 1709, in *DI* 52: 147–49.

70. Antonil, *Cultura*, 167. One thousand *arrobas* would be equivalent to something between twenty-six and thirty-two thousand pounds of gold.

71. For most of the first half of the eighteenth century, the crown relied on taxation of
slaves to collect the royal fifth in Minas Gerais. See the discussion of capitation taxes in
Chapter 6.

slaves to miners, the demographic transformation of this area of Brazil was allowed to proceed unfettered by colonial authorities. The population changes wrought by the gold rush in Brazil were as profound as the economic ones. Unlike the northeast of Brazil, which began its export economy with Indian slaves and later switched to African slaves, and unlike the captaincy of São Paulo, which developed on the basis of Indian slavery in various agricultural enterprises, the economy of the mining region developed through an initial and persistent dependence on the importation of enslaved African *men*.

The early settlers of Minas Gerais who came to make their fortunes in mining deemed it best to purchase a labor force of mostly male workers. Bras de Barros Soares, for example, was a well-to-do colonist in Sabará who had invested almost exclusively in mining. Writing his will in August 1719, Bras declared ownership of twenty-eight male slaves and only one female.[72] Numerous investments like his, repeated decade after decade, created a world of mostly male workers, in which women were at times only one-fifth, one-sixth, or even one-eighth of the slave population.[73]

In their own patterns of migration, the free colonists of Minas Gerais replicated the imbalances in the slave population. The sons of *paulista* settlers to the south, the sons of Bahian planters to the north, and aspiring men from Portugal itself streamed into the gold-bearing lands to make their fortunes as slave owners. Significantly, these men often came unaccompanied by family members other than brothers. They did not bring sisters, and they did not bring wives. Nor did White women whom they might marry readily follow these men into the frontier after mining claims were established and fortunes were accumulated.[74] Men who migrated to Sabará in the wake of Manuel de Borba Gato's discoveries often lived and died there as bachelors. Lourenço de Mello e Madureira, for example, came to the mines from São Paulo. In his 1722 will, he identified himself as a *solteiro* (bachelor) who never married. He owned twelve men and one woman.[75] Sebastião Pereira de Aguilar, who came from Bahia and is re-

---

72. Twenty-five of twenty-eight were identified as Africans; three were identified only by name. Testamento de Bras de Barros Soares, 25 August 1719, *Livro de registo de testamento* (1716–25), MOSMG, fol. 33.

73. See Chapter 2 for a discussion of sex ratios in Minas Gerais.

74. In his study of eighteenth-century emigration from the northern provinces of Portugal, Donald Ramos demonstrated that men moved alone. In those areas that supplied colonists to Minas Gerais, the numbers of women in Portuguese towns greatly exceeded the number of men. See "From Minho to Minas," 641.

75. Testamento de Lourenço de Mello e Madureira, 14 August 1722, *Livro de registo de testamento* (1716–25), MOSMG, fol. 217v.

garded as one of the principal and most successful founders of Sabará, is described in his 1716 will as a bachelor as well as owner of forty male slaves and nine women.[76] Antônio da Rocha Flores and Francisco Roiz Netto were both Portuguese men who came to Sabará as bachelors and remained so throughout their lives.[77] In its initial configuration, the population of Sabará was composed of a few male slaveholders who owned a much larger number of adult, mostly male, slaves. For the most part, these early slaveholders were White; virtually all their slaves were Black.[78]

Much of what transpired in Sabará and the other *comarcas* of the mining region over the course of the "miners' century" can be attributed to the extremely unbalanced sex ratio among African slaves forcibly imported into the mining lands as well as to the propensity of free male migrants to make their fortunes in the mines in the absence of White women of equal social standing. Neither of these patterns of migration can be regarded as natural or obvious consequences of pre-existing conditions over which individuals had little control.[79] Both patterns reflected the colonizers' ideological commitments to inequalities — the inequality of slavery as a social and economic institution and the inequality inherent in gender role assignments. Only men should be explorers and frontier settlers; only men should perform the labors of mining; only men should exercise real power and authority in a nonegalitarian regime.[80] The exploitation of enslaved women in Sabará was compounded by their assigned role in the labor force as sexual servants for male owners. In some respects, the exploitation of White women in the *comarca* was expressed in their initial absence and

76. Testamento de Sebastião Pereira de Aguilar, 27 October 1716, *Livro de registo de testamento* (1716–25), MOSMG, fol. 13. Vasconcellos names Aguilar as a *fundidor* in Sabará and Caethé. *História antiga,* 258.

77. Testamento de Antônio da Rocha Flores, 27 October 1740, *Livro de registo de testamento* (11 dezembro 1739), MOSMG, fol. 72; Testamento de Francisco Roiz Netto, 6 July 1744, *Livro de registo de testamento* (3 março 1743), MOSMG, fol. 70v.

78. The *paulistas* could have been *mamelucos,* of mixed Indian-White parentage. For a discussion of *paulista* families and the pattern of sending sons to the frontier in search of new resources and wealth, see Alida C. Metcalf, *Family and Frontier in Colonial Brazil, Santana de Parnaíba, 1580–1822* (Berkeley and Los Angeles: University of California Press, 1992).

79. Current literature on the slave trade holds that the sex ratio among slaves available on the international market was not nearly as unbalanced as the documents on slaveholding in Minas Gerais suggest. By buying a great many more men than women slaves, the early colonists in Minas Gerais evidently opted for an extremely high sex ratio among their slaves. Joseph Miller, for example, writes of a two-to-one loss of men to women from Angola in the eighteenth century. Miller, *Way of Death,* 162.

80. There is some scattered evidence that freed women worked as prospectors for gold; but slave women were not purchased to work in mining.

exclusion from the riches and power that White men hoped to gain and did gain in the rush for gold.

Male settlers in Sabará were strongly committed to the institution of slavery. They demonstrated continued support for the idea that most adult male slaves should remain as slaves for their entire lives. These men demonstrated far less commitment to the idea that women slaves should also remain as permanent slaves; they relied instead on the social and legal construction of gender roles in colonial society and on racial discrimination to keep freed women in their subordinated positions.

Despite their strong commitment to slavery, the bachelor settlers of Sabará valued their children so much that they often freed them from slavery and named them as heirs. For example, the *paulista* bachelor Lourenço de Mello e Madureira had five mulatto children by his slave woman. He freed them and requested that his mother (and heir) make sure that these children were treated as true grandchildren. Significantly, Lourenço did not free the mother of his children; he commanded her to stay with and raise his offspring.[81] The Portuguese bachelors Antônio da Rocha Flores and Francisco Roiz Netto acted in a similar fashion. Flores freed his two slave children, named them as heirs, and commanded their enslaved mother, Roza, "to serve and to raise" the children for six years.[82] Roiz Netto demanded that his slave woman, Antônia, should continue to serve as a slave to their three mulatto children for twelve years. The children were freed immediately and named as heirs.[83]

These bachelor settlers were more concerned with avoiding bequests of freedom, power, and authority to the women who had served them sexually than they were concerned about long-term transformations in the nature of slaveholding in the colony. Their sexual behavior and the manumission decisions that followed set into motion in Sabará a demographic transformation in slaveholding patterns with few parallels in Brazil and none at all in the rest of the New World. These "family-motivated" manumissions of children, in combination with other economically motivated manumissions of women slaves, helped to demolish the absolute linkage of slaveholding with whiteness. By 1805, two-thirds of the free people of

81. "[E] minha may faça que elles logrem as prieminencias de seus nettos." Testamento de Lourenço de Mello e Madureira, 14 August 1722, *Livro de registo de testamento* (1716–25), MOSMG, fol. 217v.

82. Testamento de Antônio da Rocha Flores, 27 October 1740, *Livro de registo de testamento* (11 dezembro 1739), MOSMG, fol. 72.

83. Testamento de Francisco Roiz Netto, 6 July 1744, *Livro de registo de testamento* (3 março 1743), MOSMG, fol. 70v.

Minas Gerais were non-Whites, and these non-Whites, when they could afford to, owned slaves themselves.[84] (See Chapter 5 on manumissions.)

The development of a largely non-White free society in the course of the miners' century can also be attributed in part to the accessibility of so much gold both in the mining areas themselves as well as in the urban areas, like the town of Sabará, that served as thriving commercial centers for the outlying *comarcas*.[85] For reasons that are discussed in the following chapter, both the methods of ore extraction and the strategies of marketing often put quantities of gold directly into the hands of slaves who then used it to purchase freedom. Even at the end of the colonial period, slaves born in Africa occasionally joined the ranks of the free and the ranks of slave-holders in Sabará. For example, in his will of February 1806, Jorge da Fonseca Ferreira identified himself as a *preto mina,* a Black from the Costa da Mina in Africa who had become owner to two slaves. Ferreira explained in his will that all his assets "were acquired by my own industry." The economic opportunities of the mining region had allowed him both to become free and to accumulate wealth for himself.[86]

In 1702 when Manuel de Borba Gato became Superintendent of the Mines in the *comarca* of Sabará,[87] the population of the free colonizers there was almost entirely White. Over time, however, Africans, *crioulos* (persons of African descent born in Brazil), *mulatos, pardos,* and *cabras* (various mixtures of Africans and Europeans) all appeared in the ranks of the free (or freed) and in the ranks of slaveholders.[88] It was even possible in Sabará for those still enslaved to exercise ownership of other slaves. In 1730, for example, João de Souza Sottomayor freed his slave woman Lucrecia, a native of São Thome. Lucrecia used as payment for her freedom her own Mina slave woman.[89] Although the ownership of slaves by other slaves was illegal in Minas Gerais, prohibition of this practice was not

---

84. In Sabará, slaves were 54 percent of the total population; free people were 46 percent of the total. "População da provincia de Minas Gerais," *RAPM* (1899): 294–95.

85. On quantities of gold found in Minas Gerais, see Pinto, *O ouro brasileiro.*

86. The executor "puxara para o captiveiro." Testamento de Jorge da Fonseca Ferreira, 8 February 1806, *Livro de registo de testamento* (4 março 1805), MOSMG, fol. 22.

87. At that time, the *comarca* was called Rio das Velhas; it was later renamed Sabará.

88. *Crioulos* were persons of African descent born in Brazil; Africans were often referred to, especially in earlier documents, as *pretos; mulatos, pardos,* and *cabras* were all of Euro-pean-African mixed ancestry. The meaning of the word *cabra* appears to differ according to regions in Brazil. In Sabará, the terms *pardo* and *cabra* increased in frequency in documents in the course of the eighteenth century. In particular, the term *pardo* appeared infrequently early in the eighteenth century as compared with the term *mulato.*

89. Carta de alforria, 22 July 1730, *Livro de notas* (25 de junho de 1729), MOSMG, fol. 141v.

enforced.[90] The manumission records for eighteenth-century Sabará indicate that approximately 3 percent of the manumitted adults acquired their freedom by offering as substitutes to their masters slaves of their own.[91]

The initial demographic portrait of White masters and Black slaves in colonial Sabará gave way to a society that allowed for non-Whites to be free and to victimize other non-Whites in a master–slave relationship. In 1805, more than half the *comarca* of Sabará's population of 110,000 was enslaved. Fundamentally nonegalitarian in social, economic, and political terms, the postmining boom era in Sabará provides evidence of increasing concentration of wealth in the hands of fewer slaveholders than ever before. As fewer people became wealthier and most became relatively poorer in Sabará, the acquisition of wealth (and of slaves as wealth) was not defined as the exclusive privilege of those who were of White European descent.

Just as the inequalities of a slave regime were preserved in Sabará over time, so too were those of socially constructed gender roles. The initial extreme imbalances in the sex ratios among the enslaved and free Whites diminished in the course of the century, but for neither group did these imbalances entirely disappear. The growth in the population of free women led to a significant number of women slaveholders whose behavior as owners is examined in Chapter 5. The situation for the much larger numbers of slave women in the *comarca* worsened considerably in the postmining boom era as their economic opportunities diminished and the likelihood that they would remain as slaves for life increased. For all free women in colonial Brazil, Portuguese law offered certain protections and control over communally owned property, but only if these women entered into a legal state of marriage. The precedents set by the early bachelor settlers were, however, all too enduring, and men of all races avoided marriage unless it was to an economically attractive partner who did not rank beneath them in the racial pecking order of the community. Free men continued to outnumber free women in Sabará and continued to exercise power and authority over them.

The Portuguese crown created the initial framework for the development of a slave-based gold-mining colony in the interior of Brazil. Legislative decrees linked private access to mining lands to ownership and control over enslaved labor. Crown officials maintained a steady interest in mining

90. "Estabelece que nenhum negro poderá possuir escravos ou bens," Bando do Governador D. Pedro de Almeida, Conde de Assumar, 21 November 1719, APMSC, Códice 11, fol. 282v.

91. The number of adult slaves is 681. See Chapter 5 on manumissions.

revenues and toward that end frequently expressed discontent with strategies of slave control employed by owners. They saw too much freedom
and disorder in the master-slave relationships in Sabará and objected to the
disappearance of the color line as the defining marker of who was slave
and who was free. Crown officials also identified the bachelorhood of free
men in Minas Gerais as hostile to a stable and controlled population; in
their discourse, they tended to blame the women for their lack of legal
attachments to these men.

Although the kings of Portugal had to wait two hundred years for the
dream of golden riches from the New World to be realized, the discovery
of the land of the general mines finally fulfilled at least some of their expectations. The long wait did not, however, prepare the Portuguese for
circumstances that they had not seen before: dispersed gold deposits so
easy to mine and so difficult to monopolize. Even with an anticipated labor force that would have no legal rights to speak of, the crown found that
governing a frontier colony so far from the coast of Brazil and from other
established settlements was a challenge at best. Moreover, its efforts were
frequently subverted by the free population as much as by the enslaved.

In the following chapters, the challenges that the slave society in Sabará
posed for colonial governance continue to be evident. The politics of fiscalization were often complicated by the economic and social arrangements
that grew from making gold mining and urban-based commerce profitable
for the free colonists. As some of these chapters show, even the influence
of the Catholic Church in Minas Gerais was insufficient to impose on the
population the orderliness that would have satisfied crown administrators.
The efforts of the enslaved men and women of Sabará to achieve any and
all degrees of freedom were designed to thwart colonial rulers. Their successes, discussed later, provoked considerable official dismay.

2

Patterns of Living and Working Among Slaves, Ex-Slaves, and Free Persons in Colonial Sabará

In his will of 5 October 1742, Captain Mathias de Crasto Porto, one of Sabará's early and most successful Portuguese immigrants, named his children as heirs to his estate. Although Mathias was a lifelong bachelor (in the sense of remaining unmarried), in the years 1702–36 he nonetheless had fathered four sons and three daughters.[1] In accordance with Portuguese laws of inheritance, Geremana, Joanna, and Felicianna were to inherit equally with their brothers Pantalião, Vicente, André, and Manoel.[2]

The inheritance that Mathias bequeathed to his sons and daughters had largely been built from the opportunities that a booming gold economy

---

1. Testamento de Mathias de Crasto Porto, 6 October 1742, Inventarios 1740–46, MOSMG.

2. It was not necessary for children to be legitimate to inherit. According to Portuguese law, among commoners, natural children — "offspring of individuals who might have married because law imposed no impediments to their marriage" — had the right to inherit. Linda Lewin, "Natural and Spurious Children in Brazilian Inheritance Law from Colony to Nation: A Methodological Essay," *The Americas* 48 (January 1992): 363, 366. On the distinction between natural and spurious children, see Lewin, "Natural and Spurious Children," 351–96. Female children in colonial Brazil could and did receive greater inheritances, by means of dowries, than did male children. See Metcalf, *Family and Frontier*; Muriel Nazzari, *The Disappearance of the Dowry: Women, Families, and Social Change in São Paulo, Brazil (1600–1900)* (Stanford University Press, 1991).

afforded to free men like him. The 1720 registration of slaves indicated that Porto was then master of seven slaves, not a poor man, but certainly not one of the elite masters in the region at the time.[3] When he died twenty-two years later, however, Porto's inventory revealed a vast fortune with diverse economic interests situated in several different parishes, as well as in the town of Sabará. As a measure of his wealth, the number of slaves he owned had increased from seven to ninety-four.

Both Mathias de Crasto Porto's will and the inventory of his assets are instructive as illustrations of several important features of life in colonial Sabará. His assets, described in the following pages, document the diversity of economic investments in various sectors of Sabará's economy and the necessity of slave labor for each of those enterprises. His assets also indicate that the daily lives of the numerous slaves belonging to him varied considerably according to which of Porto's businesses they labored for. Moreover, the provisions of his will and the details of the inventory reveal the multiple ways in which the personal lives of free Portuguese immigrants came to be intertwined with those of some of the slaves who served them. Partly as a consequence of the trust, respect, or affection that Mathias de Crasto Porto developed for certain slaves, he rewarded a small number of them in his will with their freedom.[4] He did not, however, free the vast majority, and these he gave as chattel to his children, whom he had fathered with the woman or women who remained nameless, unworthy even of mention in his final testament.

Other bachelor settlers in colonial Sabará, whose circumstances left them with assets to pass on to heirs such as Porto's, were more revealing in their testaments than he had been. As mentioned in Chapter 1, Lourenço de Mello e Madureira acknowledged his two mulatto sons and three mulatto daughters as the children of a slave woman whom he owned.[5] In a 1740 will, Joseph Mendes de Carvalho, also a bachelor, identified his heir as the mulatto offspring of a slave woman.[6] Inventories examined for the

---

3. "Lista dos escravos . . . para pagarem os reaes quintos de 1720 athé o de 1721," APMCMS, Código 2.

4. Inventario de Mathias de Crasto Porto, 6 October 1742, Inventarios 1740–46, MOSMG. Of the ninety-four slaves he owned, Porto freed eight in his will according to various terms. Only three were freed without owing payment to his estate.

5. Testamento de Lourenço de Mello e Madureira, 14 August 1722, *Livro de registo de testamento* (1716–25), MOSMG, fol. 217v.

6. Testamento de Joseph Mendes de Carvalho, 26 December 1740, *Livro de registo de testamento* (17 dezembro 1739), MOSMG, fol. 151. Widowers also named mulatto heirs. See Testamento de Antônio Vieyra Porto, 17 August 1740, *Livro de registo de testamento* (17 dezembro 1739), MOSMG, fol. 133.

years 1725–1808 show that among the bachelor colonists, almost 61 percent had children whom they named as heirs. When the mothers of these children were named, all were slaves or former slaves. It is therefore likely that Mathias de Crasto Porto's sexual relations had also been with slaves or freed slave women.[7]

The lengthy, richly detailed closing documents of Mathias de Crasto Porto's life provide ample clues as to the economic, demographic, social, and political circumstances that framed the opening decades of the eighteenth century in colonial Sabará.[8] For the most fortunate among Portuguese men who came to Minas Gerais, prosperity went hand in hand with increased slaveholding and diverse economic enterprises that developed from and around the central activity of gold mining. For the far less fortunate slave population, their labors were often arduous, although far from uniform, and clearly divided according to their owners' definitions of a sexual division of labor. For women slaves brought into the region by men who had migrated mostly as bachelors, sexual service, including prostitution, figured into the demands placed on them by their masters.[9]

Most slaves in colonial Sabará could not expect to be freed, either by reward or by paying to their masters the cost of their replacement. As Mathias de Crasto Porto's will and those of numerous others suggest, even the critical task of providing heirs for masters did not necessarily bring recognition or freedom to enslaved mothers. In the transfer of assets from one generation to the next, slaveholders expressed both their definition of slavery as a lifelong condition and their determination that only a few individuals should be granted manumission.

Mathias de Crasto Porto's identity as a male slave owner, along with the

---

7. The number of inventories examined was ninety-six, among which were those for twenty-three bachelors. The seven never-married women (*solteiras*) whose assets were inventoried also had children named as heirs. Inventarios, 1725–1808, MOSMG. Although the number of inventories consulted was limited to a sample of those available in the local archive, such documents are often quite lengthy. For example, the inventory of Mathias de Crasto Porto, with accompanying legal documents, made up an entire book of over 300 pages. The phenomenon of bachelors naming mulatto heirs (children of slaves or ex-slaves) was also commonly noted in books of wills (*Livros de registo de testamento*) for the years 1716–1808, MOSMG.

8. Inventario de Mathias de Crasto Porto, 6 October 1742, Inventarios 1740–46, MOSMG.

9. In his study of eighteenth-century emigration from the northern provinces of Portugal, Ramos has demonstrated that men moved alone. In those areas that supplied colonists to Minas Gerais, the number of women in Portuguese towns greatly exceeded the number of men. See Ramos, "From Minho to Minas," 641. This is not to suggest that married colonists would not also have demanded sexual services from slave women; married men were simply not the majority of migrating males.

impressive accounts of his assets, places him in the upper echelons of colonial Sabará's highly stratified social and political structure. His slaves and those of the rest of the *comarca*'s masters occupied the lowest stratum of society. The free population of eighteenth-century Sabará did not, of course, consist solely of rich male slaveholders. Some men owned far fewer assets than did Mathias de Crasto Porto, and others owned no slaves and little or nothing else of value at all.

Portuguese women did not migrate to Minas Gerais in numbers approaching those of Portuguese men.[10] The sex ratio in the free White population of Sabará was therefore seriously imbalanced from the time of the *vila*'s founding in 1711 and throughout the colonial period.[11] Among the free women who lived in the *comarca,* there were married women who owned slaves jointly with their husbands.[12] Widowed women and never-married women also owned and controlled slaves in their own right. Some free women, like free men, owned no slaves at all. The assets of Sabará's free women varied considerably in value and defined their economic and social ranking in the *comarca,* from the very rich to the very poor.

The community of free colonists in Sabará was not limited to those of European descent. The dearth of free female migrants in the gold-mining lands made it difficult, if not impossible, for male colonizers to reproduce themselves as an exclusively White elite.[13] In lieu of White heirs, as the testamentary decisions of bachelor migrants like Mathias de Crasto Porto indicated, heirs of mixed racial descent had to suffice. In addition, children born to manumitted female slaves were free. Thus, over time, the ranks of the free population were swelled with the descendants of Africans, the mixed-race descendants of Africans and Europeans, as well as freed African and Brazilian-born slaves. The available population records indicate

10. Ramos, "From Minho to Minas," 641.

11. As late as 1776, population records show that in the *comarca* of Sabará, White males outnumbered White females by a ratio of three to two (150 males per 100 females). Because these statistics included children, adult White men at this time undoubtedly outnumbered adult White women by an even greater margin. "Memoria histórica da capitania de Minas Gerais," *RAPM* 2 (1897): 511. In 1805, the demographic figures for the entire province indicated that White males still outnumbered White females by 20 percent. "População da provincia de Minas Gerais," *RAPM* 4 (1899): 294.

12. Metcalf, "Women and Means: Women and Family Property In Colonial Brazil," *Journal of Social History* 24 (Winter 1990): 277–98.

13. Male colonizers from the São Paulo region were unlikely to have been entirely of European descent to begin with; they were more likely to have been of mixed European and Indian descent. See Metcalf, *Family and Frontier.* Documentary records such as wills suggest, however, that the majority of male migrants to Sabará, Minas Gerais, were Portuguese and therefore White.

that by the third quarter of the eighteenth century, the non-Whites in the free population far outnumbered Whites in that group, and probably had done so for quite some time earlier. (See Table 2.1.)

When Mathias de Crasto Porto owned seven slaves in 1720, his holdings were not unusual. Among the almost nine hundred masters registering slave property in that year, the average number of slaves per master was 6.6.[14] More than one-half of all slaveholders owned fewer than five slaves; almost nine in ten owned fewer than fifteen. This pattern of slave distribution suggests that most masters could identify their slaves by name and sight and could well have developed some awareness of their slaves' lives. (See Table 2.2.)

Women slaveholders were more likely than men to own very few slaves. Women owners were a minority of the slaveholders (fewer than 6 percent) in 1720 and on average owned only 2.2 slaves.[15] Such women undoubtedly knew their slaves by name and like other owners of small numbers of slaves could have developed a keen awareness of their slaves' lives and personalities.

From its earliest frontier days, the *comarca* of Sabará was divided into separate areas of settlement that began as hamlets (*arraiais*) and later became organized as parishes. Several individual subdistricts made up the town (*vila*) of Sabará and the juridical seat of the entire *comarca*. In 1720, 28.4 percent of masters registering their slave property resided in the town of Sabará, and they owned 26.7 percent of the *comarca*'s slaves. The remaining owners and slaves resided in the outlying settlements. In the long term, these outlying settlements developed their own separate sense of community and during the nineteenth century became independent municipalities. Throughout the eighteenth century, however, the town of Sabará remained the largest single population center in the *comarca*. According to the slave registration of 1720, over one-third of the women owners of slaves lived in the districts of the town of Sabará.[16] (See Table 2.3 and Map 3.)

Nearly three-quarters of the *comarca*'s slaves did not live in the town boundaries of Sabará, and for many of those living both inside and outside town, personal contact with their masters was limited. Nearly 40 percent of the slaves who were registered in 1720 lived in households with fifteen

14. "Lista dos escravos . . . para pagarem os reaes quintos de 1720 athé o de 1721," APMCMS, Código 2. Number of masters is 894; number of slaves is 5,908.

15. "Lista dos escravos." Among the 894 masters registering slave property in 1720, there were 4 couples listed as joint owners; 53 owners were women, and the rest were men.

16. The exact figure is 35.8 percent.

Table 2.1. Population in the *comarca* of Sabará, 1716–1805

| Year | Number of Slaves | Number of Free Individuals | |
		Whites	Non-Whites
1716	4,905	NA	NA
1720	5,908	NA[a]	94[b]
1735	24,284	NA	576
1749	20,838[c]	NA	284[c]
1776	47,122[d]	14,394	37,878[d]
1786	55,026[e]	13,323[e]	38,394[e]
1805	60,250[e]	15,818[e]	34,557[e]

SOURCES: Declaração de Dom Pedro de Almeida e Portugal, conde de Assumar, 2 August 1718, Arquivo Público Mineiro, Secção colonial, Códice 11, fol. 275v.; "Lista does escravos . . . para pagarem os reaes quintos de 1720 athé o de 1721," APMSC, Códice 2; Boxer, *The Golden Age*, 341–46; "Memória histórica da capitania de Minas Gerais," *RAPM* 2 (1897): 511; "População da provincia de Minas Gerais," 294–95.

NOTE: NA = Not available.
[a]The available figure is for the number of slaveholders (891), not the total number of free persons.
[b]Of the 894 slaveholders listed, 51 were former slaves and therefore non-white. The figure provided indicates the number of *forros*, ex-slaves paying tax on their own persons.
[c]The decline in the number of slaves from 1735 may be due in part to a repartitioning of political jurisdictions in this period.
[d]Figures for this year were available in terms of race and sex but did not indicate the number of slaves versus free individuals. Consequently, calculations were made by using the race, sex, and status breakdowns available in the 1786 counts. The results, of course, are approximate.
[e]The 1786 and 1805 counts provided figures for the entire captaincy by race, sex, and status (no age breakdowns). The calculations here make use of the *comarca*-specific proportions available in 1776. The results are therefore approximate.

or more slaves, and more than 15 percent lived with masters who owned more than twenty-five slaves. (See Table 2.2.) For such slaves, the opportunities for achieving a personal relationship with their owners or even for attaining ready identification as an individual by them were substantially reduced. Without such recognition, slaves could not expect to escape slavery through the legal means of manumission. Thus, of the ninety-four slaves owned by Mathias de Crasto Porto at the time of his death, only three were freed without owing payments to his estate; five others were manumitted in exchange for payments of continued labor or gold.[17] For the majority of his laborers, slavery continued under new masters.

17. Inventario de Mathias de Crasto Porto, 6 October 1742, Inventarios 1740–46, MOSMG.

Table 2.2. Slaveholdings in Sabará, Minas Gerais, 1720

Size of Holding in Slaves	Percentage of Masters	Percentage of Slaves	Cumulative Percentage of Masters	Cumulative Percentage of Slaves
1–4	56.1	19.2	56.1	19.2
5–9	22.2	22.4	78.3	41.6
10–14	10.6	18.8	88.9	60.4
15–19	5.3	13.5	94.2	73.9
20–49	4.7	19.6	98.9	93.5
50–72	0.7	6.2	99.6	99.7

SOURCES: "Lista dos escravos . . . para pagarem os reaes quintos de 1720 athé o de 1721," APMSC, Códice 2.

NOTE: Number of masters is 894; number of slaves is 5,908.

For most years of the eighteenth century, household census data are not available for the *comarca* of Sabará. In lieu of such data, wills and inventories such as those of Mathias de Crasto Porto provide crucial information for detecting patterns of slave ownership and for assessing any changes over time in the slave population. Aggregate analyses of household composition and assets derived from these sources require cautious interpretation: they may under-represent Sabará's poorest colonists and others who had no need to make testamentary provisions for the transfer of their assets to heirs.[18] On the other hand, unlike the required registration of slave property in 1720, wills and inventories can reveal much more about the individual lives of colonists in Sabará (including those who owned no slaves at all) as well as the circumstances of those who lived as slaves.

The earliest collection of wills available for analysis from the *comarca* of Sabará contains documents dated from October 1716 through January 1725.[19] The rich evidence from these wills illustrates both the possibility of documentary bias toward wealthy colonists and confirmation of the existence of free colonists too poor to own slaves. Among the testators who

18. These sources do not tell us much about the poorest citizens of Minas Gerais, such as those who were the focus of Laura de Mello e Souza's *Desclassificados do ouro: A pobreza mineira no século XVIII* (Rio de Janeiro: Edições Graal, 1982).

19. *Livro de registo de testamento* (1716–25), MOSMG. These wills, and numerous others used in this and subsequent chapters, often (although not in all cases) included descriptions of the testators' assets at the time the documents were notarized. Such descriptions were similar but not identical to the inventories of assets made after the testator had died and were recorded in separate books of inventories kept in notarial offices.

Table 2.3. Location of the slave population in the *comarca* of Sabará, 1720

Locality	Number of Masters	Number of Slaves	Number of Women Owners	Number of Slaves Owned by Women
In the *vila* of Sabará:				
Arrayal Velho	64	548	6	18
Arrayal da Igreja				
Matriz	108	483	8	17
Distrito da ponte da Igreja Velha até á ponte de Capt.				
Barreto	82	550	5	12
Near to but outside the *vila* of Sabará:				
Pompeo	52	378	1	7
Roça Grande	68	520	1	3
Other localities in the *comarca*:				
Caminho Novo and Paraupeba	7	36	2	2
Capao	12	142	0	0
Congonhas	99	611	6[a]	21
Curral del Rei	35	232	3	5
Macaubas	98	514	2	6
Rio das Velhas Abaixo até as Macaubas	92	683	6[b]	9
Rapozos	71	560	7	8
Santo Antonio do Rio das Velhas Asima	95	589	5	10
Miscellaneous districts	11	62	1	1
Total	894	5,908	53	119

SOURCE: "Lista dos escravos . . . para pagarem os reaes quintos de 1720 athé o de 1721," APMSC, Códice 2.

NOTE: Seventy percent of the women owners were former slaves (*forras*).
[a]Excludes women in couples (only one in this district).
[b]Excludes women in couples (three in this district).

described assets, 5.8 percent were not slaveholders. Those who were masters each owned an average of 9.4 slaves and were therefore wealthier than the average slaveholder registering property in 1720. Whereas in the general registration of property owners made in 1720, only one in ten masters

Table 2.4.   Slaveholdings among testators, *comarca* of Sabará, 1716–1725

Size of Holding in Slaves	Percentage of Masters	Percentage of Slaves	Cumulative Percentage of Masters	Cumulative Percentage of Slaves
1–4	37.5	9.6	37.5	9.6
5–9	25.0	18.2	62.5	27.8
10–14	18.7	23.5	81.2	51.3
15–19	9.4	16.2	90.6	67.5
20–49	9.4	32.4	100.0	99.9

SOURCE: *Livro de registo de testamentos* (1716–25), MOSMG.

NOTE: Number of owners is 32; number of slaves is 302. Five slaveholders were women; they owned 27 slaves.

owned more than fifteen slaves, among the testators with slaves, nearly two in ten owned more than fifteen slaves. Moreover, these wealthier testators owned nearly one-half of all the slaves listed as assets in these documents.[20] (See Table 2.4.)

The first notarized inventories of the assets of Sabará's colonists available for analysis date from May 1725. For this study, the data available in inventories made during the years 1725–1808 have been analyzed to describe a variety of features of colonial life in Sabará, including patterns of slave ownership, household composition, material culture, economic enterprises, labor relations, and labor forces. For descriptions of slaves' lives and circumstances, these inventories often (but not always) provide crucial details about sex, age, race, places of origin, family composition, working skills, physical health (and illness). Such details affected the actual value assigned to each slave in the inventory.

The sample of inventories used in this study covers both the most prosperous period of gold mining and the period of economic decline and diversification into non-gold-mining enterprises. The inventory data (at times divided to reflect the boom and bust periods of the gold cycle) are examined for evidence of change in the circumstances of owners and slaves as the colonial society of Sabará grew in size, matured, and became less of a frontier area. In terms of the slave population, the inventories provide data for 1,378 slaves owned by 90 masters. In combination with references to additional sources and to broader demographic and economic trends,

20. Number of owners in this collection was 32; number of slaves was 302. *Livro de registo de testamento* (1716–25), MOSMG.

such a sample size provides for a significant assessment of slave life and master-slave relationships in the *comarca* of Sabará.[21]

The enormous success that Mathias de Crasto Porto enjoyed as an entrepreneur in Sabará, a success allowing him to increase his slaveholdings from seven to ninety-four, occurred sometime between 1720 and 1742, when he died. These years were ones of considerable growth in gold production in the region, a growth that coincided with an increased concentration of slave ownership in the hands of fewer masters. Inventory records for the years 1725–59, when the gold economy was thriving, indicate that almost four in ten masters owned fifteen or more slaves and that over 75 percent of the slaves belonged to owners with such holdings. From the slaves' perspective, the likelihood of being owned by masters of fewer slaves and the opportunity to develop more personal contacts with the masters had declined substantially in comparison with the opportunities suggested by either the 1720 slave registration or the testators' assets of the 1716–23 period.[22] (See Tables 2.2, 2.4, 2.5.)

Inventory records for the years 1760–1808, when the gold economy was declining and the economy was beginning to diversify, also indicate that over three-quarters of slaves belonged to masters owning fifteen or more slaves. In this latter period, however, the proportion of slave owners in this category declined; thus fewer masters held larger slaveholdings. Indeed, in the years 1760–1808, almost one in ten masters owned twenty or more slaves, and close to one-half of the *comarca*'s captives (47.6 percent) belonged to such individuals. Concomitantly, the small holders became more numerous and yet owned fewer of the *comarca*'s slaves than ever before. The period of gold's decline thus coincided with an increasing maldistribution of wealth in the *comarca*, as measured by assets in slaves.

21. Brazil is located almost entirely in the tropics. Eighteenth-century documents are fragmentary because of their long exposure to a warm and moist climate and to the ravages of insects, which consume the paper or portions of the paper. Sabará's notarial records are locally housed in a renovated eighteenth-century structure that, like all colonial buildings in the tropics, has an open-air design (no screens, no air conditioning, no heat, no moisture or insect proofing). In other colonial archives of Brazil, I have seen documents piled beneath the risers of an open-air staircase, which formed their only protection from tropical rainstorms. The operant principle guiding selection of sources is the same in all colonial archives: you examine what the bugs did not eat. Thus, the number of inventories chosen reflects the availability of these documents in the local archives and their considerable length. See note 7 above. Not all inventories examined were those of slaveholders.

22. The possible documentary bias toward over-representing wealthier colonists should not be greater in the inventories of 1725–59 than in the wills examined for the years 1719–23. The evidence thus suggests that slaveholdings became more concentrated over time.

Table 2.5. Slaveholdings in Sabará, 1725–1808

Size of Holding in Slaves	Cumulative Percentage of Masters, 1725–59	Cumulative Percentage of Slaves, 1725–59	Cumulative Percentage of Masters, 1760–1808	Cumulative Percentage of Slaves, 1760–1808
1–4	25.8	4.0	42.3	7.4
5–9	41.9	10.7	71.1	20.2
10–14	61.2	24.5	74.5	23.0
15–19	77.3	40.3	83.0	33.0
20–49	90.2	58.0	91.5	52.4
50 plus	99.9	99.8	100.0	99.9

SOURCE: A sample of 96 inventories dating from 1725 through 1808, MOSMG.

NOTE: In 6.2 percent of the inventories sampled, property holders owned no slaves. The number of slaves owned in the remaining estates was 1,378 (519 in first period, 859 in the second).

In the following descriptions of the values of various assets, it should be noted that in the mining region, as elsewhere in colonial Brazil, there was a scarcity of coin or paper specie. Unlike other areas of colonial Brazil, there was a convenient substitute for gold coins in Minas Gerais. This substitute was gold dust, which was widely used throughout the eighteenth century. Only in the last quarter of the eighteenth century did official documents begin to consistently describe the values of assets in terms of specie; before then, the value of goods was most often expressed in measured weights of gold dust, principally *oitavas* (drams), of which there are 128 in every pound.

The nonslave assets of small slaveholders, as described in wills and inventories, were very limited; the material circumstances of relatively poor colonists probably had little in common with those of rich colonists in Sabará. For example, Catherina de Paiva, a freed Black woman, declared in her will of 1721 that her possessions consisted of the value of two female slaves, one of whom had a young son. In addition, Catherina declared herself owner of some gold jewelry valued at eighty *oitavas*, which she had at that time pawned. Aside from these declared assets, this ex-slave owned nothing else of value.[23] Similarly, Thomazia de Jesus declared in her will of 1719 that she, also an ex-slave, owned one slave woman and two small slave children. In addition, she had a pair of earrings valued at

23. Testamento de Catherina de Paiva preta forra, 9 July 1721, *Livro de registo de testamento* (1716–25), MOSMG, fol. 133.

twenty-seven *oitavas*, but currently pawned for twelve. Both these ex-slave women declared in their wills that after their own deaths, the slave children were to be freed, but not the adult slaves. In the case of Catherina de Paiva, she left one of her slaves to her former master and allowed the other to pay that former master 200 *oitavas* to achieve her freedom. Thomazia de Jesus arranged for her adult slave to be sold and the proceeds to be inherited by her mother.[24]

In addition to owning at least some gold jewelry or religious ornaments, the nonrich generally had at least a couple of items of silverware, some tools, and perhaps one slave. Maria Ribeyra, a freed Black woman who died in 1737, was probably typical of the poorer but not destitute free colonists.[25] She had five young children, and she owned one slave, one horse and saddle, one gun, a pair of gold earrings, two broken silver spoons, seven pewter plates, one copper bowl, and one scythe. The slave woman Garcia was easily the most valuable of Ribeyra's assets. Although Maria's ownership of a slave, a horse, and a gun placed her in social and economic circumstances well above those of nonslave owners and of course far superior to those of slaves, her five minor children were probably left in a rather needy situation following her death. Still, they were not slaves and would not occupy the lowest position in the *comarca*'s social order.

Not all freed Black women were of such modest means.[26] In 1772, Roza de Azevedo bought property and thirty slaves valued at twenty thousand *cruzados* (more than five thousand *oitavas*). The property included a house in the parish of Pompeo with the furniture inside it, a blacksmith's forge, the tools belonging to a blacksmith, and some lands used for mining. In addition, there were several *datas* outlining mineral rights in the Sabará river, which came with the "slaves necessary for mining," and a water pump with iron chain. There were also lands for planting various food-stuffs, some cattle, pigs, and a horse. Among the slaves bought were two *crioulos*, Antonio and Lourenço, identified as blacksmiths. She also bought twenty *bateias* (wooden panning dishes), twelve *almocafres* (miner's picks), three *alavancas* (levers), all tools used in mining.[27]

24. Testamento de Thomazia de Jesus parda forra, 27 November 1719, *Livro de registo de testamento* (1716–25), MOSMG, fol. 82v.

25. Inventario de Maria Ribeyra parda forra, 9 August 1737, Inventarios: 1731–37, MOSMG.

26. Nor were all freed Black men poor. The phenomenon of freed slaves owning slaves is discussed later.

27. Escriptura de compra que faz Roza de Azevedo preta forra a Agostinho de Azevedo

In contrast with the more impoverished state of minor slaveholders, people of means such as Roza de Azevedo generally owned gold jewelry and other gold religious ornaments, silverware, and pewter ware, copper bowls, tinware, and table linens. Their furniture included beds, wardrobes, trunks, and sideboards (buffets) in addition to the tables and benches found in modest homes. Rifles, pistols, and swords were also rare in these households, although firearms of some kind were not uncommon in many poorer homes. Occasionally some musical instruments were listed in the inventories of households, and equally rarely a book or two was listed as a possession.[28]

The rich in Sabará owned substantial quantities of fine clothing and bed linens made from imported materials. In 1720, Antonio Vieira da Silva wrote his will while in bed and therefore described it in detail among the first of his assets. The bed had covers made from cloth interwoven with gold and silver threads worked into the shape of flowers and a curtain imported from India. The bedclothes were of fine fabrics imported from both India and Japan.[29] Although slaves still figured heavily as a proportion of this individual's total assets, Antonio Vieira da Silva's other property shows that he could afford more than the purchase and maintenance of a slave-labor force to do his bidding.

As might be expected, Mathias de Crasto Porto's possessions included the luxurious trappings of a man who could pay for what he wanted to own. He had a silver shaving bowl worth nearly as much as an infant slave, and he owned more than eighty silver buttons waiting to be sewn onto his clothing. He owned twenty-eight shirts of various linens imported from Britain, Holland, and India. His bed, chests, and sideboards were built of the handsome jacaranda wood; his slant-top desk came from England. His sword and his gun were adorned with silver. When he was not dressed in a dark suit, he wore a jacket made of Indian linen. He wore boots, and his socks were silk.[30]

The inventory of one of several dry goods stores that Mathias de Crasto Porto owned also indicates that other wealthy colonists in Sabará enjoyed

---

Guedes de todos os seus bens, 14 October 1772, *Livro de notas* (15 junho de 1772), MOSMG, fol. 47.

28. One book mentioned in several inventories was *Erario mineral*, by Luis Gomes Ferreyra, discussed later in this chapter.

29. Testamento de Antonio Vieira da Silva, 15 February 1720, *Livro de registo de testamento* (1716–25), MOSMG, fol. 87v.

30. Inventario de Mathias de Crasto Porto, 6 October 1742, Inventarios 1740–46, MOSMG.

sumptuous apparel. The store, located in the town of Sabará, sold many types of fabric and articles of clothing that could have been of use to only the very well-to-do. Besides hundreds of yards of ordinary cloth used for everyday clothing for masters and even clothing for slaves, there were also hundreds of yards of cloth that distinguished any wearer as a member of the elite. Among the items in Porto's store in Sabará were 56 yards of light silk, 164 yards of ordinary-weight silk, 115 yards of silk from Italy, some with edges of woven silver. There were 54 yards of Roman silk; 126 yards of velvet, some plain and some fancy; 105 yards of damask from Castille; 186 yards of black crepe; and 388 yards of taffeta. The inventory also included 93 pairs of silk socks and 98 pairs of fine gloves.[31]

The existence of such a yard goods supply in the central town of this *comarca* suggests that enough wealthy people were scattered throughout the region to make the importation of luxury items from abroad and through Rio de Janeiro worth the costs of transportation. The trade in such goods serves as additional evidence that social and economic life among the nonslave population was highly stratified. The wealthy lived a life of consumption that could not be compared to that of small slave-holders. In addition, wealthy masters managed complex business relations that further defined their economic and social standing.

As a wealthy businessman, Mathias de Crasto Porto could and often did lend funds to individuals who deposited something of value with him as collateral. He was, in effect, a pawnbroker, and among his worldly posses-sions were the pawned items left with him. Joseph Ribeiro da Costa, for example, pawned various small religious figures made of gold and valued at twenty *oitava;* in exchange, Mathias de Crasto gave him nineteen *oitavas'* worth of specie, or gold dust, or perhaps even his word as credit. Numerous other individuals also pawned gold buttons, earrings, and other jewelry, as well as miscellaneous silverware to Porto in exchange for needed funds.[32] This dependence of the less fortunate free individuals on the wealthy colonists for loans was yet another characteristic of the differ-ences separating the free colonists.

Social stratification among the free colonists created distinct experiences

31. This listing is only partial. Many of the types of fine cloth do not translate into English very well, so I chose those that did. The measurements in the inventory were made in *côvados*, each of which equals 66 centimeters or 0.72 yards. Because in the United States fabrics are sold in yards, I chose them for the translated measure.

32. It was not always clear whether Porto gave these people gold, credit, or specie, but the values pawned were ultimately expressed in *mil reis*. Thus Joseph Ribeiro da Costa's nineteen *oitavas* were expressed as 28$500.

for slaves and differentiated the lives of some groups of slaves from those of others. The relationships of slaves with their masters and with one another were heavily dependent on their owners' economic and social standing, which defined the material and demographic circumstances in which slaves lived and worked.

The absence, or relative absence, of sumptuous or even valuable material goods among slaveholders owning fewer slaves not only marked the differences between poor and well-to-do free colonists, but also reflects the enormous cost of buying slaves. Slaves were so expensive in eighteenth-century Minas Gerais that only rich masters could afford to own much else. Strong, healthy slaves commanded high prices, and their labor represented the principal costs of all economic investments in the *comarca*, including the primary activity of gold mining. In the early and most prosperous decades of gold mining, youthful male slaves could be purchased for anywhere between 150 and 250 *oitavas*, the latter figure approaching two pounds of gold.[33] Luis Gomes Ferreyra, a doctor who had lived in Sabará for twenty years, wrote in 1735 that a poor man might have to work for two or three years to save enough money to own a single slave.[34] In fact, almost no other asset that an individual could own in Minas Gerais had as high a value as a single slave. Houses in the town of Sabará and outside it as well were often no more expensive than the price of a slave. In 1721, Francisco de Souza e Moura Rolim, the local judge (*juiz ordinario*) of Sabará, sold a house to Manoel de Oliveira Barros for the price of 230 *oitavas* of gold.[35] Even the most elaborate properties in town did not cost much more than 600 *oitavas,* which at the time was the value of three strong and relatively youthful male slaves.[36] In contrast, the principal tools of mining, the *bateia* (wooden pan), the *almocafre* (miner's pick), the *alavanca* (lever), and the *enxada* (hoe), could all be purchased for less than one-half of one *oitava* of gold.[37]

---

33. For example: Escriptura de venda . . . que fez o Reverendo Padre Miguel Gomes de Araujo, 1 January 1719, *Livro de notas* (12 fevereiro 1718), MOSMG, fol. 219. In this sale, two male slaves were each sold for 245 *oitavas*, and two others were each sold for 185 *oitavas*.

34. Luis Gomes Ferreyra, *Erario mineral*, 13–14.

35. Escriptura de venda . . . que faz o Juiz Ordinario Francisco de Souza e Moura Rolim, 16 April 1721, *Livro de notas* (13 abril 1721), MOSMG, fol. 2v.

36. Mathias de Crasto Porto, one of the *comarca*'s wealthiest individuals, owned a house in Rossa Grande, valued at 800$000 or approximately 534 *oitavas*. Inventario de Mathias de Crasto Porto, 6 October 1742, Inventarios 1740–46, MOSMG.

37. Inventory of a *fazenda de loge* (dry goods store) located in Inventario de Mathias de Crasto Porto, 6 October 1742, Inventarios 1740–46, MOSMG.

The settlement of both the town and outlying parishes of Sabará had been generated as a consequence of the discovery of gold and of the efforts to extract it. The mining itself was a labor largely undertaken by slaves, although ex-slaves and other free people worked in mining sites as well. Perhaps the fact that mining tools were relatively inexpensive and mining labor was so dear made the free "miners" (*mineiros*) of Sabará such a mixed group of individuals, some close to being destitute and others fabulously wealthy. Those who were neither sometimes formed partnerships (*sociedades*) sharing the expenses and earnings of a mining enterprise. Such partnerships were undoubtedly encouraged by the fact, discussed in Chapter 1, that the size of land grants secured for gold mining was contingent on the number of enslaved laborers that a free colonist possessed. To increase the total amount of land worked by his slaves, João Barboza de Araujo, an immigrant from Portugal, created a partnership with his brother Amaro. In the parish of Congonhas and in the district of Macacos, João and Amaro had title to two mining claims.[38] In 1720, João owned sixteen male slaves, and his brother owned ten.[39] When he wrote his will in 1721, João owned little else of value besides his slaves—some silver spoons, a couple of pewter plates and a copper bowl, a couple of pigs, and some firearms.[40] Between him and his brother, however, they did have considerable labor for mining at their disposal.

The slaves bought for the purpose of working gold deposits were men or older boys. João Barboza de Araujo's will showed that he owned not a single female slave. The limited number and value of his nonslave assets suggest that he had invested his entire fortune in the male labor deemed necessary for mining. From his perspective, the equally high price of female slave labor was not a necessary expense or perhaps even affordable, because the female slave would not have been purchased to work the mines.[41] For João and his brother Amaro, women slaves were an expensive luxury that they had to live without.

It is possible that those who lent capital to colonists buying slaves for

38. Testamento de João Barboza de Araujo, 3 March 1721, *Livro de registo de testamento* (1716–25), MOSMG, fol. 165v.

39. "Lista dos escravos . . . para pagarem os reaes quintos de 1720 athé o de 1721," APMCMS, Códice 2.

40. Testamento de João Barboza de Araujo, 3 March 1721, *Livro de registo de testamento* (1716–25), MOSMG, fol. 165 v.

41. That female labor was as expensive as male labor in the early decades of the eighteenth century in this region is unquestionably true. Because of the relatively low demand for female labor in mining, the reasons for the high price of female labor are not clear.

mines did not lend for the purpose of buying females. It is also possible that claims to mineral-bearing lands were awarded on the basis of how many *male* slaves a colonist had, not on the total number of slaves he or she owned.[42] Evidence is lacking to confirm whether the overwhelming preference for male labor in mines was unwillingly foisted on Sabará's colonists by creditors or government regulations or whether such a preference simply reflected the colonists' own view of mining as the labor of men and not women.[43] In either case, colonists whose investments were principally in mining tended to be very wealthy before they decided to buy women slaves to attend to their households, personal needs, or sexual desires. For those male slaves who were bought to work in the mines, their needs and desires for personal, sexual, and family lives (which the presence of women slaves might have met) were roundly ignored.

Bras de Barros Soares was a wealthier colonist than were the Araujo brothers, and he too invested almost exclusively in mining. As mentioned earlier, in August 1719, Bras declared ownership of twenty-eight male slaves and only one female. His male slaves were almost all Africans; his woman slave Thereza was a mulatto.[44] Thereza was expecting a child, and in his will Soares freed the unborn child and provided him or her with a legacy. From the mother, he demanded payment in gold for her freedom although he set an amount considerably below Thereza's market value. The provisions of the will naturally suggest that the expected child was not that of an enslaved father, but rather the offspring of the master himself. The decision about Thereza's freedom reflects Soares' (deathbed) view that a valued freed child needed a freed mother to provide care and sustenance. The demand for gold from the mother points, however, to the limits of Soares's affection for Thereza and to her role in his life as a sexual servant. She was not a mining slave and had not been purchased for that purpose.

Colonists did not always own full title to mining claims, but instead

---

42. Nothing in the regulations suggests that the labor need be male, but we do not know how the regulations were interpreted.

43. It seems likely that an actual preference for the use of men in mining was very important in Minas Gerais. The supply of female slaves from Africa would not have been so limited as to force such an exclusive use of male labor. Miller, for example, writes of a two-to-one ratio of men to women sold into slavery from the Congo-Angola region in the eighteenth century. See *Way of Death,* 162.

44. Twenty-five of twenty-eight were identified as Africans; three were identified only by name. Testamento de Bras de Barros Soares, 25 August 1719, *Livro de registo de testamento* (1716–25), MOSMG, fol. 33.

owned or held *praças* or working rights to the mining lands of others or of a partnership. The laborers for work in *praças* were also almost entirely male. In 1768, for example, Domingos dos Santos Toledo declared that he had twenty *praças* in a mining claim, which he worked with sixteen men whom he owned.[45] In 1785, Dionysio Fernandes da Silva had five male slaves who work in the six *praças* that he held as part of a partnership in a mining claim.[46] In 1801, Tenente Coronel Antonio Brandão declared ownership of forty-three *praças* in a nearby mining site as well as mentioning mineral-bearing lands that he owned in his own right.[47] In 1806, Joze Duarte Vieira stated that in a mining *fazenda (fazenda de mineração)* in which he was partner he held thirty *praças* in addition to owning his own agricultural land. Vieira specified that he owned both mining and agricultural equipment and tools and that among his slaves were both male and female laborers.[48]

Masters in Sabará without land grants or *praças* could still have slaves who labored principally in mining activities. This situation occurred when masters hired out their slaves to others to maintain an income for themselves. Antonio Viera da Silva, owner of ten men and one woman, had been accustomed to renting his slaves to partners at the rate of one-half an *oitava* per day. Silva, who was dying in 1720, made arrangements on his deathbed for his slaves to continue to work for four years in mining and to pay 200 *oitavas* of their finds per year to their supervisor. Any additional findings would serve as income for Silva's two heirs: his wife and son.[49]

The overwhelming preference for male labor in mining sites appears repeatedly in the wills and inventories of colonists throughout the period of

45. Testamento de Domingos dos Santos Toledo, 3 June 1768, *Livro de registo de testamento* (22 maio 1770), MOSMG, fol. 43.

46. Testamento de Dionysio Fernandes da Silva, 13 June 1785 , *Livro de registo de testamento* (1 julho 1785), MOSMG, fol. 20.

47. Testamento de Thenente Coronel Antonio Brandão, 16 November 1801, *Livro de registo de testamento* (3 fevereiro 1802), MOSMG, fol. 4.

48. Testamento de Joze Duarte Vieira, 16 June1806, *Livro de registo de testamento* (4 março 1805), MOSMG, fol. 57. Vieira was not more specific about the composition of his labor force.

49. Testamento de Antonio Vieira da Silva, 15 February 1720, *Livro de registo de testamento* (1716–25), MOSMG, fol. 87v. In describing money owed to him by his *compadre*, Silva wrote: "pello ouro que cobrou (the compadre) de hum negro meu que andou na lavra do morro vermelho todo o tempo da sociedade que são 100 oitavas de ouro." And describing another debt owed: "Pello ouro dos jornais de cinco negros a saber João Banguella, João Congo, Matheus, Damião, e Pedro que andavão na lavra e faiscando o tempo de oito mezes e (davao) a meia oitava por dia o saber tres negros oito mezes e dois sete mezes e emporta tudo 456 oitavas de ouro."

this study.[50] In many agricultural or pastoral enterprises, a strong preference for male workers was also notable, although not always as extreme as that in mining operations.[51] Male slaves also predominated in the skilled and often town-based work of blacksmithing, barbering, butchering, carpentry, stonework, building, and shoemaking.[52] The preference for male labor in some town-based economic activities as well as in the mining or agricultural or pastoral sites of outlying areas meant that the sex ratios among slaves who lived or worked together could be extraordinarily unbalanced according to the economic enterprises in which their owners had invested.

The assets of Mathias de Crasto Porto illustrate that the investments of one particular slave owner and their locations shaped the demographic circumstances of his slave-labor force. In Rossa Grande, a parish located only a few kilometers from the town of Sabará, Porto owned seven different buildings, including an expensive two-story home situated across from the central church of the parish (Igreja Matriz). He also owned another two-story home in that parish, a dry goods store, a butcher shop, two blacksmith shops, and two other smaller residences, one of which was rented to the local priest. In this parish alone, Porto had twenty-three slaves, one of whom was a barber, another a blacksmith, and a third a shoemaker. Somewhere in the parish, he also kept twenty head of cattle.[53]

Rossa Grande was the parish of Porto's principal residency, and here the sex ratio among his slaves was the most balanced. Among his adult slaves were ten men and six women. He also owned two boys and five girls. Among his slaves born in Africa, Porto owned eight men and only one woman. None of the children were Africans, and all were offspring of the

---

50. As one more example, Manoel das Neves Ribeiro owned title to three mining claims in 1732. Among his slaves were twenty-two men, one woman, and her two children. Testamento de Capitão Manoel das Neves Ribeiro, 22 August 1732, *Livro de registo de testamento* (17 dezembro 1739), MOSMG, fol. 63.

51. There was some overlap in the use of slaves both in mining and nonmining activities. Padre Felix da Silveira, for example, used his slaves in mining, but also owned one-quarter interest in a sugar mill. In 1767, he owned twenty-five men and two young *crioulla* girls. Testamento de Padre Felix da Silveira, 27 January 1767, *Livro de registo de testamento* (4 julho 1766), MOSMG, fol. 39.

52. Slaves working as blacksmiths were found in both urban and outlying settlements.

53. Inventario de Mathias de Crasto Porto, Inventarios 1740–46, MOSMG. The values for the two-story residences were the highest I have seen in this *comarca*, 800$000 and 500$000 respectively. The total value of these buildings centrally located in this parish was 2:080$000 (the *oitava* being worth 1$500 at this time, this figure equals 1,387 *oitavas*).

woman slaves whom he owned or had owned. Among the adult slaves, two couples were identified as married.

In the parish of Curral del Rei, Mathias de Crasto Porto owned a *fazenda* on which there was a mill for grinding manioc into flour, and more important, a mill to grind sugar cane (*engenho de moer cana*). The sugar mill came with all the usual equipment and a carpenter's shop to keep everything in repair. In the nearby district of Capam, Porto's slaves also worked at gold mining; the inventory listed the typical tools for such activities, including a large hammer-like device of iron used to grind stones in the search for gold. Between the mining and cane cultivation, Porto employed an additional fifty-six slaves.[54]

Among these fifty-six slaves, only six were women; only one was a child. The remaining slaves were men. Among the African slaves working in these two outlying areas of the *comarca*, forty-two were men; only three were women. The descriptions of these slaves and the low values assigned to some indicate an aging labor force with many individuals suffering from crippling afflictions to their feet, the loss of an arm, or old age.[55] The presence of only three married slave couples and only one child under-scores the character of this slave-labor force as one that was never pur-chased for the purpose of being able to reproduce itself. The initial pur-chase of so many men and so few women would never have allowed for a natural increase in the slave population.

In the district of Bento Pires, Porto had fewer slaves, and the tools in-cluded in this listing suggest that the land was largely uncultivated. There was, however, a mill of some type along with yet another residence. The most important aspect of this particular property was that on it Porto kept 150 head of cattle, presumably for use in the various butcher shops he owned in the urban centers.[56] To care for these cattle, Porto owned six men and two women. Among these slaves there was one married couple, but no children.

In the parish of Congonhas, Porto was one of four partners in a mining operation there. The value of his portion of the partnership was not high

54. Inventario de Mathias de Crasto Porto, Inventarios 1740–46, MOSMG. The *fazenda* at Curral del Rei was valued at 2:400$000, and the Capam property had a value of six thousand *cruzados* (1:920$000). This amount did not include slaves who were listed with their individual values.

55. Fourteen of the fifty-six were described as crippled or having bad feet (*aleijados* or *malfeito dos pés*). Five others were described as old (*velhos*).

56. The value of the cattle alone was 1:102$000.

and did not constitute one of his major investments. Just as valuable in Congonhas for Porto was another *corte de carne,* or butchering establishment, which was described as having its own corral for livestock and a separate store area in which to conduct sales. Another building in Congonhas also owned by Porto was used as some type of store.[57] No slaves owned by Porto were listed as living in the parish of Congonhas.

In the town of Sabará, Porto owned yet another building used as a butchering shop. This one was somewhat larger than the others; it had a corral in which the beasts were slaughtered and a tile-covered shed nearby in which meats were probably hung. The building also had a yard in which bananas and oranges grew. The basic equipment for the shop included a *machado* (ax) with which to kill animals, a large set of scales with an iron arm, which could weigh large quantities (having weights up to eight pounds), and a small set of scales used for weighing the quantities of gold exchanged as payment on sales. The large scales with their wooden plates were quite valuable and represented 8 percent of the value of the entire butcher shop.[58]

Porto owned seven additional buildings in the town of Sabará, all located on the most important streets. One was rented as a residence, another served as a second butcher shop in town, two were dry goods stores, and one served as a wet goods store. The two others were not identified for any particular use, but each had a yard, and one had a stable in back. Seven male slaves served Mathias de Crasto Porto in his holdings in Sabará; they worked either in the butcher shops or in the various stores. Five of these seven slaves were Africans.[59]

The daily lives of the many slaves belonging to Mathias de Crasto Porto clearly varied considerably according to which of his businesses they provided labor for. Some of the slaves working in Rossa Grande, where Porto maintained his personal residence, undoubtedly served as house servants; others worked in his stores or tended cattle. The slaves most likely to be working side by side with significant numbers of fellow captives were those occupied in Porto's sugar plantation in Curral del Rei or in his mining fields in Capam. The number of slaves required for working in his

57. The value of the partnership in the mining site was 70$000, and the values of the butcher shop and store were both 80$000.

58. The scales used in Sabará were valued at 6$000; the shop as a whole had a value of 75$000. In Congonhas, the scales were even more valuable, perhaps larger and newer, and were valued at 12$000.

59. Inventario de Mathias de Crasto Porto, Inventarios 1740–46, MOSMG.

various butcher shops and stores was quite limited, but these few individuals were the most likely captives to have considerable daily contact with the free colonists and urban dwellers of the *comarca*. The large numbers of Mathias de Crasto Porto's slaves imply that not many of them could have had sustained personal contact with their master, but their distribution among various sectors of Sabará's economy suggests that for some of his slaves daily contact with nonslaves was more frequent than would have been the case had they all lived in a strictly plantation-oriented economy. (See Table 2.6 for a summary of Mathias de Crasto Porto's assets.)

Mathias de Crasto Porto's stores and shops are indicative of the commerce that had developed in the *comarca* in conjunction with the gold-mining economy. The earliest evidence for the strength of this commercial activity comes from tax collections for the Royal Fifth. The 1720 collection of the fifth included a tax on shops and stores of various sizes and activities. The tax records in that year indicated that there were forty-four *vendas* and *lojas*[60] registered in the district of the Igreja Matriz, the area of the *vila* of Sabará centering on the largest and most important church in the town. In another *vila* district that ran from the Old Church bridge to the bridge named for Captain João Velho Barreto, there were another thirty-nine *vendas* and *lojas*. In the Arrayal Velho, the third district of the *vila* of Sabará, there were five more *vendas* and *lojas*. Thus the total number of shops in the town of Sabará was eighty-eight. In the other outlying parishes and districts of the *comarca*, there were fewer shops; the total number for those localities outside town was thirty. The town represented the center of commercial activities in the *comarca*.[61]

Owning a shop from which to sell goods in Sabará was not necessarily an indicator of significant wealth, but many who did were slaveholders as well. Almost 70 percent of the individuals who were taxed for ownership of one of these shops were also taxed for owning slaves. All but five of the registrants were men, although this fact says little about who actually did the selling of goods. Of the five women registrants, four were freed Black

---

60. *Vendas* were much smaller enterprises than were *logeas* and were usually associated only with the sale of wet goods (*molhados*). The *logeas* were certainly larger and more store-like and sold a variety of both wet goods (*molhados*) or dry goods (*secas*). One aspect of the fifth collection at this time, which made it a particularly regressive tax, was that the amount paid for *vendas* and *logeas* was the same for all regardless of size: ten *oitavas* of gold. Registrants therefore did not specify whether they were paying on a *venda* or a *logea*.

61. "Lista dos escravos . . . para pagarem os reaes quintos de 1720 athé o de 1721," APMSC, Códice 2.

Table 2.6.   Assets and slaves belonging to Mathias de Crasto Porto, 1742

Parish	Assets	Number of Slaves
Rossa Grande	4 houses Dry goods store Butcher shop 2 blacksmith shops 20 head of cattle	23
Curral del Rei	Plantation for cane and manioc Sugar mill	56 (plantation and
Capam	Goldfields	mine slaves)
Bento Pires	Uncultivated land 150 head of cattle	8
Congonhas	Mining land Butcher shop Store	0
Town of Sabará	2 dry goods stores 1 wet goods store 2 butcher shops 2 other buildings	7
Total		94

Source: Inventario de Mathias de Crasto Porto, 6 October 1742, MOSMG.

women, and the fifth was a slave women. The tax on the latter's *venda* was paid by her master.[62]

Twenty-five years later, in 1745, the presence of women as sellers of goods in the town of Sabará was far more obvious; manumissions had no doubt resulted in a growing number of women who lived as marketers. Of those individuals in town who did business requiring the registered use of scales and weights to measure payments in gold dust, thirty-four were women, and sixty-five were men.[63] The majority of these women worked in *vendas de molhados*, but three of them were registered as bakers, and one was a seller of bananas. Seven were slaves, five were identified as freed slaves, and the remainder were probably freeborn.[64] The fact that slaves,

62. "Lista dos escravos . . . para pagarem os reaes quintos de 1720 athé o de 1721," APMSC, Códice 2.
63. "Aferições de pesos e medidas," APMCMS, 16a. The year 1745 is chosen here only as a reflection of the available records relating to verifications of weights and measures.
64. It is possible that some women who were not identified as freed slaves in this context were definitely identified as such in another type of document such as a will or baptismal record.

through the registration of their own weights and measures, were certified by the colonial government to conduct business in town suggests that they were not simply extensions of their masters' person and authority. Were that true, a master such as Manoel Rodrigues de Almeida would have registered weights and measures in his own name, rather than have his slave Josepha do so in her own right. The arrangement of slaves registering on their own indicates that they operated more or less independently of masters in commercial transactions and that they were not customarily supervised by their masters when selling goods. Such independence indicates that masters and slaves must have come to an agreement over how profits, and how much of them, would be returned by the slave to the master. Such an agreement did not require that masters and slaves negotiate on equal terms, but slaves probably had more bargaining power in such a relationship with the master than in situations where slaves worked in closely supervised activities.

There were of course other tradespeople and artisans in town in addition to the hawkers of dry goods, food, and drink. Just in the period from 1735 to 1736, more than a dozen artisans were issued licenses to practice their trade in the town of Sabará. These included Manoel Lopes who was a carpenter, Manoel Duarte who was a miller (*celeiro*), and Manoel Pinto Fernandes who was a blacksmith. In addition, there were two tailors, Estevão Ferreyra Braga and Manoel João, and two cobblers, Manoel Dias da Costa and Manoel Pereyra. One man named Manoel D'Orta also worked as a cutler, and two men, Manoel de Couto Souza and Manoel da Costa Pontes, were goldsmiths.[65] Numerous other tradespeople in town included stone masons and the barber, who usually also carried the title of *sangrador*, for lending his services to those who needed or requested to be bled.[66]

Slaves also worked as artisans in Sabará and were valued for their special skills. When such slaves were sold in the *comarca*, they were identified by their trade and therefore commanded a higher than average price. For example, among the property sold by Antonio Fernandes Rozado in 1782 were two slave blacksmiths named Francisco and Lourenço.[67] In 1756, Francisco da Silva Forte sold fifteen slaves among whom were a barber, a carpenter, and an overseer.[68] Mathias de Crasto Porto's earlier employment

65. Cartas de exame dos officios, APMCMS, Códice 8.
66. Carta do officio de Sangrador, 16 April 1766, APMCMS, Códice 37, fol. 39v.
67. "Escriptura de compra e venda de huma fazenda," 28 May 1782, MOSMG, *Livro de notas* (16 janeiro 1782), fol. 37.
68. The slaves were identified as "Jozé barbeyro, Jozé corabani carapina, and Jozé con-

of slaves in butcher shops and the growth of butchering establishments in the second half of the eighteenth century also point to the use of Sabará's slaves in other skilled jobs whenever necessary.

As the gold production declined and the economy of Sabará was diversifying, the raising of cattle in the region became much more significant. Accompanying the increased importance of cattle raising was a rise in the number of *casas de corte* in and around the town of Sabará. These establishments were part butcher shop and part slaughterhouse, sites where people brought livestock to be slaughtered and sold as meat. Beginning in 1775, the colonial government, to raise funds, required that owners of the *casas de corte* pay for a license.[69] The registration of these enterprises indicates that there were many of them located on many of the most established streets of the town of Sabará. In 1775, seventeen licenses were granted for *cortes* in the town of Sabará, with several individuals paying for more than one. Some of these shops were run by ex-slaves, such as Luis Ribeiro, a freed *crioulo,* whose *corte* was located directly in front of Sabará's oldest church, Nossa Senhora do O. Anna Francisca Xavier de Sam Payo was also an ex-slave with a *corte* in town. Other shops were clearly owned by free individuals but managed by their slaves.[70]

Between 1775 and the end of the century, the number of licenses issued varied from year to year with an average number of 13 being recorded. Most of the registrants were men, fewer than 1 in 5 of the licensees was a woman. The numbers of freed slaves registering for licenses was fairly small: only 3 men and 6 women out of a total of 158. As with the town venders, the registrants for *casas de corte* were occasionally slaves. Marianna, for example, was a slave of Josefa da Costa, and she operated a *corte* in the years between 1788 and 1792. In a similar fashion, Antonio da Costa, slave of Josefa da Costa Sampayo, was licensed to operate a *corte* three times during the years between 1782 and 1790.

Although the total proportion of women licensed for *cortes* was less than 20 percent, their presence was significant in an occupation that in European countries and their colonies was mostly reserved for men. Among the most successful *cortes,* those operating for five years or more, the proportion of licensed women rose to over 30 percent.[71] In the six *cortes* that remained in operation for more than ten years, three, or half

---

tremestre" in Escritura de compra e venda, 22 May 1757, *Livro de notas* (3 julho de 1756), MOSMG, fol. 134.

69. Registo da licença para os cortes, APMCMS, Códice 28.

70. Registo da licença para os cortes, APMCMS, Códice 28.

71. Nineteen *cortes* operated for five years or more; of these, six were operated by women.

the licensees, were women. Two of these women, Anna Fernandes Tavares and Anna Francisca Xavier de Sampayo, were both ex-slaves.

Slave owners determined not only the actual work that slaves performed and where and with whom such work was performed but also the conditions under which the slaves performed it. As the discussion of occupations for slaves suggests, conditions of work could vary considerably according to whether the slave was a man or a woman, a miner or a marketer, an artisan or a manual laborer, a domestic servant or a sexual servant, a town dweller or a rural resident. One characteristic of the working conditions of slaves in the *comarca* of Sabará, which emerges from the arrangements detailed in wills, inventories, and other forms of property transfers, is that many slaves, in different occupations, performed their work in exchange for remuneration, often in the form of gold. Of these many slaves who performed work in exchange for cash rewards, slave owners expected that a few would save enough to buy their freedom from owners at a price equivalent to their market value. When masters did not wish to grant manumissions to individuals, they still made contractual arrangements with slaves, which allowed their laborers to accumulate and spend a cash income and to exercise some control over their daily work and lives.

The numerous male slaves working in goldfields were among those who performed their tasks in exchange for the possibility of earning an income of their own. Padre Martinho de Barros, who advised the king on methods of tax collection in the mines in 1724, observed that slaves engaged in mining customarily paid their masters the sum of one-half of an *oitava* of gold per day and could keep what remained of their day's findings.[72] Masters apparently did not always enforce a strict work regime in the mines as long as their slaves paid them a daily sum. In addition to the fact that slaves engaged in commercial activities in the *comarca* could often work unsupervised, those who worked in the principal industry of the region — gold mining — also seem to have had considerable freedom from close supervision in their daily work.

Masters could also choose to reward individual slaves with arrangements that would provide them with greater autonomy and assets of their own. In 1716, Sebastião Pereira de Aguilar owned forty-nine slaves among whom were forty men and nine women. Aguilar described his slave Andre as one "to whom I gave permission to acquire his own goods [to possess

---

72. "Voto do Padre Martinho de Barros sobre o quinto do ouro das Minas Geraes," 6 February 1724, AHU, Minas Gerais, Documentos avulsos. Unpaged document found in the uncatalogued collection on Minas Gerais.

them] and to control them as long as I lived in the mining region, and leaving the mines, I would allow him half of these goods so as to live with his wife, the other half of the goods being mine." Aguilar made similar arrangements with two others of his male slaves.[73]

Slave owners also expected that women as well as men slaves would be able to earn an income and accumulate savings. This expectation underlies the practice of setting a price for the manumission of both women and men and in many cases limiting the number of years in which a slave had to accumulate the necessary sum.[74] In colonial Sabará, a slave for whom a manumission price had been set by his or her owner was referred to as *cortada* or *cortado*, and such slaves were sometimes granted more freedom from supervision than were slaves for whom no manumission price had been set.[75] Evidence is not available to determine what proportion of slaves who were *cortados* were freed. The annual rate of actual manumissions for slaves in Sabará was quite low — under 1 percent per annum. The decisions of masters to set manumission prices (i.e., *cortar* a slave) therefore should be considered as a strategy employed by owners primarily to achieve cooperation from slaves and perhaps as a source of income that might not otherwise be forthcoming. (See Chapter 5 for a more complete discussion of manumission practices.)

Those owners who wished to make it more feasible for their slaves to pay their way out of slavery could offer better working conditions, a longer or unspecified period in which to pay the necessary price, or (more rarely) a lower price for freedom. In 1740, for example, Maria de Freytas set the price of her slave Anna Mina at 100 *oitavas* and gave her two years to pay that amount. In instructions to her executors, she wrote that Anna should be given "all the liberty possible to acquire the 100 oitavas."[76] The previously discussed 1719 decision of Bras de Barros Soares to set a price

---

73. ". . . ao qual dei licença para adquerir seus bens (pessuirlos) e administrarlos em quanto eu estivesse nas minas, e deixandoas lhe permeteria a metade dos bens que tivessem para vivir com sua mulher com quem he cazado, sendo minha a outra metade dos dittos bens." Testamento de Sebastião Pereira de Aguilar, 27 October 1716, *Livro de registo de testamento* (1716–25), MOSMG, fol. 13.

74. The practice is observable both in the provisions of wills and inventories and in the records of letters of manumissions for slaves who successfully paid their price of manumission.

75. Slaves in colonial Brazil did not have the legal right to demand that the price of manumission be set by their masters. Alternative spellings for *cortado* were *coartado* and *quartado*. Manumission practices are discussed at length in Chapter 5.

76. Testamento de Maria de Freytas, 6 August 1740, *Livro de registo de testamento* (17 dezembro 1740), MOSMG, fol. 94v.

for his slave woman Thereza did not limit the number of years that she had to pay for her freedom. He also demanded an amount much lower than her market value as a reflection of the non-income-producing work of raising a newborn child who was in all likelihood his own.[77] Still, Soares's demand for payment in gold from his slave woman was a recognition of the fact that in her work as a slave she, like many other slaves in the region, did earn an income and might be able to accumulate some savings.

The contractual arrangements between slaves and owners in Sabará allowing for some remuneration for the work performed clearly did not apply uniformly to every slave and did not change the fact that conditions of work still varied considerably. The daily lives of those who worked in mining were, by all accounts, considerably more difficult than those of slaves who resided in town selling goods or working at a trade. Closely supervised or not, the process of searching for gold or working in mining sites represented backbreaking labor. Slaves worked nearly all the day, filling *bateias* with heavy mixtures of gravel and water. When not standing panning for hours in water, slaves were digging canals and pits and carrying earth and other supplies from one place to the next in wooden boxes borne on their heads.[78] Even when the work of slaves led to some form of remuneration, the ordinary labors of mining were exhausting and could be both hazardous and unhealthy.

Extraction of gold in Sabará depended, as noted, entirely on access to water. Patterns of rainfall therefore had serious consequences for working conditions. Although the average annual rainfall in Minas Gerais is somewhere between one and one-half to two meters, yearly variations are such that twice that amount is possible. Two-thirds of the yearly rainfall comes between December and March.[79] As a consequence, the rivers and streams in the region are wide and shallow during the dry season; in the rainy months they often reach flood stage and run swift and treacherously deep. Under these circumstances, the rechanneling of watercourses necessary for advanced forms of mine development was not easy and often meant the loss of much equipment and time when flood waters destroyed canal proj-

77. Testamento de Bras de Barros Soares, 25 August 1719, *Livro de registo de testamento* (1716–25), MOSMG, fol.33. "[E] ella a corto em baixo preço pelo trabalho que ha de ter em criar o seu filho o filha."

78. Luis Gomes Ferreyra reported that slaves did sometimes work in underground mines, and he described these as ranging in depths from 50 to 100 *palmas* (palms) deep and in lengths reaching up to 700 *palmas*. See Ferreyra, *Erario mineral*, 2.

79. Dorr, "Physiographic, Stratigraphic, and Structural Development of the Quadrilátero Ferrífero, Minas Gerais, Brazil," 1A.

ects.[80] Such periodic patterns of destruction meant that slaves spent many hours rebuilding and redigging channels and canals.

Luis Gomes Ferreyra, a doctor in residence in Sabará during the first decades of the eighteenth century, wrote of countless deaths among slaves working in mining and described in detail the physical problems encountered by slaves engaged in such work.[81] He attributed many of their illnesses, particularly the tendency to suffer from respiratory diseases, to the conditions of mining: working in water or in a damp underground pit, sweating in a climate where with wet feet it was easy to become chilled. Slaves working underground often stayed there all day, to work, to eat, and even to sleep.[82] Ferreyra attributed many digestive problems to slaves eating badly cooked food, only twice a day, late at night, and then right after sleeping.[83] He was critical of masters' treatment of their slaves, not simply because he believed neglect increased a master's losses of laborers. When describing the treatments for illnesses, he had a special warning for slave masters: "And I advise that if the patient is a slave that he be given a good blanket, warm shelter, and sufficient food, as in these matters, many masters of slaves are remiss and they will have to account to God for it."[84] Ferreyra's advice reflected the fact that temperatures in the region could fall to uncomfortably cold levels even in a semitropical environment. His suggestions also indicate the likelihood that most slaves he encountered were not given adequate food, clothing, or shelter by their owners.

According to Ferreyra, respiratory illnesses were quite common in the mines, and many slaves died. The diseases struck laborers so swiftly that a master could lose his most valuable assets in a matter of days or even in twenty-four hours.[85] With the likelihood of slaves dying off suddenly, mas-

---

80. Eschwege, *Pluto brasiliensis*, 1, p. 44.

81. "Morrem escravos sem numero," Ferreyra, *Erario mineral*, 1.

82. "[O]s pretos, porque alguns habitao dentro da agua (como sao mineyros, que minerao nas partes bayxas da terra, e veyos della), outros feytos-toupeyros minerando por baixo da terra, huns em altura de fundo cincuenta, oitenta, e mais de cem palmas; outros pelo cumprimento em estradas subterraneas, muito mais, que muitas vezes chegão a seiscentos e a setecentos: lá trabalhao, lá comem, e lá dormem muytas vezes;" Ferreyra, *Erario mineral*, 2.

83. Ferreyra, *Erario mineral*, 12.

84. "E advirto que se o doente for preto se lhe dé boa cobertura, casa bem recolhida, e o comer de boa sustancia, que nisto peccao muitos os senhores de escravos de que hao de dar conta a Deos," Ferreyra, *Erario mineral*, 31.

85. Writing in *Erario mineral* about "pontadas sem complicações": "esta doença era muito commua, e que morriao tantos escravos, e se perdia tanto ouro em poucos dias," 13; and also "vendo que hum pobre trabalhava dois e tres annos para lucrar hum [slave], e que o perdia em poucos dias ou bem 24 horas," 14.

ters could probably not expect their slave force to remain alive for many years. Martinho de Mendonça, who briefly served as governor of Minas Gerais, wrote in 1734 that owners did not expect slaves bought as young men to be fit for more than twelve years of labor.[86]

It was Ferreyra's experience that slaves from different parts of Africa reacted differently to illness. He noted that Cobu and Angola slaves became very listless when ill, whereas Mina slaves did not. In general, Ferreyra thought that Blacks were more robust than Whites and that they admitted to illness only when they were half dead. Of course, sickness was a luxury that slaves could not afford, and they perhaps had little faith in their masters' ability or intention to cure them of their ills.[87] This point was suggested by Ferreyra himself in his discussion of *formigueyros,* a parasitic infestation in the soles of the feet, which also manifested itself as tumors on hands, arms, legs, and fingers. He observed that *formigueyros* in the feet of slaves was very difficult to cure because masters would not give their slaves time off from work.[88]

An intelligent and inquisitive physician, Ferreyra strongly believed that the conditions in which people lived and worked were related to the types of illnesses that abounded in the mining region. He noted that respiratory illness (*pontadas*) was not exclusively a disease found in Black slaves, but one shared by many Whites who lived in circumstances that paralleled the deprivations suffered by slaves. He therefore wrote: "All that has been written about *pontadas* should be understood to apply not only to blacks, but as well to whites who work in the same tasks as blacks, or almost the same; as they work as overseers of mining sites, or agricultural lands, or at other jobs while barefoot, living poorly, eating poorly, with inadequate clothing, always damp, and sweaty, etc., these Whites can be cured of pontadas using the same methods applied to blacks."[89] Ferreyra's com-

86. Martinho de Mendonça de Proença, "Reflexões sobre o sistema da capitação," ca. 1734, cited in Boxer, *The Golden Age,* 174. In examining parish records in nearby Ouro Preto, Ramos found a mortality rate for slaves of 8.2 percent annually. Thus slaves could have expected to live for twelve years. There is insufficient evidence available to calculate mortality rates for slaves in the *comarca* of Sabará. I did not encounter death registers in either the local or state archives. On the other hand, there is little reason to believe that conditions would have been better there than in Ouro Preto. See Ramos, "A Social History of Ouro Preto: Stresses of Dynamic Urbanization in Colonial Brazil, 1695–1726" (Ph.D. diss., University of Florida, 1972), 221.

87. Ferreyra, *Erario mineral,* 54.

88. Ferreyra, *Erario mineral,* 358.

89. "Todo que fica escrito a respeyto das pontadas se entenderá não so a respeyto dos pretos, se nao tambem a respeyto dos brancos, que se exercitarem o mesmo officio dos

ments indicate that the distinctions between the conditions of at least some Whites' lives and those of Black slaves were not very noticeable.

Ferreyra's other observations about disease also indicate that Whites in the mining region shared both material deprivation with Blacks and an extremely marginalized status, at least in terms of education and upbringing. In another section of his treatise, he advises that in dealing with both *pretos* and *brancos rudes* (Blacks and uncouth Whites), one had to repeat information about treatments often and carefully as both these groups of people were rustic and therefore fickle in nature (*agrestes e variavel*).[90] This Portuguese-born doctor thus confirms the evidence from other sources that the White population included both wealthy masters and poor, uneducated itinerants. His observations augment the picture of Sabará's free society as highly differentiated.

The slave population in colonial Sabará was quite complex as well. The vast majority of the adult slaves working in the *comarca* were of African origin. Inventories for the years 1725–59 show that 88 percent of adults were Africans; in the years 1760–1808, over three-quarters of slaves listed in Sabará's inventories were still of African origin. For the Portuguese colonists in eighteenth-century Brazil, the most important sources for Africans were the *Costa da Mina*[91] and the west-central area of Congo-Angola. During the years 1760–1808, the numbers of Africans originating in the Congo-Angola region increased relative to those identified as Minas. Before 1760, Mina slaves had outnumbered Congo-Angola slaves two to one. After 1760, Congo-Angola slaves made up a majority of Sabará's African slave population (53 percent). (See Tables 2.7 and 2.8.)

As the earlier discussion of the use and preference for male labor in the gold-mining region indicated, aggregate analyses of slaveholdings show that the sex ratio among African adults working in Sabará was severely skewed. Among slaveholdings examined in the years 1725–59, there were over five times as many men from the Costa da Mina as there were women from that region, and there were more than six times as many men from the Congo-Angola region as there were women from that part of Africa.

---

pretos, ou quasi o mesmo; como he o serem feytores de lavras, ou roças, ou andarem em outros ministerios descalços, com ma ordem de viver ou mal comidos, mal enroupados, molhados, suados, etc., que estes se curarao de pontadas pelo mesmo methodo que os pretos," Ferreyra, *Erario mineral*, 54.

90. Ferreyra, *Erario mineral*, 20.

91. The *Costa da Mina* was a term applied by the Portuguese to an area extending from the Gold Coast to the Bight of Benin.

Table 2.7
Race, ethnicity, or place of origin for adult slaves in Sabará, 1725–1759

	Men	Women	Total
Brazil			
Crioulo	21	13	34
Mulato	5	5	10
Pardo	0	0	0
Cabra	4	0	4
Subtotal	30	18	48
Africa			
Cabo Verde	6	1	7
Costa da Mina	181	35	216
Nago	2	1	3
São Tomé	0	1	1
Congo/Angola	90	14	104
Cobu	12	2	14
Monjollo	2	0	2
Other	5	2	7
Subtotal	298	56	354
GRAND TOTAL	328	74	402

SOURCE: Inventarios, 1725–59, MOSMG.

NOTE: Sex ratio among adults of known origin was 443. Among those originating in Africa, it was 532. Among those originating in Brazil , it was 166.

The overall sex ratio among African slaves in these years was 532 males per 100 females.[92] (See Table 2.7.)

Slaveholdings in the years 1760–1808 show that the sex ratio among adult Africans remained severely imbalanced and in fact became worse

92. Francisco Vidal Luna and Iraci del Nero da Costa also found a very high sex ratio in the neighboring *comarca* of Serro do Frio (also part of Minas Gerais). There the slave registration of 1738 indicated that free slave owners (owning 90.1 percent of all slaves) owned slaves in the following proportions: 86.6 percent were men, and 13.4 percent were women, a sex ratio of 6.5 (650 men per 100 women). In their study, the number of slaves was 7,134. "A presença do elemento forro no conjunto de proprietários de escravos," *Ciência e cultura* 32 (July 1980): 840. Bergad has similarly found imbalances in the sex ratio among African slaves in Mariana, Minas Gerais, in 1750 (792/100). The presence of creoles was greater in Mariana and produced a composite sex ratio there of 329/100. See Bergad, "After the Mining Boom," *LARR* 31:1 (1996): 67–97. This configuration of slaveholding may be unfamiliar to scholars who rely on figures deriving from the African slave trade to the New World. See note 43 above. During the California gold rush of the nineteenth century, the average sex ratio in the western United States was 278.9 and in some gold-mining counties was as high as 3,329. Sherman L. Ricards, Jr., "A Demographic History of the West: Butte County, California, 1850," *Papers of the Michigan Academy of Science, Arts, and Letters* 46 (1961): 474.

Table 2.8
Race, ethnicity, or place of origin for adult slaves in Sabará, 1760–1808

	Men	Women	Total
Brazil			
Crioulo	60	56	116
Mulato	10	6	16
Pardo	1	1	2
Cabra	6	4	10
Subtotal	77	67	144
Africa			
Cabo Verde	2	0	2
Costa da Mina	144	25	169
Nago	15	0	15
São Tomé	3	0	3
Congo/Angola	214	22	236
Cobu	9	0	9
Monjollo	3	0	3
Other	7	0	7
Subtotal	397	47	444
GRAND TOTAL	474	114	588

SOURCE: Inventarios, 1760–1808, MOSMG.

NOTE: Sex ratio among adults of known origin was 416. Among those originating in Africa, it was 844. Among those originating in Brazil, it was 115.

than in the earlier period. Among the Mina slaves (who had become a minority of the total African population in these years), there were still over five times as many men as women (576 men per 100 women). Among Congo-Angola slaves, there were close to ten times as many men as women. Among African adults listed in inventories for these years, the overall sex ratio had risen to 844 males per 100 females. (See Table 2.8.)

The presence of Brazilian-born adult slaves in Sabará's slaveholdings served to improve the overall sex ratio among adults because among them there were more women. Brazilian-born slaves were, as stated, more numerous in the post-1760 period than in earlier decades, and the sex ratio among them was more balanced in these later years as well.[93] For the entire period (1725–1808), the composite sex ratio among adult slaves was therefore approximately four to one.[94] (See Tables 2.7, 2.8.)

93. Bergad has found a much larger proportion of creole slaves in late eighteenth-century Mariana, 54 percent of slaves inventoried in 1795. See Bergad, "After the Mining Boom," 67–97.

94. From 1725 to 1759, the adult sex ratio was 443; from 1760 to 1808, that ratio was 416.

Despite the formidable obstacles to the natural increase of slaves, which the colonists of Sabará created by purchasing so many more male slaves than females and by using almost exclusively male labor in the mining sites of the region, the inventories of colonists include listings of slave children, virtually all of whom were Brazilian born.[95] The overall sex ratio in the population of child slaves was balanced, a fact that suggests that these children were also born locally.[96] In the years 1725–59, 82 percent of the children were *crioulos*, born in Brazil of two Black parents who were either African or *crioulo* slaves. Almost 13 percent of the children were *mulatos*, of African and European descent.[97] The remainder of the children were also of mixed racial background and were identified as *cabras* or *pardos*.[98]

In the second half of the eighteenth century, the proportion of children in the sample slave population increased very little — from 16 to 18.3 percent of the total.[99] Among these children, however, the *crioulos* had become less numerous (76.7 percent) and *mulatos* somewhat more numerous (16.6 percent) than in the earlier decades. The remainder of the children were identified as *cabras* or *pardos*. The increase in the percentage of children of mixed descent in slaveholdings was a reflection of the declining interest among slaveholders in manumitting their own offspring or the offspring of their relatives. This change in the behavior of slaveholders can be related to demographic changes among them and is discussed more fully in Chapter 5.

Aggregate analyses of the sex ratios among African adults, *crioulo* adults, or child slaves offer significant observations about the overall composition of the slave population in Sabará and the purchasing choices of masters, but are less revealing about the individual experiences of slaves. Most slaves did not, in fact, live in households where the average sex ratio for any particular group prevailed. In 1775, for example, Maria *crioula*

95. Sixteen percent of slaves listed in inventories of 1725–59 were children. The number of slaves was 517.

96. Inventories did not always specify who the mothers of the children were, but the nature of the listings in which children are often named near the names of women also suggests that these children were born locally and not purchased.

97. The children of two *mulato* parents were also *mulatos*.

98. The exact meaning of these terms is not clear, although both words indicate a person of mixed racial descent. *Cabra* was a term more commonly used by owners originating in the northeast of Brazil. The number of children listed in inventories for these years was 83.

99. In the years 1760–1808, the number of slaves listed in inventories was 774, 142 of whom were children.

and Izabel *crioula* lived in the household of Gracia Rodrigues de Bom Fim, a freed Black woman.[100] These two therefore lived in an entirely female household. More commonly, as noted earlier, slaves such as those of Domingos Alves do Couto lived only with other men. João Mina, Antonio Mina Gago, Gonçallo Angolla, and Matheus Angolla were the only slaves belonging to this master in 1767.[101] No uniform sex ratio dominated slave-owning households, and in most cases the sex ratio among adult slaves was less extreme than that indicated by the aggregate numbers.[102] Slave owners were therefore less likely than one might think to have observed that the overall sex ratio among adult slaves in the *comarca* was as imbalanced as was indeed the case.

From the perspective of the slaves and in terms of what would most likely encourage a natural increase in the slave population, what mattered was of course where most adult slaves actually lived. The vast majority of the slaves from Sabará's sample households lived where the sex ratio among adults was equal to or greater than two males per female. More than one-half the adults (54.9 percent) lived in households where the sex ratio was greater than four men per woman, and another 4.3 percent lived in single-sex households. These data confirm that most enslaved men in Sabará lived where it was not possible for them to establish a relationship with a slave woman living in the same quarters. The numbers of slave families with children were therefore, as noted in the holdings of Mathias de Crasto Porto, quite limited.[103]

Slaveholders in Sabará also complicated the relationships that slaves could forge with one another by deliberately acquiring slaves of various African national or ethnic identities. In no case was there a household where all the slaves were Minas or Angolas, or even all *crioulos*. Masters commonly owned slaves from diverse backgrounds. Slaves could and did choose to foil the intentions of masters to prevent alliances among themselves in households. They even married (when this was permitted) partners of different African origins. For example, Felix Banguela and Paula Mina were a married slave couple belonging to Manoel de Sousa de Oli-

---

100. Inventario de Gracia Rodrigues de Bom Fim, 1 May 1775, Inventarios, 1770–79, MOSMG.

101. Inventario de Domingos Alves do Couto,1767, in Inventarios, 1760–69, MOSMG.

102. Among all households examined in the years 1725–1808, in approximately 50 percent the sex ratio was less than three men per woman or even better (i.e., more balanced).

103. These data are also derived from an aggregate analysis of inventories in the years 1725–1808.

veira and his wife Eugenia da Silva in 1749. Their four young *crioulo* children were listed among the assets of this couple along with eight other African slaves (two Banguela men, four Mina men, one São Thome woman, and one Banguela woman).[104] In 1743, Manoel Lopes Machado and his wife also owned a slave couple of diverse African backgrounds: Izabel Angolla was married to Lucas Courano.[105] In 1742, Joseph Gomes Alves Abram owned a married slave couple, Antonio Cobu and Maria Angolla, who had four young *crioulo* children.[106]

As this chapter's opening discussion of bachelor colonists suggested, another important variable shaping the experiences of slaves in their households was the fact of their owner being a man or a woman. Women owners (unmarried and widowed) were far less common than were men owners in the early decades of the eighteenth century, but their smaller numbers of slaves were better known to them. Men owners (married and unmarried) were the rule in the *comarca*, and in their larger slaveholdings men slaves risked a significant lack of contact with their master or other free colonists; women slaves risked sexual servitude and bearing their master's children.

The household inventories for the years 1725–59 and 1760–1808 indicate that slaveholding patterns of men and women colonists dramatically changed as the eighteenth century progressed. Men who were not co-owners (i.e., had no spouses) owned over 40 percent of the slaves in the sample population before 1760, but only just over 20 percent in the post-1760 period.[107] Women who had never married and women who acquired authority over property holdings through widowhood were a small minority among slaveholders before 1760.[108] In the years 1760–1808,

104. Manoel de Sousa de Oliveira, 25 June 1749, Inventarios, 1747–49, MOSMG.

105. Inventario de Manoel Lopes Machado, 13 January 1743, Inventarios, 1760–69, MOSMG.

106. Inventario de Roza Maria da Cunha, 4 June 1742, Inventarios, 1740–46, MOSMG.

107. These inventories may well over-represent the presence of married couples in the free population; there is a correlation between wealth, marriage, and the likelihood of having a will or inventory. For a discussion of low rates of marriage elsewhere in Minas Gerais in the same period, see Ramos, "Marriage and the Family in Colonial Vila Rica," *HAHR* 55 (May 1975): 212; Ramos, "Single and Married Women in Vila Rica, Brazil, 1754–1838," *Journal of Family History* 16:3 (1991): 261–82.

108. In the wills examined for the years 1716–25, the presence of women owners was somewhat greater than in the 1720 slave registration or in the sample of inventories from 1725–59. Women owners represented 15.6 percent of the testators and owned 8.9 percent of the slaves. *Livro de registo de testamento* (1716–25), MOSMG. (See Table 2.4.) Luna and Costa also found women owners quite uncommon in Minas Gerais during the first half of the

however, such women became owners of nearly one-fourth of the child slaves and over one-fifth of women slaves in the sample slave population.[109] These women, who in the years 1725–59 owned and controlled only 2.3 percent of the sample population of slaves, held seven times as many slaves in the 1760–1808 period (16.2 percent of total slave population in the sample). The increase in the presence of women as slaveholders thus coincides with the previously mentioned growth in smaller slaveholdings in the *comarca* and the development of an even wider gap between the assets of richest slaveholders and the poorest. (See Tables 2.5, 2.9, 2.10.)

Another aspect of the experiences of slaves in the *comarca* of Sabará was the likelihood of encountering the presence of *forros* or manumitted slaves. The presence of ex-slaves in the free population not only raised the issue for slaves of becoming freed but also demonstrated the prospect of ex-slaves' becoming slave owners themselves. The 1720 collection of the Royal Fifth required that *forros* pay a tax on their own persons as well as

Table 2.9. Demography of slaveholdings in Sabará, Minas Gerais, 1725–1759 (Percentages)

Owners	All Slaves	Children	Women	Men
Women 10.0	2.3	0	7.5	1.5
Men 23.3	40.4	18.1	31.1	48.4
Couples 66.6	57.2	81.9	61.3	50.1

SOURCE: Inventarios, 1725–59, MOSMG.

NOTE: The number of slaveholders is 30 (3 women, 7 men, 20 couples). The number of slaves is 517 (341 men, 93 women, 83 children). Of 3 women owners, 2 were widows; 1 of 7 men owners was a widower.

eighteenth century. In the years 1743–45, only 3.95 percent of slaveholders listed in *Livros de assento de óbitos* were women. Their data come from both the *comarca* of Sabará and the capital of Minas Gerais, Vila Rica. Luna and Costa, "A presença do elemento forro," 838.

109. Although married women owned property (including slaves), they, unlike widows or the never-married, had limited control over it. Portuguese law made husbands the heads of household and the managers of household property, the so-called *bens do casal*. Through marriage, men controlled the enslaved property of women. For a concise discussion of the authority of women over property in colonial Brazil, see Metcalf, "Women and Means," 277–98.

Table 2.10. Demography of slaveholdings in Sabará, Minas Gerais, 1760–1808 (Percentages)

Owners	All Slaves	Children	Women	Men
Women 18.9	16.2	24.6	22.7	12.2
Men 27.5	20.8	24.6	24.2	18.8
Couples 53.4	62.9	50.7	53.0	69.0

SOURCE: Inventarios, 1760–1808, MOSMG.

NOTE: The number of slaveholders is 58 (10 women, 16 men, 32 couples). The number of slaves is 774 (500 men, 32 women, 142 children). Of 10 women owners, 5 were widows; 3 of 16 men owners were widowers.

on the slaves whom they owned.[110] The registration lists for the tax collected in that year named ninety-four individuals as *forros,* among whom fifty-one were slave owners.[111] For example, Thereza Pinta, who lived in the district of the Igreja Matriz, was listed as paying the tax for her own person because she was an ex-slave. Another freed slave woman named Marta who lived in the *vila* of Sabará paid tax on her four slaves and on herself as well. The fifty-one *forros* who owned slaves were masters of a total of ninety-nine individuals. The largest number of slaves owned by an ex-slave was eight, and these were owned by Daniel Pereira Tavares, a *forro* living in the district of Raposos. The remaining *forros* all owned four or fewer slaves and so were in the ranks of the small slaveholders who formed the majority of masters at that time. (See Tables 2.2 and 2.11.)

In comparison with the number of slaves registered in Sabará in 1720 (5,908), the number of ex-slaves was very low, less than 2 percent of the total slave and ex-slave population (94/6002 = 1.56%). From the slaves' perspective, then, the likelihood of becoming freed probably appeared to be no more than a remote possibility.[112] For women slaves, however, the

110. *Forros* paid the same amount for themselves as they did for each slave owned. "Lista dos escravos . . . para pagarem os reaes quintos de 1720 athé o de 1721," APMSC, Códice 2.
111. It is not known whether freed children were exempt from this registration, but none was listed at the time.
112. This calculation does not take into account the possibility that freed male slaves may have been more likely than freed female slaves to leave the *comarca* or the possibility that mortality among freed male slaves may have been higher than that among freed female slaves. The conclusion drawn from this calculation is therefore tentative.

Table 2.11. Freed slaves and slave ownership in the *comarca* of Sabará, 1720

Non-slave Owners		Slave Owners					
Forros	Forras	Forros	(No. of Slaves)	Forras	(No. of Slaves)	Forro Couples	(No. of Slaves)
12	31	10	(28)	37	(68)	2	(3)

SOURCE: "Lista dos escravos . . . para pagarem os reaes quintos de 1720 athé o de 1721," APMSC, Códice 2.

NOTES: Total number of freed slaves was 94; 51 (54 percent) were slave owners. Total number of slaves owned by former slaves was 99. *Forras* represented almost 70 percent of women slave owners in the *comarca* and owned 57 percent of slaves owned by women.

possibility of being freed was less remote. In the slave population, the data on sex ratios show that women were very much a minority; among adult *forros,* however, women represented the vast majority of the group — 74.4 percent in 1720. If the sex ratio among slaves of testators in the years 1716–25 (516 males per 100 females) approximated that in the 1720 slave registration, then only 1,144 of the 5,908 slaves registered were women. In this case, the freed slave women represented almost 6 percent of the total slave and ex-slave female population (70/1214 = 5.76%). In other words, perhaps as many as 1 in 17 slave women was freed in the first decades of the mining era in Sabará.[113] In contrast, the same type of calculation made for men would indicate that only 1 out of every 200 slave men was freed.[114]

The presence of close to 100 *forros* in 1720 was undoubtedly significant both to Sabará's slaves and to its free White slaveholders, although perhaps for very different reasons. The role of *forros* as masters was so common that one out of eighteen slaveholders was an ex-slave. The fact that *forros* so readily chose to become masters may explain why, in this part of Brazil, the free Whites eventually were totally outnumbered by the population of free non-Whites. (See Table 2.1.) In many slave societies of the

113. It was quite likely that the slave population was 90 percent African in 1720, if not more so, because there were fewer Brazilian-born slaves in the inventories analyzed in the first half of the eighteenth century than there were in the second half. Because the inventories indicated that only 18% of the total number of slaves were Brazilian born, it is logical to assume that this figure was lower in the period preceding the analysis of inventories. An estimate of six to one male to female among African slaves is consistent with the data found in inventories. The number of Brazilian women in 1720 was also estimated based on the figures from inventories showing that men outnumbered women 121/100.

114. If there were 4,900 men in 1720, then 23 *forros* divided by 4,923 is .5 percent.

New World, particularly in the United States, there was much apprehension among the White populations when it appeared that they were going to become minorities relative to the population of slaves. With this fear came an accompanying suspicion toward manumitted slaves and an increasing curtailment of the possibilities for manumission. The lives of ex-slaves were also increasingly monitored and restricted by White authorities.[115] If, however, in the mining region of Brazil, Whites could readily expect that a large percentage of manumitted slaves would identify with the master class and seek to join it, there was less reason to fear a free non-White population and little motivation to prevent its growth in the region. It is one thing to fear the growth of a servile population (whether slave or free) that appears to be resisting or rejecting the existing social structure[116] and another to fear the growth of a free, albeit non-White population that seeks not to overthrow but to participate in the slave society as masters of slaves.

The potential fears that White male slaveholders in Sabará might have had about *forros* competing with them for mining lands or other coveted riches in the *comarca* were undoubtedly eased by their decisions to free far fewer men than women. One result of such a pattern of manumission decisions was that three-quarters of the ex-slaves who were slave owners in 1720 were women, not men. In fact, women who were former slaves were 70 percent of all the women slaveholders listed in 1720. These women slaveholders were, as noted earlier, concentrated in the urban centers of the *comarca* and supported themselves (through slaves) in occupations associated with commerce and marketing. They did not often directly compete with White men in the more alluring and lucrative gold-mining sector of the economy, which had first attracted free immigrants to the *comarca*. The small numbers of slaves owned by these women did not allow the *forras* to present much of an economic threat to owners of much larger slaveholdings. (See Table 2.3.)

The phenomenon of *forros* as masters of slaves continued throughout the eighteenth century. In the 1720 registration lists of slave owners in Sabará, freed slaves represented 5.7 percent of all masters. Among properties inventoried in the years 1725–59, 12.1 percent of the owners were *forros*. The inventories of properties in the years 1760–1808 listed 9.5

---

115. See, for example, Peter H. Wood, *Black Majority: Negroes in Colonial South Carolina from 1670 Through the Stono Rebellion* (New York: W. W. Norton & Co., 1974), chap. 8.

116. See Edmund S. Morgan, *American Slavery, American Freedom: The Ordeal of Colonial Virginia* (New York: W. W. Norton & Co., 1975).

percent of the owners as *forros*.[117] The children of *forros* who were masters eventually joined the ranks of slaveholders and were identified as free non-Whites. With such individuals added to the numbers of *forro* masters in the period 1760–1808, the proportion of non-White propertyholders among the inventories examined rises to 15.8 percent.[118] Female ex-slaves continued to outnumber male ex-slaves in the role of slaveholders throughout the period of this study.[119] *Forras* also continued to represent a large proportion of the women who owned slaves in Sabará.[120]

By the nature of their normative and formulaic character, the wills of individuals who were former slaves in the *comarca* of Sabará reveal only some of the differences that marked the lives of such people from those who had arrived willingly in Brazil as free colonists. Instead, these documents demonstrate, and perhaps overemphasize, how strongly freed slaves could have identified with the culture and mores of their former owners, the Portuguese colonists. It is, of course, difficult to know how representative of all freed slaves the will-writing freed slaves were and how they felt about having their lives recorded and defined in such a wholly Portuguese and non-African format as a formula-defined will. That such wills exist at all does, however, serve as evidence of the Portuguese interest in incorporating some former slaves into the world and culture of the masters, even if such an interest could not be fully realized.

The wills of former slaves were all of individuals converted to Catholicism, or at least accepted as converts to Catholicism, and probably represent the lives of those who mostly successfully demonstrated an ability to live and work according to Portuguese-defined norms. These individuals were, after all, those who owners felt could be safely freed from slavery and whose new status would not pose a threat to free colonists in the *comarca*. It therefore should not be surprising to see that some of these ex-slaves and their children followed so closely in the footsteps of their former masters.

As mentioned in Chapter 1, Jorge da Fonseca Ferreira was a freed Black

117. In the years 1725–59, four of thirty-three properties had former slaves as owners. Two properties were owned by unmarried women, two were owned by *forro* couples. In the years 1760–1808, six of sixty-three properties were owned by *forros* (five women and one man, no couples).

118. In addition to six properties owned by *forros* in the years 1760–1808, four more were owned by free *pardos* (free persons of mixed racial descent). In two cases, the owners were unmarried women; in two other cases, the owners were couples. 10/63 = 15.8 percent.

119. See note 113 above.

120. In the inventories dated 1760–1808, *forras* constituted 50 percent of the women who owned slaves.

slave from the Costa da Mina living in Sabará in 1806. A bachelor like Mathias de Crasto Porto before him, Jorge nonetheless had one son by an African woman named Antônia Xavier, also from the Costa da Mina. This son became his heir to his assets. In his decisions about his own slaves, Ferreira freed one named Joaquim Angolla on his death and set a manumission price for another slave named Lourenço. Ferreira's executor was instructed to give Lourenço two years to pay his price, and if the slave failed to produce the required sum, Lourenço would be returned to captivity.[121]

Joze Carvalho was a freed slave and native of the Costa da Mina. He was baptized in the parish of Sabará and remained a lifelong bachelor. In his will of 1789, Carvalho named his son Benedito Carvalho as his heir and set manumission prices for three male slaves. He left a small sum to the local Catholic brotherhood to which he belonged. Carvalho also arranged to pay his executor for his work in caring for the estate and carrying out testamentary decisions. As payment, he gave to his executor another slave named Joze Mozambique.[122]

In 1771, Caetano Fernandes da Silva, a former slave and native of the Costa da Mina, named Manoel de Crasto Porto (Mathias's son) as the executor of his estate. He identified his former master as Gonçalo Fernandes and declared that he had paid 256 *oitavas* (two pounds) of gold for his freedom. Caetano stated that he had had a son, Vitorio, during his time in captivity, but now both his son and the mother were dead. He named two friends as heir and alternative heir; the latter was also a former Mina slave.[123]

Silva had been quite successful in his role as slaveholder in Sabará. He owned ten men, eight women, and one child among whom were a mix of Angolas, Minas, and *crioulos*. His assets included a tile-roofed house, several other dwellings, some forested land, a large *bananal* (banana grove), soap-making equipment, two spinning wheels, saddle and reins, and tools used in mining. Silva freed six of his slaves in his will, but the remainder were to continue their captivity as laborers for his heir.[124]

Barbara de Oliveira was an elderly freed *crioula* who had been born in northeastern Brazil, in Bahía. She and her daughter had at one time been

121. "[P]uxara para o captiveiro." Testamento de Jorge da Fonseca Ferreira, 8 February 1806, *Livro de registo de testamento* (4 março 1805), MOSMG, fol. 21v.

122. Testamento de Joze Carvalho, 14 August 1789, *Livro de registo de testamento* (18 janeiro 1791), MOSMG, fol. 181.

123. Testamento de Caetano Fernandes da Silva, 27 February 1771, *Livro de registo de testamento* (22 maio 1770), MOSMG, fol. 156v.

124. Testamento de Caetano Fernandes da Silva, 27 February 1771, *Livro de registo de testamento* (22 maio 1770), MOSMG, fol. 156v.

owned by Manoel de Oliveira, but both were freed by Oliveira's daughter who had inherited them. In 1766, Barbara de Oliveira declared that although she herself had never married, among her heirs were her *parda* daughter Francisca dos Anjos, her married granddaughter Anna, and Anna's two sons. Like other slaveholders in Sabará, Barbara de Oliveira carefully considered which of her slaves to free and under what circumstances. In the case of some of the smaller slave children, she freed them outright (on her death) and left each a small legacy. She did not dispose of her entire *terça* (the one-third of her estate that she could bestow as she wished) in gifts to slaves. Of other slaves, including children, she required the payment of their value in exchange for manumission. In this way, she increased the size of her own children's inheritance.[125]

Other freed woman slaves who wrote wills were also slaveholders. In 1763, Luiza da Souza, who was a marketer in town, owned just one slave woman and her daughter. In 1761, Luiza Pereira do Lago owned seven men and two women. In 1752, Maria da Costa and her husband (also a *forro*) together owned five slaves. In their wills, both Luiza da Souza and Maria da Costa stated the names of their former owners and the prices paid to them for their own manumissions (170 and 256 *oitavas* of gold respectively).[126] The fact that all three of these women had once been slaves and had struggled to escape the bonds of captivity did not apparently deter them from assuming the role of owners themselves. In fact, in assuming the role of slaveholders, they undoubtedly protected themselves and their families from any threat of re-enslavement that freeborn colonists may have posed. The best proof to others that one was no longer a slave or enslaveable was surely to become a master.

Conclusion

The slave society in the gold-mining region of eighteenth-century Sabará was complex for reasons relating to the nature of the economic activities that took place there and to the demographic portrait of both the free and slave

125. Testamento de Barbara de Oliveira, 10 August 1766, *Livro de registo de testamento* (4 julho 1766), MOSMG, fols. 93–105.
126. Testamento de Luiza da Souza, 24 March 1763, *Livro de registo de testamento* (28 março 1760), MOSMG; Testamento de Luiza Pereira do Lago, 12 January 1761, *Livro de registo de testamento* (28 março 1760), MOSMG, fol. 182.; Testamento de Maria da Costa, 2 August 1752 (*Livro de registo de testamento*, 28 março 1760), MOSMG, fol. 178.

populations. An overwhelmingly male slave-labor force was employed in diverse activities located in and around various small nuclear settlements, one of which was large enough to constitute a fair-sized urban and commercial center. Men and women slaves worked in the town of Sabará as artisans, venders, and manual laborers in the tasks presented by city life. They served as bearers of wares, layers of stone for streets and houses, and slaughterers of livestock in butchering establishments. It was mostly men slaves who worked in mining sites located on or near the watercourses that wove their way through and around the various parishes. Both men and women slaves also worked, as did many free people, on agricultural or grazing lands and produced food, meat, and rum for the local population.

In Sabará, slaves lived in a world where ex-slaves, if not numerous, were not uncommon and where free people were not necessarily, or even frequently White. They lived in a world where masters were commonly male and White, but not exclusively so, and where a man or woman born in Africa and sold into slavery could, after years of hard labor and some luck, become the master of another African. Most slaves in Sabará were not lucky, however, because, although the range of economic activities in the region was large in comparison, say, with a sugar plantation area, the most palatable, respectable, or lucrative jobs for slaves could absorb only a small proportion of the laboring population. In other words, a few slaves worked as barbers, butchers, bakers, and blacksmiths, but most worked standing in water all day panning for gold.

From the perspective of masters, living in Sabará was probably very different from what they knew or imagined to be true about masters of slaves elsewhere in colonial Brazil. Compared with the sugar plantation areas of Bahia, many more masters in Sabará had access to only a very modest number of slave laborers. Many masters and free individuals without slaves had few material possessions of any kind; their life savings were molded into religious figures that would be pawned for cash or credit when a pressing need arose.

Also from the perspective of the masters, their relationships with slaves may have been much less formal than might be expected in slave societies exclusively devoted to inflexible agricultural regimes. Most masters in Sabará probably got to know most of their own slaves on terms more personal than those in rural Bahia where nearly two-thirds of the masters owned ten or more slaves and nearly one-half owned more than twenty.[127]

127. Schwartz, *Sugar Plantations in the Formation of Brazilian Society,* 464. In Sabará, in the years 1760–1808, 71 percent of masters owned fewer than ten slaves. See Table 2.5.

The commercial activities in town also required that masters in Sabará delegate more unsupervised responsibility to slaves than they would have on a sugar plantation. Labor arrangements in mining sites provided slaves with limited remuneration for their work and (in some instances) less supervision than was characteristic of plantation life.

The frontier quality of life in this region, and the economic activities associated with mining and an urban environment, allowed at least some free individuals and even some slaves to vastly transform their social and economic standing while living in Sabará. The described cases of the successful freed slaves are among the most outstanding examples of the potential for individual success and transformation, but there were numerous others of equal or greater importance.

Mathias de Crasto Porto had come to the mines of Brazil early in the eighteenth century, perhaps even in the last years of the seventeenth century. Through his decisions and behavior as a slave owner, he contributed to a larger process of social and demographic change in a number of significant ways. In 1743, for example, at least one of Porto's manumitted African slaves, Manoel da Costa, became master in his own right of a young slave named Joze of the Courano nation.[128] Mathias de Crasto Porto's original decision to manumit Manoel da Costa necessarily preceded Costa's transformation from slave to master.

Mathias de Crasto Porto's sexual behavior and consequent decisions about mixed-race offspring probably had an even larger transformative impact on the development of the colonial social structure than his manumissions of a small number of slaves. Because he was a bachelor and had fathered no children in a legal marriage, he was able to name seven natural sons and daughters as sole heirs to one of the largest fortunes in the *comarca*, if not in the entire captaincy of Minas Gerais. Thus, in 1742, the children of slaves, or ex-slaves, became landlords of the local priest in the parish of Rossa Grande. Mathias de Crasto Porto's own tremendous success as an individual colonist in Sabará had served to define his offspring, not as mixed-race outcasts among a free White elite, but rather as fully recognized members of the free society.

The slave society of Sabará was therefore complex in ways that extend beyond the issues of a diverse economy or opportunities for improving an individual's economic standing. It was complex in the fact that in Sabará,

---

128. Testamento de Manoel da Costa, 25 June 1743, *Livro de registo de testamento* (3 março 1743), MOSMG, fol. 63.

the traditional European definitions of the "correct" social order were stretched as the frontier mining colony required. Such stretching was perhaps facilitated by the fact that in a mining economy chance alone could transform an impoverished and marginalized individual into a wealthy person of high social status. The transformation of social status that slaves, ex-slaves, free non-Whites, and Whites experienced in colonial Sabará was evident in many different personal and societal relationships shared by masters and slaves. These relationships are discussed in the following chapters.

3

Man, Woman, and Church in Colonial Sabará

Man, woman, and child: all who lived in colonial Minas Gerais encountered and engaged the influences and practices of Portuguese Catholicism. Freeborn, slave, and freed, European and African alike; everyone, at some point, was apt to accept, reject, or transmute these influences and practices as they filtered into the developing frontier society. The Catholic Church was an unavoidable aspect of Portuguese culture and of Portuguese colonialism. There were, however, clear limits to church influence in the ordinary lives of the colonists; ample evidence demonstrates that Catholicism was not an omnipotent force in the mining region. Higher-ranking clergy could sometimes scarcely control the behavior of lower-ranking clergy, much less effectively police the entire flock.

In colonial Sabará, among the rich and the poor, the powerful and the powerless, there was a willing embrace of much Catholic ritual, as well as ready acceptance and rapid growth of church-sponsored organizations dedicated to mutual aid, burial ceremonies, and community life. As evidence of their piety and enthusiasm for religious ceremony, individuals donated large sums of money to fund the building and decoration of magnificent baroque churches typical of the major parishes throughout the *comarca* as well as the entire captaincy.

In the boundaries of the *vila* of Sabará alone, the following churches epitomized eighteenth-century baroque style: Igreja do Carmo, Igreja de Nossa Senhora da Conceição, Igreja das Mercês, Igreja de Nossa Senhora do O, Igreja de São Francisco, and the Igreja do Rosário, which was begun in the eighteenth century but never completed. These churches are located in a series of large open plazas connected to one another by narrow, winding cobblestone roads that climb the northern banks and hillsides of the Sabará river near where it meets the wider Rio das Velhas. Along with the administrative buildings in the *vila,* one for the Intendant of the Mines and another for the municipal council (and local jail), these churches were the largest structures ever built in the *vila* in the colonial period. They provided Sabará with a lasting architectural and community identity. Today, they remain as impressive monuments to the influence of Catholicism and baroque architecture in the eighteenth century. (See illustrations)

Participation in various Catholic ritual practices was an important way for colonists in Sabará to demonstrate their social status in the community. Funeral processions, for example, could be elaborate affairs that illuminated social connections. The prestige accorded to a man or woman could be measured by which brotherhoods in Sabará he or she belonged to and how many brotherhoods were represented at his or her funeral procession. Devout Catholics donated considerable sums of money to the church to pay for masses to be said for their own souls or the souls of others in purgatory.[1] The brotherhoods also spent large sums on celebrations of feast days, saints' days, holy days, and the public processions that went with such occasions. Brotherhoods were organized to represent the needs and interests of slaves, and ex-slaves as well. From cradle to grave, free, freed, and enslaved colonists of Sabará all experienced the influence of Catholicism in their lives.

As I hope to demonstrate in the course of this chapter and the next, Sabará's colonists did not, however, accept all the tenets of official Catholicism. As elsewhere in eighteenth-century Minas Gerais, there was considerable diversity in the responses of slaves and free or freed people to the clergy's effort to make good Catholics of one and all. As everywhere in the mining region, in Sabará it was impossible for the church to achieve its objective of ending concubinage or institutionalizing marriage among cohabiting adults.

---

1. According to Catholic teachings, the souls of the dead in purgatory required the prayers of the living to ascend into heaven. In practice, the Church required the "donation" of money in exchange for masses to be said on behalf of the state of these souls.

The widespread rejection of the legal and sacramental state of marriage in Sabará represented a significant departure from the official teachings of the Roman Catholic Church in the eighteenth century. In a free population that in other respects might be characterized as demonstrating deep devotion, lasting respect, and solid financial support for the Catholic Church, customary beliefs — not church doctrine — prevailed in the practice of sexual relationships and sexual partnerships. Customarily, legal marriages between social unequals and between White men and non-White women were deemed both unnecessary and inappropriate. The primary beneficiaries of such beliefs were White men. Non-White women could experience considerable victimization in nonmarital sexual relationships with White men because women had no property rights in these relationships and no other forms of legal recourse.

The final testaments of Sabará's colonists provide ample evidence of the strong sense of Catholic identity and faith that could prevail in the community; they also indicate the various ways that individual beliefs or attachment to church doctrine could and did vary. As mentioned in Chapter 2, the formulaic structure and opening paragraphs of eighteenth-century wills tended to underscore and perhaps even overemphasize the degree to which an individual testator (especially a former slave) identified with European culture and religion. These opening paragraphs and their patterned language do not serve as sufficient evidence that a testator was a fully Lusified (acculturated) colonist or an adherent to all or most Catholic precepts. Testators in Sabará were, for the most part, illiterate, and it is therefore not in the patterned language of wills (produced by scribes and bound to a formulaic template) that one can discern an individual's preference or commitment to social and religious values.[2] What informs my discussion of the variability of individuals' commitments to Catholic practices and to a Catholic colonialism based on slavery are the distinct and unique features of each will recorded in the sections and the language revealing a testator's individual provisions and bequests. The nature and size of testamentary bequests and provisions varied from one testator to the next, and it is through an examination of these diverse statements that the otherwise formula-bound documents yield a scarce glimpse into the lives of testators and their social, economic, and religious practices. Wills also often reveal significant personal information, such as the social origins, community status, and race of a testator.

In keeping with customary beliefs, the individual bequests and provi-

2. See page 83.

Nossa Senhora da Conceição, Sabará, Minas Gerais. (Courtesy of the University of New Mexico, Latin American and Iberian Institute, Brazil Slide Series)

Gold leaf interior of Nossa Senhora da Conceição, Sabará, Minas Gerais. (Courtesy of the University of New Mexico, Latin American and Iberian Institute, Brazil Slide Series)

Nossa Senhora do O, Sabará, Minas Gerais. (Courtesy of the University of New Mexico, Latin American and Iberian Institute, Brazil Slide Series)

Painted gold leaf interior of Nossa Senhora do O, Sabará, Minas Gerais. (Courtesy of the University of New Mexico, Latin American and Iberian Institute, Brazil Slide Series)

sions examined in the wills reveal that unmarried adults who were not celibate considered themselves and were considered by others to be as Catholic as anyone else. In his final testament of 1742, Mathias de Crasto Porto, lifelong bachelor and father of seven children, professed himself to be a Christian, provided clear instructions for his rites of Christian burial, and granted legacies both for the numerous church-sponsored organizations to which he had belonged and for masses to be said for his soul. As a member of the Third Order of St. Francis, a prestigious lay brotherhood, Mathias followed custom and called for his body to be shrouded in the habit of that order. In addition, he requested that his body be buried in the principal church of Rossa Grande where he was a parishioner and where fellow parishioners in good standing were customarily laid to rest.[3]

In his testament, Mathias de Crasto Porto called for the customary funeral procession in which the members of "all of the brotherhoods of which I am a brother" would accompany his body to its final resting place. As a rich man, Mathias could afford to leave legacies to help sustain these organizations. In fact, he left fifty drams of gold to each of the following seven confraternities: Nossa Senhora de Monserrate, Nossa Senhora do Rosário, Santa Quitéria, Almas, Santo Antônio, São Sebastião, and São Francisco Xavier in the Matriz of Rossa Grande.[4] He also left to the brotherhood of the Santíssimo Sacramento of Rossa Grande fifty drams of gold for the purchase of certain ceremonial items.[5]

The sums of gold that Mathias de Crasto Porto left to the brotherhoods of his choice can be viewed, in some respects, as donations to organizations that served as the arms of the Catholic Church in the captaincy. These gifts therefore represent indirect donations to the church as a larger institution.[6] Portuguese laws of inheritance allowed that all individuals

3. Testamento de Mathias de Crasto Porto, 6 October 1742, Inventarios 1740–46, MOSMG.

4. These brotherhoods are listed in the order in which he named them. Mathias de Crasto Porto did not suggest that any of these were from outside Sabará or Minas Gerais, in places such as Bahia or Rio, which other testators tended to mention when true. In my view, they were probably all locally based organizations. The number and ubiquitousness of lay brotherhoods in Minas Gerais are discussed in detail in Caio César Boschi, *Os leigos e o poder: Irmandades leigas e política colonizadora em Minas Gerais* (São Paulo: Editora Atica, 1986).

5. The ceremonial items were described as the *pavilhão do [sacrano]*, which I think should read *pavilhão do sacrário* and which refers to cloths or curtains that decorated a venerated location served by the brotherhood (possibly in the church itself).

6. Boschi has argued in *Os leigos e o poder* that the brotherhoods were both an arm of the church and an arm of colonial authority in Minas Gerais.

could freely dispose of one-third of their estates while the remaining two-thirds were to be divided equally among all heirs.[7] From the one-third, or *terça*, Mathias could deduct the funds for these donations.[8]

Like innumerable other colonists in the eighteenth century, Mathias de Crasto Porto also used his *terça* to donate money to the Catholic Church in more immediate ways. The fees allocated for masses to be said for one's soul put gold or currency directly into the hands of local clergy. In Mathias's case, he asked for two thousand masses to be said for his soul at the cost of two drams of gold each.[9] The number of masses he asked for was exceptionally high in comparison with the numbers requested by other testators in colonial Minas Gerais, a reflection no doubt of both his wealth and his interest in securing his own salvation.

The practice of allocating *terça* funds for masses was widespread among Sabará's testators in the eighteenth century; individuals could choose to have the masses said for the souls of others as well as for themselves. In his will of 5 October 1790, Captain João Lopes Freire requested that a large number of masses be said after his death. Three hundred fifty were for all the souls in purgatory. One hundred fifty masses were "for the souls of all my slaves who have died." In addition, he allocated sums for three hundred masses to be said in his native parish in Portugal for his parents, brothers, and sisters. Captain Freire was a wealthy man in 1790; he claimed ownership of considerable landholdings, mining claims, and fifty-five slaves in his final testament.[10]

In addition to forwarding the spiritual goal of achieving salvation, the purchasing of masses served the purpose of financing the material existence of the clergy. Many colonists in Minas Gerais did not, however, want all the funds that they dedicated to the church to be linked to a specific number of masses or perhaps to the livelihoods of local clerics. For donations that were less identifiable both in terms of quantity and immediate destination, individuals chose the mechanism of naming their own souls as heirs or as the only heir to their estates. By this means, the Catholic

---

7. Lewin, "Natural and Spurious Children," 351–96. See also above, Chapter 2, note 2.

8. It was also from the *terça* that the value of his manumitted slaves would be deducted.

9. In almost all other wills examined, the customary fee for such masses was one-half of a dram of gold. Testamento de Mathias de Crasto Porto, 6 October 1742, Inventarios 1740–46, MOSMG.

10. "[P]elas almas de todos os escravos que me tem morrido," Testamento de Capitão João Lopes Freire, 5 October 1790, *Livro de registo de testamento* (18 janeiro 1791). MOSMG, fol. 157v.

Church in eighteenth-century Minas Gerais was enriched over and over as countless colonists of Sabará and elsewhere tied their hopes for salvation to testamentary bequests.

In keeping with Portuguese law, the souls of the colonists could not inherit at the expense of the living, for example, children or other qualified heirs.[11] In such circumstances, a testator could name his or her soul as heir only to the *terça* or to a fraction of it. Mathias De Crasto Porto himself named his soul as the recipient of what remained from his *terça* after all his other bequests had been deducted.[12] Ten years before, in 1732, Captain Manoel das Neves Ribeyro allocated half of his *terça* to his soul.[13] Bras de Barros Soares, the unmarried Portuguese immigrant to the mines who owned the twenty-eight male slaves and one female slave discussed in Chapter 2, named his father as his heir in 1719 and gave his entire *terça* to his soul.[14]

Some individuals at the time of their final testament had no living heirs to name. In most of these cases, the testators chose their soul to be their one and only universal heir. Francisco Gonçalves Pinheiro was a bachelor immigrant from the Madeira islands who lived in the *vila* of Sabará. He owned three adult men, one adult woman, a gun, and a few other household wares. In March 1719, he declared his soul as the heir to his estate.[15] In June 1740, Izabel Pinheyra, a former slave and a widow, had no living heirs. In her will, she also named her soul as her only heir.[16] Similarly, in January 1767, the cleric Felix da Silveira declared that as a priest he was unmarried and had had no children. He owned twenty-five adult men, two young *crioulas,* some land and a house, gold-mining equipment, and one-fourth of a *engenho* for making sugar. All this he bequeathed to his soul.[17]

In granting bequests to their souls, colonists in Sabará were in fact donating their assets to the Catholic Church. When these colonists were slave

11. Lewin, "Natural and Spurious Children," 351–96. See also above, Chapter 2, note 2.

12. Testamento de Mathias de Crasto Porto, 6 October 1742, Inventarios 1740–46, MOSMG.

13. Testamento de Manoel das Neves Ribeyro, 22 August 1732, *Livro de registo de testamento* (17 dezembro 1739), MOSMG, fol. 63.

14. Testamento de Bras de Barros Soares, 25 August 1719, *Livro de registo de testamento* (1716–25), MOSMG, fol. 33.

15. Testamento de Francisco Goncalves Pinheiro, 24 March 1719, *Livro de registo de testamento* (1716–25), MOSMG, fol. 7.

16. Testamento de Izabel Pinheyra, 4 June 1740, *Livro de registo de testamento* (17 dezembro 1739), MOSMG, fol. 79v.

17. Testamento de Padre Felix da Silveira, 27 January 1767, *Livro de registo de testamento* (4 julho 1766), MOSMG, fol. 39.

owners (as was the case for all the individuals just named), they eschewed the opportunity to manumit their slaves and increased the slaveholdings of the Catholic Church itself.[18] Even the former slave Izabel Pinheyra wanted to use her slaves' market value as a donation to the church, rather than awarding them their freedom as gifts after her death. Izabel owned two slave women, each of whom had children. In her testament of 1740, she set manumission prices for her slaves, including one not yet born. Izabel's slave Maria was required to pay to the estate fifty drams of gold for her freedom and was given one and one-half years to produce this sum. Maria's child was freed outright. Izabel's other slave woman, Domingas, was far less favored in her owner's declarations. Domingas was to pay 128 drams of gold for her freedom, which was in fact the price that Izabel Pinheyra had paid for own freedom years before.[19] Domingas, at that time pregnant with a third child, also had to pay 64 drams for each of her first two children. If the third child lived, Izabel Pinheyra requested that the mother pay to her estate one-fourth of a pound of gold (32 drams) to free the newborn from slavery.[20] By this latter provision, Izabel was able to maximize her charitable donation to church coffers.

What happened to the slaves and other assets of Sabará's colonists after they were donated to the church is not clear. Some were probably sold off at auction, but we do not know for certain.[21] There is no available evidence to suggest that the church did not accept the bequests of testators, and the practice of naming one's soul as heir continued in wills throughout the eighteenth century.[22] Considerable evidence suggests that church officials did not free slaves donated to them through these gifts.[23] The dona-

18. In those cases of individuals without qualified heirs, there was no legal obstacle to freeing all their slaves in their final testament; where qualified heirs existed, owners could not disinherit them and could only have chosen to deplete the value of their *terça* with gifts of manumission.

19. In one pound of gold there were 128 drams or *oitavas* in Portuguese.

20. "[E] pella criança que tem no ventre, sahindo viva, uma coarta," Testamento de Izabel Pinheyra, 4 June 1740, *Livro de registo de testamento* (17 dezembro 1739). MOSMG (book 3), fol. 80v.

21. There may be records of church finances in ecclesiastical archives, but I have not yet seen citations for such documents in the works of those who have used such archives extensively.

22. See, for example, Testamento de Anna Maria da Conçeição, 29 November 1795, *Livro de registo de testamento* (20 janeiro 1797), MOSMG, fol. 59v. Such wills as this one may have been invalid although uncontested. The legal right to name the soul as an heir came under attack from Pombaline legislation beginning in 1769.

23. No known documents of manumission suggest that the Church freed slaves. See below Chapter 5, note 5. No church records that suggest that in Brazil church officials opposed

tions of slaves and other assets were meant as expressions of piety and as gestures of hope that the enrichment of one's church might lead to individual salvation.

Colonists of Sabará did not have to name the Catholic Church as their heir of last resort. Nonrelatives could be named as heirs instead. Thus the transfer to the Church of slave ownership and of the value of slaves owned was a conscious choice on the part of Sabará's men and women testators. The bequeathal of slaves as an act of piety and the acceptance of such bequests are stark reminders of the pervasiveness and unquestioned acceptability of slavery as a social and economic institution in colonial Brazil. For Izabel Pinheyra, herself an ex-slave, there was no incongruity in the act of setting a price in gold for an enslaved fetus. For the Catholic Church in Minas Gerais, there was no sin in accepting a donation of property in the form of a newborn child.

The degree of piety that an individual felt or felt the need to express in the form of a charitable donation to the Church varied considerably in Sabará. Some people left relatively few of their assets to the Church. Caetano Fernandes da Silva, a freed Mina slave who wrote a will in February 1771, made the far less common choice of naming a friend, rather than the Church, to inherit the bulk of his wealth. Caetano had been married to a freed Black woman named Mariana, but she had died and left him a widower. During his enslavement, Caetano had had a son, Vitorio, by another woman. The son and mother had both died earlier. How Caetano made his living is not entirely clear, although it seems likely that he did both mining and farming. What is clear, however, is that Caetano had been quite successful; in 1771, he claimed to own ten men, eight women, and one child. Of these slaves, Caetano freed outright three men, two women, and the child. Without any living relatives, Caetano Fernandes da Silva named a friend, Antônio Gonçalves, as his heir. Gonçalves was to own the remaining nonmanumitted slaves in the estate.[24]

The 1771 will of Caetano Fernandes da Silva reproduces the formulaic

---

slavery or opposed it by freeing their own slaves. Numerous historians have noted that the Catholic Church in Brazil was not opposed to the enslavement of Africans. See Fernandes, *O negro no mundo dos brancos*, 63; Eduardo Hoornaert, *Formação do catolicismo brasileiro (1500–1800)*, 2d ed. (Petrópolis: Vozes, 1978); Hoornaert, "The Catholic Church in Colonial Brazil," in Leslie Bethell, ed., *Cambridge History of Latin America* (Cambridge: Cambridge University Press, 1984), vol. 1, 541–56; Boschi, *Os leigos e o poder*, 155.

24. Testamento de Caetano Fernandes da Silva, 27 February 1771, *Livro de registo de testamento* (22 maio 1770), MOSMG, fol. 156v.

features of all such documents of the period and in doing so stresses some of the universal aspects of Catholicism in the lives and deaths of Sabará's colonists. Like Mathias de Crasto Porto before him, Caetano professed himself to be a true Christian who was fearful of death and concerned for his soul "on the path to salvation." Just as Porto had done, Caetano asked to be buried in the church of his home parish of Raposos, in the company of the brotherhood to which he belonged. He arranged for masses to be said for his soul and for the souls of those who had been dear to him. On the other hand, the specific bequests and provisions of Caetano's will reveal information about his own economic circumstances, religious commitment, and relationship with his slaves. A man of more modest fortunes than Porto had been, Caetano asked for one hundred masses for himself, one hundred for his deceased wife, fifty for his brother, and fifty for another woman, Luzia de Barros, perhaps the mother of his son. Like Captain Freire, Caetano Fernandes da Silva also expressed concern for the souls of his slaves by arranging for twenty-five masses to be said on their behalf. In addition, he called for twenty-five more masses to be said for all souls in purgatory.[25]

Caetano Fernandes da Silva made just one donation that went beyond the purchasing of masses. He promised to pay for the painting of two walls in a church in his parish of Raposos. The value of this work was seventy-four drams of gold. Although such a gift was certainly a significant act of charity, Caetano's gifts of manumission for six of his slaves were considerably more valuable.[26] Moreover, his decision to leave the remainder of his estate to a friend, not to his soul, deprived the Catholic Church of a much larger legacy.

Fernandes da Silva's outright gifts of manumission to nearly one-third of his slaves and his unwillingness to have the others handed over to the Church (and possibly to immediate auction) suggest a stronger sense of identification with his captives than most owners in colonial Sabará commonly demonstrated. We will probably never know precisely why this was so, but his decisions were undoubtedly shaped by his own experience as an enslaved African.[27] Caetano was both a convert to Catholicism and a con-

---

25. The price for these masses was one-half dram of gold each.

26. In view of prices in the period, it is safe to say at least six times more valuable. There was no indication that his adult slaves were very old or infirm and therefore worth very little.

27. Caetano had paid two pounds of gold for his freedom. Testamento de Caetano Fernandes da Silva, 27 February 1771, *Livro de registo de testamento* (22 maio 1770), MOSMG, fol. 156v.

vert, in some respects, to Portuguese culture and its slave-driven economy. His identification of himself as a Christian and a slaveholder suggests that he had rejected neither the religion of his oppressors nor the economic system in which he had first played a role as a victim and later the role of victimizer. On the other hand, his individual and unique testamentary provisions also suggest that his embrace of slavery and of Catholicism was more limited than that of Izabel Pinheyra's. He was far more generous to more of his slaves than she had been to nearly all of hers. Izabel's donation to the church was completely at the expense of her captives' immediate and possibly future freedom. In deciding on her substantial and expensive (as well as final) act of piety, Izabel Pinheyra simultaneously demonstrated a solid commitment to slavery.

For governors and high church officials in Minas Gerais, simultaneous expression of piety as a good Catholic and of commitment to the social and economic stratifications that were inherent in a slave society represented the ideal behavior to be wished for in every free or freed person in the colony. Such ideal behavior was, however, often lacking, as often from the ranks of those who were wealthy and White as from the ranks of those who were poor and non-White. From the perspective of both church and crown officers, the colonists (including the clergy) were often not nearly Catholic enough: they were corrupt and immoral and lived in open defiance of official church precepts, especially those pertaining to the importance of marriage and the prohibition against concubinage. Commitments to gold and slavery and the material, sexual, and other personal perquisites derived from them often outweighed any commitment to Christ or a Catholic way of life.

As the individual provisions of final testaments discussed here suggest, although the colonists of Sabará were indeed not entirely observant of official tenets, they nevertheless lived according to most Catholic customs and in an environment where no other religion was officially tolerated. At various moments in time, therefore, they were enthusiastic participants in Catholic rituals, generous contributors to monumental baroque structures that glorified the saints, Christ, and Christendom in general, and avid practitioners of a locally based Catholicism that placed a particular emphasis on membership in lay brotherhoods.

Brotherhoods were ubiquitous in colonial Minas Gerais.[28] The historian

---

28. In Portuguese, the words *irmandade* and *confraria* are regarded as interchangeable or near equivalents. In English, these organizations are referred to as brotherhoods, confrater-

Caio Boschi has identified well over 250 *irmandades* founded in the captaincy during the eighteenth century.[29] These organizations were lay religious associations open to both men and women; they recruited their members from all sectors of society. Although the brotherhoods were not segregated according to sex, membership in some was restricted according to race, class, and even purity of blood.[30] Others were open to all regardless of race, class, ethnic background, or status (slave versus free).[31] According to A. J. R. Russell-Wood, common to all brotherhoods in colonial Brazil was an emphasis on the practice of Christian virtues and the demonstration of corporate responsibility for the welfare of members in need of alms, medical aid, provisions, clothes, and burial.[32] When funds permitted, brotherhoods sometimes expressed a commitment to charitable assistance for the poor and sick.[33] All lay brotherhoods, regardless of their particular orientation, were officially authorized by church authorities in Portugal and were governed according to approved statutes.[34]

It has been argued that brotherhoods in colonial Minas Gerais were even more significant in that captaincy than elsewhere in Brazil partly because of the history of crown restrictions on the presence of clergy in the mining region.[35] When the gold rush began at the end of the seventeenth century, gold-seeking and unscrupulous clergymen had joined the ranks of those streaming into the mining region. These clergy quickly earned a reputation for active participation in contraband trade, an unwillingness to pay any Royal Fifths, and failure to attend to their religious obligations to

---

nities, and sodalities. Third Orders (*Ordens Terceiras*) were (and are) a form of lay brotherhood usually associated with stricter admission requirements.

29. Boschi, *Os leigos e o poder*. See appendices for extensive listings of extant brotherhoods in the captaincy.

30. A. J. R. Russell-Wood, "Prestige, Power, and Piety in Colonial Brazil: The Third Orders of Salvador," *HAHR* 69:1 (1989): 61–89. Purity of blood refers to applicants not having ancestors who were of Moorish or Jewish background, p. 67.

31. Patricia Mulvey, "Slave Confraternities in Brazil: Their Role in Colonial Society," *The Americas* 39 (July 1982): 39–68.

32. See chapter 8, "Collective Behavior: The Brotherhoods," in Russell-Wood, *The Black Man in Slavery and Freedom*.

33. The Santa Casa de Misericórdia was a lay brotherhood dedicated to charitable works, including providing hospitals for the ill. See Russell-Wood, *Fidalgos and Filanthropists: The Santa Casa de Misericórdia of Bahía, 1550–1755* (Berkeley and Los Angeles: University of California Press, 1968).

34. The body of statutes that governed the brotherhoods was called a *compromisso* and had to be approved in Portugal by the Mesa de Consciencia e Ordens. Mulvey, "Slave Confraternities in Brazil," 44.

35. See Boschi, *Os Leigos e o poder*, 23.

the population. According to Charles Boxer, "Ten years after the gold rush had begun, it was alleged in 1705 that not a single priest in Minas Gerais took an active interest in the religious needs of the people."[36] In 1711, the Portuguese crown responded to the complaints against the clergy by banning all unauthorized clergy from the region and prohibiting the establishment of any regular orders in the captaincy.[37]

The ban against unauthorized clergy, and against the regular orders in particular, left the Catholic Church with few resources at hand for developing its presence in the mining region. The lay brotherhoods in Minas Gerais thus not only provided a means through which individuals could express a religious identity but also, in practice, took on the responsibility of attending to the performance of Catholic rituals by contracting with individual clergy to perform the sacraments for their members. Moreover, the brotherhoods were responsible for the cultivation of general religious activity in the mining region, and in this regard they are credited with building virtually all the churches in the captaincy.[38]

The brotherhoods in the *comarca* of Sabará actually predate the official founding date of the *vila* of Nossa Senhora da Conçeição de Sabará. Associations dedicated to Santa Quitéria, Santo Antônio de Bom Retiro, and the Santíssimo Sacramento already existed when the *vila* was established by the governor in 1711.[39] In just another decade, testators writing wills in Sabará claimed membership in or made donations to sixteen different brotherhoods. Dozens more brotherhoods were founded in the *comarca* of Sabará throughout the course of the eighteenth century.[40] Wealthy colonists

36. Boxer, *The Golden Age*, 54.
37. Boxer, *The Golden Age*, 54.
38. Boschi writes on the importance of the *irmandades* in Minas Gerais: "Por seu turno, a Igreja não teve tempo e nem condições para se impor, como instituição, no novo território. Nos primeiros tempos, sua ação foi desencontrada, individualizada. Quando poderia se estabelecer, o Estado a impediu, através de toda uma legislação restritiva. Assim, não restou à Igreja outro recurso senão o de atrelar-se às associações leigas, mais para a prática de seus ofícios do que para uma política evangelizadora. Até mesmo a construção dos templos não ficou sob a sua responsabilidade. Foi também obra de leigos." *Os leigos e o poder*, 23.
39. *Os leigos e o poder*, 23.
40. In the appendices, Boschi lists thirty-six brotherhoods identified in the boundaries of the *comarca* of Sabará (using localities named in the 1720 listing of slave holders; see Table 2.3). Boschi, *Os Leigos e o poder*, 218–19. Some *irmandades* that I have encountered in wills examined (for example, Lugares Santos de Jerusalem, sometimes called Santos Lugares de Jerusalem or even Santa Casa de Jerusalem) do not appear in his listing, and thus his figures represent the minimum number of brotherhoods in the *comarca* extant during the eighteenth century. In looking for evidence about *irmandades* in the *comarca* of Sabará, I have examined a sample of wills dating from 1719 to 1806. The sample size was approximately 200.

tended to belong to more than one and often made small bequests even to those to which they did not belong. Individuals who were less wealthy belonged to fewer *irmandades,* and many belonged to one or none. (See Table 3.1.)

The brotherhoods to which people belonged in Sabará were, as elsewhere in Minas Gerais, an indication of social status and race. Catherina de Payva, a freed Black woman, stated in 1721 that she was a member of the brotherhood of Nossa Senhora do Rosário dos Pretos, an organization open to Whites, but particularly associated with a membership composed of slaves and freed slaves, be they mulattos, *crioulos,* or Africans.[41] Caetano Fernandes da Silva, the freed African slave discussed earlier in this chapter, also claimed membership in this brotherhood in 1771.[42] Chapters of the brotherhood of Our Lady of the Rosary of the Blacks existed in nearly every settlement in the *comarca,* and in the captaincy as a whole, there were at least sixty-two branches.[43] According to Patricia Mulvey,

Table 3.1. *Irmandades* extant in the *comarca* of Sabará, 1719–1723

Almas
Lugares Santos de Jerusalem
Nossa Senhora do Amparo da Matriz de Sabará
Nossa Senhora do Bom Sucesso
Nossa Senhora da Conceição
Nossa Senhora de Nazaré
Nossa Senhora da Piedade
Nossa Senhora do Rosário
Nossa Senhora do O
Santa Quitéria
Santíssimo Sacramento
Santo Antônio
São Caetano
São João
Santos Passos do Senhor
Virgem Maria Santíssima

SOURCE: *Livro de registo de testamentos* (1716–25), MOSMG.

41. Testamento de Catherina de Payva, preta forra, 9 July 1721, *Livro de registo de testamento 1716–25,* MOSMG, fol. 133. See also Mulvey, "Slave Confraternities in Brazil."
42. Testamento de Caetano Fernandes da Silva, 27 February 1771, *Livro de registo de testamento* (22 maio 1770), MOSMG, fol. 156v.
43. *Os leigos e o poder,* 187.

Black brotherhoods pooled meager resources to bury the dead, performed charitable works of mercy, purchased the freedom of some slaves, advanced loans to others for that purpose, and provided legal counsel to slaves.[44] Our Lady of the Rosary was just one of many brotherhoods in colonial Brazil open to non-Whites, but it was by far the most common one in Sabará and in Minas Gerais as a whole.[45]

Another brotherhood in Sabará, which appears to have been associated with slaves and freed slaves, was called Lugares Santos de Jerusalem.[46] Ignacia Ferreira da Silva, a freed Black woman, identified herself in 1786 as a sister of this association.[47] Some individuals who were obviously White gave small legacies to Lugares Santos but did not claim membership in it.[48] Mathias de Crasto Porto was one of these individuals. In 1742, he gave 300$000 to "Santos Lugares de Jerusalem" and specified that half of that sum was "for the slaves."[49] The other Whites who gave to this brotherhood, like Mathias de Crasto Porto, indicated some affinity or closer relationship to their own slaves than did noncontributing Whites. For example, Captain João Lopes Freire, who gave money to Lugares Santos in 1790, also donated masses for his slaves' souls, and Lieutenant Colonel Antônio Brandão, who made a donation in 1801, named his son by an African slave woman as his only heir.[50]

Some lay brotherhoods were reserved for Whites only.[51] The Third Orders of São Francisco and Nossa Senhora de Monte de Carmo had statu-

44. "Slave Confraternities in Brazil," 40.

45. Patricia Mulvey identified 35 distinct brotherhoods open to non-Whites in Brazil. Mulvey, "Slave Confraternities in Brazil," 66–68.

46. Sometimes it appeared as Santos Lugares de Jerusalem, sometimes as Santa Casa de Jerusalem, and even as Irmandade de Jerusalem.

47. Testamento de Ignacia Ferreira da Silva, 18 November 1786, *Livro de registo de testamento* (27 janeiro 1801), MOSMG, fol. 129.

48. Testamento de Thenente Coronel Antônio Brandão, 16 November 1801, *Livro de registo de testamento* (3 fevereiro 1802), MOSMG, fol. 4.; Testamento de Capitão João Lopes Freire, 5 October 1790, *Livro de registo de testamento* (18 janeiro 1791), MOSMG, fol. 157v.; Testamento de Mathias de Crasto Porto, 6 October 1742, Inventarios 1740–46, MOSMG.

49. Testamento de Mathias de Crasto Porto, 6 October 1742, Inventarios 1740–46, MOSMG.

50. Testamento de Thenente Coronel Antônio Brandão, 16 Novembro 1801, *Livro de registo de testamento* (3 feveiro 1802), MOSMG, fol. 4.; Testamento de Capitão João Lopes Freire, 5 October 1790, *Livro de registo de testamento* (18 janeiro 1791), MOSMG, fol. 157v.

51. Julita Scarano, "Black Brotherhoods: Integration or Contradiction?" *Luso-Brazilian Review* 16 (Summer 1979): 1–17.

tory restrictions prohibiting admissions of non-Whites.[52] The brotherhood of Santíssimo Sacramento, which was not a Third Order, was also strongly identified as a Whites-only association.[53] In colonial Sabará, membership in the prestigious Third Orders was relatively common among the well-to-do. Without question, however, the brotherhood of Santíssimo Sacramento was one of the most frequently cited associations in eighteenth-century wills. The other most commonly cited brotherhood in Sabará's wills was called Almas, or Santas Almas. Almas drew its membership from all sectors of the population, and its primary function appeared to have been that of a burial society.

The internal histories of brotherhoods in Minas Gerais are not well known, and in the *comarca* of Sabará, no studies of individual organizations exist at all.[54] It is therefore difficult to state with certainty much about the internal workings of these associations or their changes over time. It is certain that the lay brotherhoods in Sabará were numerous and that they were successful in accomplishing their goals of building monumental baroque churches and of attending to the burial of the dead. Membership in these associations affirmed the social and economic standing of individuals in the community; the segregated nature of the brotherhoods both reflected and reinforced social and racial hierarchies in the *comarca*.

The Black brotherhoods of Our Lady of the Rosary and that of similarly configured associations in the *comarca* undoubtedly provided their members with some degree of social status — even for the enslaved.[55] In Sabará, the variety of individual provisions made by Black brotherhood members in regard to their own slaves does, however, make it difficult to generalize about whether the typical member of such an association sought member-

52. Most of the time, Nossa Senhora de Monte de Carmo appeared as Nossa Senhora do Carmo. See also Russell-Wood, "Prestige, Power, and Piety," 61–89.

53. Scarano, "Black Brotherhoods," 1–17.

54. Scarano has produced a study of a Black brotherhood in the eighteenth-century diamand district in Minas Gerais: *Devoção e escravidão: A irmandade de Nossa Senhora do Rosário dos pretos no distrito diamantino no século xviii,* 2d ed. (São Paulo: Companhia Editora Nacional, 1978). Boschi's work *Os leigos e o poder* is a larger discussion of brotherhoods throughout eighteenth-century Minas Gerais, but as he admits, sources with which to write internal histories of these brotherhoods are scarce. Zorastro Viana Passos does refer to documents of the *irmandades* in Sabará in his discussions of the building of the churches and commissions for sacred art in those churches. See *Em tôrno da história do Sabará,* vol. 1 (Rio de Janeiro: Spahn/Mec, 1940) and vol. 2 (Belo Horizonte: Imprensa Ofcial de Minas Gerais, 1942).

55. Scarano has made this point for the same brotherhood in Diamantina. See *Devoção e escravidão.*

ship principally as a way of establishing community ties among fellow non-Whites or as a way of demonstrating an acceptance of the existing hierarchies of a slave regime and of slavery itself. For example, Caetano Fernandes da Silva was a freed African slave owner and member of Nossa Senhora do Rosário; in 1771, he freed outright nearly one-third of his slaves and gave none of the rest to the Church.[56] Ignacia Ferreira da Silva, a freed slave woman and member of the brotherhood of Jerusalem, in 1786 bequeathed her own house to her slaves and arranged for their eventual freedom.[57] Neither of these testamentary provisions would lead one to equate membership in a Black brotherhood with complete social or religious conformity. On the other hand, in 1791, Maria Rodrigues de Almeida, a Rosary member who was the daughter of an ex-slave woman and a free Black man, bequeathed one of her slaves to her mother.[58] Such a bequest does suggest acceptance of slavery as an economic and social system.

As organizations, the Black brotherhoods in Sabará did not overtly challenge slavery. Slaves who joined had first to seek permission of their masters, and as these brotherhoods were not closed to Whites, there were often Whites in leadership positions in the organizations.[59] Moreover, although Patricia Mulvey, Julita Scarano, and others have suggested that Black brotherhoods played an important role in helping slaves to secure their manumissions, the documentary evidence in Sabará does not support this argument. Among recorded manumissions in notary records, evidence of the role of brotherhoods in providing funds to slaves seeking manumission is virtually absent, and cases in which the brotherhoods freed slaves whom they had purchased from "bad" masters are more apocryphal than real.[60]

If the available evidence does not support a view of lay brotherhoods in Sabará as sites of contestation over social and racial hierarchies or other

56. Testamento de Caetano Fernandes da Silva, 27 February 1771, *Livro de registo de testamento* (22 maio 1770), MOSMG, fol. 156v.

57. Testamento de Ignacia Ferreira da Silva, 18 November 1786, *Livro de registo de testamento* (12 julho 1786), MOSMG, fol. 129.

58. Testamento de Maria Rodrigues de Almeida, July 1791, *Livro de registo de testamento* (18 Janeiro 1791), MOSMG, fol. 85.

59. "[A]s irmandades de negros nao combaterem a ordem escravocrata. Por essa razao, foram consentidas e emulada."; Boschi, *Os Leigos e o poder*, 155. Scarano also points to the presence of Whites in the Black brotherhoods, particularly in the positions of treasurer or secretary that would require a person to be literate. See *Devoção e escravidão*.

60. Mulvey, "Slave Confraternities"; Scarano, *Devoção e escravidão*. See Chapter 5 on manumissions.

power relationships inherent in a slave society, it is also problematic to suggest that these associations were powerful social instruments that effectively increased the likelihood of social or religious conformity in their constituencies. Among members of the very popular Black brotherhoods in Sabará, *individual* expressions of solidarity along racial and ethnic lines and across the barrier of slavery survived throughout the colonial period in the form of testamentary provisions that subverted the slave system by freeing captives.

For the White and well-to-do in Sabará, memberships and donations to lay brotherhoods also continued to be evident into the early nineteenth century. For example, Lieutenant Colonel Antônio Brandão provided legacies to five brotherhoods in his 1801 will: Almas, Santíssimo Sacramento, Jerusalem, Nossa Senhora do Carmo in Vila Rica, and Nossa Senhora do Rosário of the Whites in Brumado. Brandão's participation in and contributions to three Whites-only brotherhoods (Santíssimo Sacramento, N. S. do Carmo, N. S. do Rosário dos Brancos) were a reflection of his wealth and status in the *comarca* and of his legitimate birth in Portugal. Affiliation with these exclusive associations did not, however, bind Antônio Brandão to a standard of personal sexual behavior and religious conformity much emphasized by the Catholic Church in colonial Minas Gerais and deemed highly desirable by crown officials as well. Brandão was a bachelor, and like countless Portuguese bachelors before him in Sabará, Antônio's only fruitful sexual relationship had been with an African slave woman. Lieutenant Colonel Brandão named as his only heir Joaquim Brandão, the *pardo* (mixed-race) son of Joanna Angola, his slave. She had clearly been his concubine.[61]

Antônio Brandão's wealth and status as a White slaveholder and his participation in several prestigious lay brotherhoods in the captaincy demonstrate his important standing in the social and economic hierarchies of colonial Sabará. On the other hand, his lifelong status as a bachelor, his evident concubinage with at least one African slave woman, and the sympathetic acknowledgment of a freed slave child as his heir also speak to his own adherence to social and sexual practices roundly condemned by church and administrative officials. His behavior—and that of equally wealthy, powerful, and avowedly devout men—serves to explain one his-

61. Testamento de Thenente Coronel Antônio Brandão, 16 November 1801, *Livro de registo de testamento* (3 fevereiro 1802), MOSMG, fol. 4.

torian's observation that "[i]t is difficult to think of mineiro society subordinating itself faithfully to the designs of orthodox Catholicism."[62]

The phenomenon of concubinage was in no way unique to the *comarca* of Sabará; it also existed throughout the mining region. In his study of family life in colonial Minas Gerais, the historian Luciano Raposo de Almeida Figueiredo concluded that the institutionalization of legal marriage in the mining region was "unattainable."[63] In his demographic studies, Donald Ramos has found that even at the end of the colonial period in Vila Rica, the capital of Minas Gerais, only 23.4 percent of the free adult women (over the age of twelve) had ever been married.[64] It is likely that such figures held true for Sabará and other *comarcas* in the captaincy. Referring to the mining region in 1725, the Portuguese Overseas Council stated: "The majority of the residents of those lands do not marry because of the free and easy ways in which they live."[65]

According to the historian Muriel Nazzari, marriage in colonial Brazil generally occurred between equal partners. Men expected "to marry women who were their equals or their superiors, especially in wealth."[66] Sabará's inventory records (examined in Chapter 2) do indicate, in fact, that marriages among wealthy slaveholders were common even if not universal.[67] An alternative to marriage among equals was concubinage, a sexual relationship outside marriage, which was both illegal and condemned by the Catholic Church.[68]

62. Boschi, "As visitas diocesanos e a Inquisição na colônia," *Revista brasileira de história* 7 (March 1987): 155.

63. Luciano Raposo de Almeida Figueiredo, "Barrocas familias: Vida familiar em Minas Gerais no seculo XVIII" (master's essay, Univerity of São Paulo, 1989), 125.

64. In 1804, free adult women made up 55.3 percent of the free population in Vila Rica. Ramos, "Single and Married Women," 264.

65. Quoted in Ramos, "Single and Married Women," 261.

66. Nazzari, "Concubinage in Colonial Brazil," 107. See also Nazzari, *Disappearance of the Dowry*.

67. See Tables 2.9 and 2.10. In the years 1725–59, 57 percent of the slaves were owned by couples; in the years 1760–1808, almost 63 percent of the slaves were owned by couples.

68. Fráncisco Torres Londoño, "Público e escándoloso: Igreja e concubinato no antigo bispado do Rio de Janeiro" (Ph.D. diss., University of São Paulo, 1992), 12. Other studies of Brazilian family life discussing concubinage include Nazzari, "Concubinage in Colonial Brazil"; Elizabeth Anne Kusnesof, "Sexual Politics, Race, and Bastard-Bearing in Nineteenth-Century Brazil: A Question of Culture or Power," *Journal of Family History* 16:3 (1991): 241–60; Ronaldo Vainfas, *Trópico dos pecados: Moral, sexualidade, e Inquisição no Brasil* (Editora Campus, 1989); Maria Beatriz Nizza da Silva, *Sistema de casamento no Brasil colonial* (São Paulo: University of São Paulo, 1984); Luna and Costa, "Devassa nas Minas Gerais; Observações sobre casos de concubinato," *Anais do Museu Paulista* 31 (1982): 221–33.

In discussions of sexual relationships outside marriage in Brazil, it is, of course, possible to employ other terms such as the English phrase *consensual union* or the Portuguese term *amasia* (mistress or lover), which both imply a certain degree of equality between partners. In the following analysis of sexual relationships outside marriage in colonial Sabará, there are, however, evident *inequalities* of both race and class in the majority of relationships that I describe. In only a minority of cases is there evidence to suggest that terms connoting equality in the relationship are appropriate. I agree then with the historians Muriel Nazzari, Luciano Raposo de Almeida Figueiredo, Francisco Londoño, and others that concubinage is the appropriate term for unequal sexual relationships outside marriage and that women in such liaisons were concubines.[69] As all three point out in their own studies, *concubine* and *concubinage* were also the terms used by contemporaries for these relationships.

The Council of Trent (1554–63), which had first condemned concubinage and threatened those engaged in it with excommunication, also provided a mechanism for overseeing the morals of both parishioners and local clergy. The Council called for intermittent episcopal visits to the various dioceses. Bishops could appoint visiting clergymen to tour the parishes, interview the faithful, and impose discipline and orthodoxy on the errant. In colonial Minas Gerais, episcopal visits from appointed Visitors became a regular (if not always well-announced) feature of religious life in the various *comarcas*. Luciano Figueiredo has identified a minimum of fifty-three episcopal visits that took place in the mining region between 1721 and 1802.[70] Some Visitors stayed only a month in the mining region; others remained for a year and traveled through forty different localities in the captaincy.[71]

Thus it occurred in Sabará on the fifteenth of January in 1734 that Jacinto Pacheco Ribeiro, a free and single male, was fined three *mil réis* for having committed the sin of keeping a concubine in his home. Appearing

---

69. Nazzari, "Concubinage in Colonial Brazil," 108; Londoño, "Público e escándoloso"; Figueiredo, "Barrocas familias."

70. Figueiredo, "Barrocas familias," 48.

71. Figueiredo, "Barrocas familias," 46. See also Boschi, "As visitas diocesanos," 151–84. The church laws regulating episcopal visits in Minas Gerais were formulated as part of a larger code that outlined how tridentine reforms would be enacted in Brazil and was entitled *Constituições primeiras do Arcebispado da Bahía, feitas e ordenadas pelo ilustríssimo e reverendíssimo senhor Sebastião Monteiro da Vide bispo do dito arcebispado, e do conselho de sua Magestade, propostas e aceitas em o synodo diocesano que o dito senhor celebrou em 12 de junho do anno 1707* (São Paulo: Typografia 2 de dezembro, 1853).

before the Reverend Doctor Lourenço Jozé de Queiroz Coimbra, an appointed Visitor to the *comarca* of Sabará from the Holy Office of the Inquisition in Lisbon, Pacheco was ordered to expel the concubine from his home in two days to avoid the further penalty of excommunication. The concubine, identified as Anna *parda,* was also called before the visiting cleric; she confessed to her own sinfulness and was in turn fined three *mil reis.* Anna, however, did not pay the sum required. Instead, Jacinto Pacheco Ribeiro paid the combined fee of six *mil réis.* This act was more than a matter of largesse — Anna was his own slave.[72]

When the Reverend Doctor Coimbra arrived in Sabará, he immediately became the supreme ecclesiastical authority, and the objectives of his visit were outlined in an edict distributed to all local authorities (civil as well as clerical). Such edicts called for the banishment of "vices, sins, abuses, and scandals" and for vigilance of the spiritual and temporal well-being of the population. Such an edict typically also demanded that all parishioners and clergy should appear before the Visitor within twenty-four hours of its posting either to confess to their own failings or to denounce the "public and scandalous" sins of fellow members of the community.[73]

Concubinage was so common in the *comarca* of Sabará in 1734 that of the 237 individuals called to answer for their various sins before Lourenço José de Queiroz Coimbra between the months of January and September, 221 (93.2 percent) either had to pay fines for engaging in an "illicit communication" or were admonished for participating in the practice with a man or woman.[74] The penalties imposed by the visiting cleric indicated that many individuals continued to engage in concubinage despite the Church's condemnation of the practice. Indeed, almost 20 percent of the persons fined for concubinage in 1734 had been condemned and fined for

---

72. Cúria Municipal de Belo Horizonte, Lourenço José de Queiroz Coimbra, *Livro segundo dos termos que ha de servir nesta visita ordinaria desta comarca de Sabará e Pitanguí,* Vila Real, 24 de dezembro 1733, fols. 1v, 4. According to Figueiredo, a number of episcopal visits in Minas Gerais were carried out by clergy like Queiroz Coimbra who also served as agents of the Portuguese Inquisition in Brazil. In colonial Minas Gerais, there was not a systematic presence of Inquisition tribunals as occurred elsewhere in Brazil. Figueiredo, "Barrocas familias," 75–76.

73. Boschi, "As visitas diocesanos," 162–64.

74. Cúria Municipal de Belo Horizonte, *Livro segundo dos termos.* Twenty-one individuals were warned as opposed to actually fined. This is 9.5 percent of the total. In examining similar sources for the year 1737, which included individuals from a number of parishes in the *comarca* of Sabará, Luna and Costa also found that concubinage was the single most prevalent crime among the accused (87.43 percent of 350 cases). "Devassa nas Minas Gerais," 227.

it previously. Over 5 percent of those who appeared before Dr. Queiroz Coimbra were cited for their "third lapse" into concubinage.[75] For these second and third offenders, the fines imposed were double and triple those of first-time sinners. The willingness of Sabará's residents to withstand repeated condemnation and increased fines for their sins indicates both the limits of the Catholic Church's ability to shape moral behavior in the region at this time and the important place that concubinage held in the social structure of the *comarca*.

Although serial relationships with women, in which men have one concubine after another, may have been quite ordinary for men in this *comarca*, instances of males having multiple concubines were rare.[76] (By *serial*, I mean having one concubine, ending that liaison, starting another, ending it, starting anew, and so on.) For most men, having a concubine did not signify having a second woman in addition to a wife. Only 6 of the 142 males (4.2 percent) mentioned in the pastoral records were married.[77] Concubinage was thus largely an alternative to marriage, not a practice that took place in addition to it. For some individuals, this situation may have been due to the fact that legal marriage was difficult to arrange because, as recent immigrants to the mining region, the residents of Sabará could not easily demonstrate that they were single to the local church authorities as required by canon law. Legal marriages also required payments of sometimes considerable fees to local clergy.[78]

Such bureaucratic obstacles to marriage were quite real, but they do not adequately explain why rich and powerful men could not or did not choose to overcome such obstacles.[79] Lieutenant Colonel Antônio Brandão (discussed earlier) was a well-connected and wealthy member of the community in Sabará and a member in good standing of several prestigious lay brotherhoods. It is unlikely that any bureaucratic fees or paperwork could have impeded his desire to marry a woman of his choosing. His woman, however, was an African slave from Angola, and a marriage to her would

75. Luna and Costa, "Devassa nas Minas Gerais," 227.
76. Bento Cardoso, single male, was fined in April 1734 for having two concubines, both his slaves. Cúrio Municipal de Belo Horizonte, *Livro segundo dos termos*, fol. 88.
77. For the year 1737, Luna and da Costa found that 84.6 percent of the men were single. "Devassa nas Minas Gerais," 227.
78. Ramos, "Marriage and the Family," 212; Silva, *Sistema de casamento*, 50–56, also argues that bureaucratic and financial requirements were obstacles that lowered rates of marriage in colonial Brazil.
79. Vainfas, *Trópico dos pecados*, 84, argues against the view that colonists failed to marry because of legal and financial impediments.

definitely have been one of unequals. By Portuguese law, through marriage, the slave Joanna would have gained both legal rights and *half* of his community property.[80] Concubinage, unlike marriage, allowed Brandão to pass on his entire estate to his mixed-race child without having to share a fixed percentage of it with his non-White sexual partner. Concubinage thus could have been preferable to marriage in colonial Sabará because it fulfilled an economic desire to maximize the inheritance of a man's children and a concern to limit access to wealth and status in the community to White (or whiter) women.

Quieroz Coimbra's investigation of sins in Sabará also brought to his attention the transgressions of his fellow clergymen. On 28 March 1734, Father Antônio de Macedo Rego was fined for his first lapse into concubinage with his slave Maria.[81] Earlier that month, fellow priest Melchior Cardozo de Aguiar had been officially warned "to put out of his house" such women as he kept there. Father Melchior accepted his warning and promised to make amends promptly.[82] Later that year in September, Father Joseph Lobo Barreto was also admonished "to put out of his house" Thereza das Flores, a *parda* woman, "for the imminent danger" that living with her (*de portas adentro*) caused.[83] The transgressions of the local clergy suggest that such priests would have been of little use to the Church as local enforcers of the official tenets of Catholicism on sexual behavior.

The phenomenon of concubinage included but was not limited to situations of masters establishing sexual liaisons with their own slave women. Although most of the slave women condemned (87.2 percent) were concubines of their own masters, slaves made up only one-third of all the women cited. The majority of the women (51.3 percent) were freed slaves.[84]

---

80. According to the *Ordenações filipinas*, the Philipine Code, on the marriage of a woman to a man, she becomes half-owner of all their possessions, and he does as well. When her husband dies, the woman keeps her half, and the children automatically receive two-thirds of the husband's assets. The husband can dispose of the remaining one-third of his assets as he wishes in a will. If a man was not married, the size of the estate going to his children might well be doubled, particularly if his wife had brought nothing of value into the marriage. *Ordenações do Senhor Rey D. Affonso V* (Coimbra: Real Imprensa da Universidade, 1786), livro iv, título 12.

81. Cúrio Municipal de Belo Horizonte, *Livro segundo dos termos*, fol. 56.

82. "[Q]ue lancasse fora de sua caza as mulheres que nella tem." Cúrio Municipal de Belo Horizonte, *Livro segundo dos termos*, fol. 48.

83. Cúrio Municipal de Belo Horizonte, *Livro segundo dos termos*, fol. 120v. The phrase "De portas adentro" implies a sexual relationship, even in modern usage.

84. Luna and Costa found that in 1737 53.9 percent of accused women were freed slaves and 27.1 percent were slaves. "Devassa nas Minas Gerais," 227.

The remaining women mentioned were all free and identified either as married, widowed, poor, Indian, or as co-parents with the male cited.[85] (See Table 3.2.)

The records of 1734 indicate that, in addition to rich White men, men of lower social status, non-Whites, and even some slaves were also condemned for concubinage. For example, Balthezar do Valle, a freed bastard, lived in concubinage with a slave woman, Maria Gomes, who belonged to another free male. Tax records from 1720 show that Valle was himself a slave owner, but he had not been very prosperous and owned only two slaves.[86] Bento Luis, a Black slave belonging to one of Sabará's wealthiest masters, Colonel Antonio de Sá Barboza, was also condemned for his relationship with another slave, Josepha Mina, who actually belonged to a different owner, a freed *parda* woman.[87] Colonel Barboza himself did not escape the notice of the Visitor, and he was fined for living with Maria de Souza, a freed *crioula*.[88] The wealthy Barboza was matched in his transgression by an even wealthier man who, according to the 1720 tax records, owned the most slaves in the *comarca*.[89] Master of seventy-two slaves fourteen years before, Colonel Jozé Correa de Miranda appeared before his churchman on 7 September 1734 to pay a fine of nine *mil réis* to

Table 3.2
Women living as concubines, *comarca* of Sabará, 1734

	Number	Percentage
Freed slaves	74	51.3
Slaves	47	32.6
Free	22	15.3
Unknown	1	0.7
Total	144	99.9

85. Co-parentage describes the relationship between godparents and biological parents of a baptized child. They were forbidden to marry one another or have carnal relations under canon law.

86. Cúrio Municipal de Belo Horizonte, *Livro segundo dos termos*, fol. 22v; "Lista dos escravos . . . para pagarem os reaes quintos de 1720 athé o de 1721," APMCMS, Códice 2.

87. Cúrio Municipal de Belo Horizonte, *Livro segundo dos termos*, fols. 80v, 75. In 1720, Barboza owned fifty-one slaves. "Lista dos escravos . . . para pagarem os reaes quintos de 1720 athé o de 1721," APMCMS, Códice 2.

88. Cúrio Municipal de Belo Horizonte, *Livro segundo dos termos*, fols. 98v, 99v.

89. "Lista dos escravos . . . para pagarem os reaes quintos de 1720 athé o de 1721," APMCMS, Códice 2.

absolve himself from his "third lapse" into concubinage.[90] This time, Miranda's companion was Joanna Victoria, a free, single, White woman. This lapse was Joanna's first into concubinage, an indication that Miranda's previous alliances had involved someone else.[91] All these women were themselves cited and fined for concubinage by the Church's spokesman, Dr. Queiroz Coimbra.[92]

The examples cited here indicate that in terms of wealth, race, and social status the practice of concubinage in colonial Sabará involved the rich as well as the poor, Whites and non-Whites, slave and free. Relationships of equals or near equals do appear in the records of those condemned, but in the vast majority of instances, the relationships appear to have been between men of higher social standing and women of inferior position. Social or racial inequality characterized the liaisons between most of the men and women condemned.

In contrast to the characteristics of women concubines, very few men condemned for concubinage were former slaves or slaves (7 percent). Only eight (5.6 percent) of the men were *forros* or ex-slaves, and only two (1.4 percent) were slaves themselves. The female partners of the eight *forros* and the two male slaves were either *forras* or slaves themselves.[93] Four of the *forros* had *forras* as concubines; four had slaves as concubines. One of the enslaved men had a *forra* as a partner; the other had a slave as a partner. For these men and women, it is possible that bureaucratic impediments to legal marriage were not easily surmounted and that their relationships were those of social and racial equals who were simply unable to marry.

For the much larger number of cases of men who were born free, unequal relationships were more characteristic: these (presumably) White men often established relations with non-White women.[94] Nearly three-

90. "Lista dos escravos . . . para pagarem os reaes quintos de 1720 athé o de 1721," APMCMS, Códice 2. Cúrio Municipal de Belo Horizonte, *Segundo livro dos termos*, fols. 104v, 113.

91. Cúrio Municipal de Belo Horizonte, *Livro segundo dos termos*, fol. 104v.

92. Cúrio Municipal de Belo Horizonte, *Livro segundo dos termos*, fols. 23v, 75, 98v, 104v.

93. Four of the *forros* had *forras* as concubines; four had slaves as concubines. One of the men slaves had a *forra* as a partner; the other had a slave as a partner.

94. Population records for 1735 do not indicate the exact number of Whites in Sabará, but at that time *forros* were specifically identified as such for tax purposes. Those not so identified were presumably of European origin or were Whites born in Brazil. For the second half of the eighteenth century, it is not safe to assume that the majority of those born free in Minas Gerais were also White. See Table 2.1.

quarters of the enslaved concubines were identified as *pretas*, a label that indicated color (Black) as well as origin (African)[95] Of those enslaved concubines who were not Africans, those of mixed race outnumbered *crioulas* (Blacks born in Brazil). *Pardas, cabras* (both are progeny of Blacks and Whites), and *mestiças* (Indian and White progeny) made up more than four-fifths of the Brazilian-born concubines. Because at this time mixed-race female slaves did not constitute so large a proportion of the Brazilian-born slaves in Sabará,[96] their over-representation among the concubines probably reflects the desires of White males for women closest in appearance to themselves. This preference for whiter concubines provides some indication that White males in Sabará were both race conscious and racist; to the degree that it was possible, they avoided liaisons with darker women. (See Table 3.3.)

Among the freed slave women who were concubines, close to one-half (47.3 percent) were born in Brazil, and nearly two-thirds of those were individuals of mixed race. Both figures reflect the fact that in the popula-

Table 3.3
Race of enslaved female concubines in Sabará, 1734

Race of Slaves	Number	Percentage
Pretas	35	74.4
Crioulas	2	4.2
Pardas	6	12.7
Cabras	2	4.2
Mestiças	1	2.1
Carijó[a]	1	2.1
Total	47	99.7

[a]Indian.

95. At this still early point in the eighteenth century, most slaves referred to as *pretas* or *pretos* were Africans and labeled as such to distinguish them from the Brazilian-born slaves known as *crioulas* and *crioulos*. The records reflect a certain amount of carelessness on the part of the recorders: they did not bother to note the African origin of all these slaves. Nonetheless, *crioulo* was a label of distinction, indicating greater value, and perhaps greater esteem; it was reserved for those born in Brazil.

96. Inventories of households examined for the years 1725–44 indicated that 76 percent of the enslaved women were African; *crioulas* represented 50 percent of the remaining non-African female slaves, and this percentage increased as the eighteenth century progressed. See Tables 2.7 and 2.8 for an overall view of racial and ethnic categories in eighteenth-century Sabará.

tion of freed slave women in Sabará there were more *crioulas* and individuals of mixed parentage than in the population of enslaved women. The increased proportion of Brazilian-born individuals among Sabará's ex-slaves resulted from the overall advantages held by Brazilian-born slaves (in particular, children) over African slaves in becoming manumitted.[97] The prevalence of mixed-race ex-slaves among those condemned for concubinage again suggests a strong sense of race consciousness among White men and indicates that darker women were not sought after as concubines as much as the whiter women in Sabará were. (See Table 3.4.)

Because so many of Sabará's concubines were ex-slaves or slaves, women who were Black or of mixed race formed the vast majority of those accused by the Catholic Church (84 percent). Because the men accused were mostly free (93 percent) and therefore more likely to be White, the relationships of concubinage in Sabará were characterized by much inequality. These free men enjoyed the highest social ranking in the community whereas their concubines were viewed as particularly inferior for reasons of both status and race. As Muriel Nazzari has noted, such inequality gave the men involved considerable power and freedom, much more of both than they would have had in a married state.[98] Still, it should be noted that men in Sabará did not attempt to maximize the inequalities that concubinage afforded them. They clearly preferred women who resembled them in appearance (were whiter or lighter) and women who were born in Brazil, spoke Portuguese, and were knowledgeable about Portuguese cul-

Table 3.4
Race of freed slave concubines in Sabará, 1734

Race	Number	Percentage
Pretas	39	52.7
Crioulas	13	17.5
Pardas	12	16.2
Mulatas	3	4.0
Cabras	2	2.7
Mestiças	1	1.3
Bastardas[a]	4	5.4
Total	74	99.8

[a]Bastards, presumably also of mixed descent.

97. See Chapter 5 on manumissions.
98. Nazzari, "Concubinage in Colonial Brazil," 119.

ture and customs in the colony. The very characteristics of these preferred women would have gained them somewhat more respect or standing in the slave society of Sabará. Knowledge of the Portuguese language and culture would surely have also enhanced any available opportunities to improve the conditions of their concubinage.

The phenomenon of concubinage and the preference for women who were acculturated and more nearly White were related consequences of the relative absence of White women in colonial Sabará.[99] The absence of White women did not necessarily translate directly or immediately into power and freedom for the non-White women who served in their stead. The absence of White women did not compel White men to marry non-Whites and thus provide to non-White women the legal standing and property rights that marriage would have provided. In addition, manumission records in Sabará do not indicate that enslaved concubines, having been involved in sexual unions with their masters, were then regularly rewarded for their services, or for their affections, with the gift of freedom.[100] It was more likely that a good number of mixed-race children of enslaved concubines would be freed outright by their masters/fathers.[101] These children would then provide an important source of growth for the population of freed people of mixed racial descent (and future concubines) in Sabará.

As long as free White men continued to outnumber free White women, legal marriage did not become universal in Sabará. Demographic records for the captaincy of Minas Gerais in 1786 and 1805 demonstrate that even at the end of the eighteenth century, White males outnumbered White females by 20 percent.[102] Surveys of the records of episcopal visits throughout Minas Gerais, which took place between 1721 and 1802, also indicate that during this period such visits continued to focus on the sexual practices and mores of the population and that accusations of and fines for concubinage continued to represent the vast majority of the sins of the

99. Demographic records for the year 1776 indicate that White males continued to outnumber White females in the *comarca* of Sabará by a ratio of three to two (150 males per 100 females). "Memoria histórica da capitania de Minas Gerais," *RAPM* 2 (1897): 511. Records for the entire captaincy of Minas Gerais in 1786 and 1805 show that even at the end of the eighteenth century, White males outnumbered White females by 20 percent. In 1786, there were 121 White males per 100 White females, and in 1805, there were 118 White males per 100 White females. "População da provincia de Minas Gerais," *RAPM* 4 (1899): 294.

100. See Chapter 5. Most adult men and women paid for their manumissions; gifts of freedom were not uncommon, but more regularly applied to small children.

101. See Chapter 5.

102. "População da provincia de Minas Gerais," *RAPM* 4 (1899): 294.

population.[103] Concubinage involving both slave and ex-slave women continued to serve as a substitute for marriage, although White males were not prohibited from marrying such women.

The phenomenon of concubinage, which cut across social and racial categories in colonial Sabará, is so suggestive of inequality between the men and women involved that the women involved (and especially the slaves) were unlikely to have much choice about establishing such a relationship. How, after all, could a poor Black ex-slave woman say No to the attentions of a free White male? Who, in a community governed by White men, would have defended her, if she refused a particular man or any man at all? Concubinage in Sabará in the eighteenth century provides evidence of the power that free White men held over the lives and bodies of the darker women who lived in proximity to them.

This is not to argue that all such liaisons were devoid of affection; some of these relationships were loving and perhaps even mutually rewarding. Francisco Dias Rebello, for example, was denounced in 1730 for keeping a *mulata* slave woman as a concubine whom he "treated as his wife and mistress of his house." In turn, Rebello sent his legal wife off to the woods to find firewood, wash laundry, and prepare corn.[104] Because some concubines did benefit from the relationship, some women may even have chosen to pursue or promote such arrangements.[105]

The unions of men and women in situations of concubinage were, if nothing else, fruitful, as the parish records of the baptisms of infants reveal. Significantly, these children were not systematically cut off from the free White community in Sabará. They acquired permanent connections to both White and non-White free adults through the acquisition of godparents. The character of the phenomenon of concubinage in Sabará is perhaps reflected in the fact that the children of such extramarital and mixed-race unions were not entirely separated from the White community, even if they were born into slavery. If the institution was primarily a coercive one in which men of one race coldheartedly exploited vulnerable women of another, then, strangely enough, concubinage also motivated the establishment of voluntary, ritualistic social relationships, such as godparentage and co-parentage, which linked adults of different races to one another and to the mixed-race infants born of those relationships. God-

---

103. "Não havia livros de culpas em que as condenações decorrentes da prática da mancebia ocupassem menos de 85% em media." Figueiredo, "Barrocas familias," 64.

104. Figueiredo, "Barrocas familias," 110.

105. Nazzari, "Concubinage in Colonial Brazil," 119.

parents acted on behalf of godchildren, no matter what their color. Thus, at least some social relationships derived from concubinage cut across racial categories in a positive way, were voluntary in nature, and served to harmonize relations between Whites and people of color in Sabará. The following chapter focuses in more detail on the children of Sabará, baptisms of slaves, and the rituals of godparentage.

4

Slave Baptisms and Godparentage in Colonial Sabará

In the formula-bound opening passage of her will of 2 January 1761, Luiza Pereira do Lago, an African woman from the Costa da Mina, declared herself to be a true Christian, a believer in the holy Catholic faith and in the Holy Mother Church of Rome. She commended her soul to the Holy Trinity and called for the intercession on her behalf of the Virgin Mary, all the saints of the celestial court, her guardian angel, Saint Anthony, Saint Anne, and Saint Michael the Archangel. She expressed hope that as a believer her soul would be saved, not for reasons of her own worthiness but for that of the only son of God, Jesus Christ.[1]

Although I have argued in both Chapters 2 and 3 that the formulaic openings of eighteenth-century wills are insufficient proof of a testator's religious values or commitment, in the case of Luiza Pereira do Lago, the unique individual provisions and bequests that she made in her will confirm her adherence to a Catholic identity in colonial Sabará. Luiza Pereira do Lago had been a slave at the time of her adult baptism in the city of

---

1. "Em esta fé espero salvar a minha alma não por meus merecimentos mais pellas de santíssima paixão do unigénito filho de deus." Testamento de Luiza Pereira do Lago, 2 January 1761, *Livro de registo de testamento* (28 março 1760), MOSMG, fol. 182.

Bahía in northeastern Brazil. In 1761, she had paid her market value to her former master, Manoel Luis Pereira, and was no longer a slave. A resident of the parish of Raposos in the *comarca* of Sabará, Luiza was a member of the local branch of the brotherhood of Our Lady of the Rosary for Blacks and a supporter of the Chapel of Santa Ana in Raposos. She bequeathed ten drams of gold for decorations of the principal altar in that chapel and ten more for a side altar dedicated to Saint Michael. She left fifteen drams for the brotherhood of Manos de Madre and ten each for the brotherhoods of Santa Casa de Jerusalem and Santíssimo Sacramento. Leftover funds from the disposable third of her estate were to purchase masses to be said for her soul.[2] Although Luiza did have some savings in the form of gold jewelry, her estate consisted principally of the house in which she lived and nine slaves (seven men, two women).

Although Luiza Pereira do Lago had never been married, she did have two daughters: Esperança and Maria, both identified as *pardas* or children of European and African descent. As Luiza was an African, the father(s) of her children had probably been White, and she had been a concubine. Luiza stated that her daughters were both married and provided the names of the husbands: Manoel Ferreira da Rocha and Antônio Martins Netto. Neither of these men was identified as an ex-slave or a person of color, and it is possible that both were White. Although Manoel Ferreira da Rocha no longer lived with Esperança and his whereabouts were unknown, Antônio Martins Netto lived with Maria in an outlying settlement.[3] Respectable married women, Esperança and Maria were both to inherit from their mother's estate the majority of her slaves.

From the viewpoint of both the Portuguese crown and the Catholic Church, the conversion of this African slave woman to Catholicism was successful and highly desirable. Making Christians of slaves in Catholic Brazil, unlike in Protestant North America or in the Caribbean, was not considered threatening to the social order.[4] Luiza Pereira do Lago's enthu-

---

2. All the brotherhoods she mentions were the local branches founded in Raposos.

3. Of Esperança's husband, Luiza declared: "se aubzentou."

4. According to Albert J. Raboteau, slave owners in North America initially believed that christianizing slaves would result in their legally being freed. In addition, slaveholders feared that Christianity would make their slaves proud and rebellious. The economic profitability of slaves was also more important to masters there than was their being catechized. *Slave Religion: The Invisible Institution in the Antebellum South* (New York: Oxford University Press, 1978), 98–105. See also Wood, *Black Majority*, 133–35. Michael Craton, writing of slaveholders in the British West Indies, also observed that these masters argued that Christianity was unsuitable for the limited capacities of Negro slaves and that missionaries incited cate-

siasm for church-sponsored organizations, her donations to church coffers, and her own transformation from slave to slaveholder (and from concubine to mother of *married* daughters) provide evidence that, at least in some cases, conversion could lead to social conformity.

Slave owners in colonial Brazil nonetheless were not all equally devout Catholics and did not always or uniformly comply with the Church or crown demands that the tenets of Catholicism should, to some or any degree, apply to the enslaved. Slave owners ignored exhortations that holy days should be observed and were deaf to protests against slaves working on Sundays. Masters did not respond to demands that all slaves be properly catechized or allowed to marry. They did not agree with arguments that married slaves should not be parted from one another. Converting adult slaves to Catholicism or allowing those who had converted to freely practice their religion was expensive and inconvenient for slaveholders in Brazil. Time spent in religious activities reduced the profits of the masters because these activities diverted slaves from their labors.[5]

If all owners were not in favor of slaves becoming observant Christians, neither were they systematically opposed to slaves being baptized. Many, if not most, slaves in colonial Sabará thus eventually became at least nominal Catholics, and, as the specific passages and bequests of Luiza Pereira do Lago's will suggest, an untold number embraced Catholic beliefs with enthusiasm. The few surviving baptismal records from Sabará allow a number of observations about adult slave conversions, their baptisms, and the resultant godparent relationships that followed conversions. Perhaps the most significant observation is that godparent relationships established among adult converts to Catholicism differed from those created by parents for enslaved children baptized at birth. These differences in turn suggest that the motivations behind the decisions of slaves to accept conversion for themselves or for their children were complex and reflected an ongoing struggle between owners and slaves for control over the converted slaves' lives and the community connections among slaves, which becoming Christians helped to foster.

chized slaves to rebel. *Testing the Chains: Resistance to Slavery in the British West Indies* (Ithaca: Cornell University Press, 1982), 241. Emília Viotti da Costa also discusses the role of missionaries in slave rebellions in *Crowns of Glory, Tears of Blood: The Demarara Slave Rebellion of 1823* (New York: Oxford University Press, 1994).

5. See selected passages of *Constituições primeiras*, in Robert E. Conrad, ed., *Children of God's Fire: A Documentary History of Black Slavery in Brazil* (Princeton: Princeton University Press, 1983), 154–63.

In this chapter, I explore the contestation of goals or interests that are represented by variations in the patterns of baptismal records in early colonial Sabará. These variations reflect much more than the phenomenon of devout slaveholders leading men, women, and child slaves to the baptismal font in pious acts designed to assure eternal salvation for both owner and their human property. Without denying the role of religiosity in baptisms, I suggest that these variations show that enslaved men, enslaved women, and their owners all interpreted the worldly outcomes of baptisms differently and attempted to manipulate their interests in these outcomes accordingly.

Although it is likely that most slaves in Sabará were at least nominally Catholic by the end of the eighteenth century, what proportion of the slaves were Christian in the early decades of the mining boom is not clear.[6] Some African slaves destined for Brazil were reportedly baptized en masse before arriving in the colony. Adult slave baptismal records in Sabará indicate, however, that not all who arrived in the mining region had been christened earlier. Throughout Minas Gerais, slave owners initially failed to meet a requirement to present their slaves to the local parish for baptism within one year of their arrival in the region.[7] In 1719, the king of Portugal was said to be extremely displeased by the news that such a large number of the slaves in Minas Gerais lived and died without ever having been baptized. The governor of Minas Gerais responded to the king's complaint by ordering local parish priests to seek out unbaptized slaves and promptly christen them.[8]

Although it is not possible to determine the effect of the governor's orders in the comarca of Sabará, the evidence that slaves were baptized comes from various sources. The wills of numerous former slaves such as that of Luiza Pereira do Lago attest to the individual experiences of adult slaves becoming Christians. The popularity and numbers of lay brother-

6. One reason for this change was an increase in the proportion of slaves in Minas Gerais who were born there. Bergad has argued that the proportion of creole slaves increased significantly in Mariana toward the end of the eighteenth century. "After the Mining Boom," *LARR* 31:1 (1996): 67–97.

7. Schwartz cites Henry Koster, *Travels in Brazil,* 2 vols. (Philadelphia, 1817), 199, to support the statement that by the end of the eighteenth century, slaves from Angola were baptized en masse before coming to Brazil whereas those from Mina were not. See *Sugar Plantations in the Formation of Brazilian Society,* 411.

8. "[D]iz que o rei está desgostosissimo ante as noticias que tem do grande numero de escravos que vivem e morrem nas Minas sem baptismo," Dom Pedro de Almeida, Conde de Assumar, to Vigarios das varas das minas, 23 September 1719, APMSC, Códice 11, fol. 151v.

hoods in Sabará dedicated to slaves and ex-slaves are also indications of slave baptisms; one obvious requirement of membership was to be a baptized Roman Catholic. In the late eighteenth century, lists of members of a chapter of the Lady of the Rosary for Blacks in a neighboring *comarca* indicated that almost 70 percent of those admitted to the brotherhood were slaves.[9] It is likely that the chapters of Black brotherhoods in Sabará were similarly configured.

The Catholic Church attracted certain individuals from the slave and ex-slave communities not only through the organization of the brotherhoods, but also through the significant opportunities it provided for various kinds of artistic expression. Highly skilled artists and artisans, among whom were slaves and freedmen, helped in the construction of the magnificent baroque churches built in Sabará and the other major mining towns of the captaincy. One of the best-documented examples of a mulatto artisan in colonial Minas Gerais is that of António Francisco Lisboa, the sculptor known as O Aleijadinho, who was born in the 1730s and was the creator of much church art in mining towns throughout the region. In Sabará, his sculptures include the pulpits, choir, and doorway of the Igreja do Carmo.[10]

The Catholic Church also provided opportunities for musical performances. On the occasion of religious festivals, musical performances were often given, and the musicians present were often local individuals: slaves, ex-slaves, and their descendants prominent among them.[11] If they had arrived in the region as adults, some of these individuals might have sought membership in the Church through baptism.

The number of surviving parish baptismal registers for the *comarca* of Sabará is extremely limited. Those that do exist are from first half of the eighteenth century and confirm that not all adult slaves arriving in Sabará were already baptized. The names of children born as slaves and those of adult slaves are both recorded in these registers, and together these two

9. Scarano, *Devoção e escravidão*, 115, 133. This is an approximate figure given missing pages from the membership books. Between 1779 and 1800, Scarano found 139 ex-slave members versus 314 slaves. Individuals identified as Whites were also members, but their numbers were very low.

10. Lisboa was the illegitimate son of the Portuguese master carpenter and architect Manuel Francisco Lisboa and his slave Isabel. He would have been baptized as a Christian at birth. Russell-Wood, *The Black Man in Slavery and Freedom*, 101.

11. Germain Bazin, *L'Architecture religieuse baroque au Brésil*, 2 vols. (Paris: Plon, 1956); Passos, *Em torno da historia de Sabará*; Curt Francisco Lange, "A música barroca," in *História geral da civilização brasileira*, ed. Sérgio Buarque de Holanda (São Paulo: Difel, 1977), vol. 2, 121–44.

groups made up over 80 percent of all baptisms. Adult baptisms alone constituted over one-half of the registered baptisms. Thus for at least the early decades of the mining boom, the conversion of adult slaves to Catholicism was a significant activity that took place in the *comarca* itself. (See Tables 4.1 and 4.2.)

Baptismal records provide tantalizing but all too brief details about the individuals involved. Only the names of the baptized, the parents, and the godparents were required. Sabará's records also identified the legal status (free, freed, or slave) of the participants and often provided indications of legitimacy or illegitimacy (for children), marital status (for adults), and color—if not White. For example, on 8 June 1727, a child named Gonçallo was brought to the Mother Church (Igreja Matriz) in Sabará to be baptized. Gonçallo's mother was a freed Black woman named Antônia; his father's name was unrecorded. He entered into the religious community of Sabará as an illegitimate, freeborn member. His godparents, charged with the responsibility of contributing to the child's spiritual as well as material welfare, were also members of Sabará's community. His godfather was João de Olanda Porto, almost certainly a free White male, and his godmother was Joanna, a Black slave woman who served another free man, Domingos de Crasto.[12]

Gonçallo's identity as an illegitimate child was hardly unique in the baptismal records of Sabará. In the first six months of 1727, twenty-four free and freed children were baptized in the Matriz of Sabará. Twelve were boys, and twelve were girls. The records of ten of these children did not

Table 4.1. Baptisms in Sabará, 1 January–29 June 1727

	Freeborn	Freed	Slaves
Boys	11	1	9
(Illegitimate)	(2)	(1)	(9)
Girls	8	4	13
(Illegitimate)	(3)	(4)	(12)
Men	0	0	44
Women	0	0	7
Totals	19	5	73

SOURCE: Cúria Municipal de Belo Horizonte, Registo de batizados.

12. Cúria Municipal de Belo Horizonte, *Registo de batizados, 1726–1740*, vol. 2, n. p.

Table 4.2.   Baptisms in Sabará,
4 October 1731–29 September 1732

	Freeborn	Freed	Slaves
Boys	13	2	25
(Illegitimate)	(6)	(2)	(24)
Girls	19	2	30
(Illegitimate)	(5)	(2)	(30)
Men	0	0	65
Women	0	0	42
Totals	32	4	162

SOURCE: Cúria Municipal de Belo Horizonte, Registo de batizados.

provide the name of the child's father, an indication that more than 40 percent of the nonslave children were illegitimate.[13] (See Table 4.1.) For example, on 23 May 1727, Roza, daughter of Joanna Correa and "unknown father," was baptized. A few weeks before, on 20 April, Barbara, the daughter of Anna de Andrade, a freed Black woman, was baptized. Barbara's father was not even mentioned in the registration of the event. Other illegitimate children were also baptized without the names of either of their parents registered. Thomé, for example, was an *exposto*, an abandoned child left at the house of Dom João de Castro e Sotomayor,[14] who must have decided to care for the child and have him baptized as well. Abandoned children were also left in the care of less well-to-do people. Florencia, for example, was an *exposta* in the care of Paula, a freed Black woman, when she was brought to be baptized. Paula's economic position

13. Curia Municipal de Belo Horizonte, *Registo de batizados, 1726–1740*, vol. 2, n. p. If no male was recorded in the baptismal registration, illegitimacy was assumed. Legitimate children were generally identified through the naming of their father and *his wife*, in that order. In four cases, both parents were named although they were not clearly identified as married. In one of these cases, the child was clearly labeled as legitimate (as in "Josepha, legitimate daughter of João Goncalvez and Maria de Araujo, 3 March 1727"). In the three other cases, the child was not clearly labeled as illegitimate (as in "João, innocent son of Florencia, slave of Caetano de Souza, 12 January 1727") or as legitimate. I have made the assumption that, in an eighteenth-century baptismal registration, if both parents were named and no contradictory labels existed, then the child was indeed legitimate. If I am wrong, then thirteen of the twenty-four children registered were illegitimate, rather than ten.

14. The title of Dom could have indicated nobility and in all likelihood signified great wealth and social standing in the *comarca*.

in Sabará was almost certainly inferior to that of Dom João; most freed slaves remained persons of humble means.[15]

Five of the illegitimate children baptized were the children of slave women and freed at the time of their baptisms; of these, four were girls, and one was a boy. Their manumissions suggest that their owners may have felt kindly toward the mothers and freed the (albeit less valuable and mostly female) infants as a reward for good services. These masters could well have been the fathers of these slaves. It is also possible, however, that these masters did not wish to provide food to raise children and thus passed the responsibility for doing so onto the female parent. Because no male declared his paternity for these five children, it remains uncertain whether the freed slaves were fathered by their own masters or by other men.

The prevalence of concubinage in eighteenth-century Sabará meant, of course, that the births of illegitimate but free children like Gonçallo were common in this community. The difficulties that slaves faced in establishing church-sanctioned unions is also evident in the almost total absence of legitimate births among enslaved children. (See Tables 4.1 and 4.2.) Social historians of the eighteenth and nineteenth centuries have noted that proportions of illegitimate births in Brazilian communities varied from 5.5 to 65 percent of all births. For the second half of the eighteenth century in urban São Paulo and urban Rio de Janeiro, scholars have found illegitimacy rates between 30 and 45 percent.[16] In Vila Rica, the capital of Minas Gerais, 65 percent of all births between 1760 and 1800 were illegitimate.[17] Illegitimacy in Sabará thus had its parallels elsewhere in the colony.

Gonçallo's baptismal registration does not identify his race, but in view of his mother's identity as a freed slave, he was either Black or mulatto. The race of children freed at baptism was sometimes implied by other details of the written record. On 27 July 1732, Domingos Dias de Crasto of the district of Lapa brought a young boy named José to the local church to be baptized. José, the son of Josepha, a slave woman belonging to

---

15. In general, freed slave women are referred to in documents as having humble jobs, a small number of slaves, and smaller amounts of property. See Chapter 2.

16. Maria Luiza Marcílio, *A cidade de São Paulo: Povoamento e população, 1750–1850* (São Paulo: Pioneira, 1974), 159; Renata Pinto Venâncio, "Nos limites da sagrada familia: Ilegitimidade e casamento no Brasil colonial," in Vainfas, ed., *História e sexualidade no Brasil* (Rio de Janeiro: Graal, 1986), 114–18; Kusnesof, "Sexual Politics, Race, and Bastard-Bearing in Nineteenth-Century Brazil," 241–60; Nazzari, "Concubinage in Colonial Brazil," 107–24.

17. Costa, *Vila Rica: Populacão 1729–1826* (São Paulo: IPE/USP, 1979), 227.

Crasto, had been born a slave. Domingos Dias de Crasto recognized the child as his own son, and José was baptized on this day as a freed and illegitimate child.[18] Not identified as otherwise, it is most likely that Domingos de Crasto was a White man, and therefore his son José was a mulatto.[19]

The enslaved children freed at their baptisms were without doubt fortunate, particularly in comparison with other slave children in Sabará who remained captives. These freed children did not, however, enjoy a social status equal to that of the freeborn and legitimate children of the *comarca*. Even the mulatto child José, whose father had acknowledged his paternity, would have been looked down on as a non-White. It is not clear, however, just how serious the consequences of illegitimacy were for freed children, especially because between one-fourth to one-third of the children born to free mothers in Sabará were also illegitimate.[20]

Gonçallo's godparents, one a free White male and the other an enslaved Black woman, were significant reflections of his own likely economic and social position in Sabará. Although it was common for child slaves and children freed at birth to have godfathers who were free White males, legitimate children did not have godparents who were enslaved or who had once been slaves.[21] The slave status of Gonçallo's godmother was a

18. Cúria Municipal de Belo Horizonte, *Registo de batizados, 1726–1740*, vol. 2, n. p: "27 July 1732, José, son of Domingos Dias de Crasto and of Jozepha, his slave, as free." Under the circumstances of the mother's being named a slave of the father and with no contradicting evidence, it is reasonable to assume that the two parents were not married. The child was therefore illegitimate.

19. Individuals who were persons of color were identified as such in the registrations: "20 April 1727, . . . Barbara, daughter of Anna de Andrade, freed Black"; "31 August 1732, . . . Bartholomeu, son of Thereza, slave of Domingos da Sylva, freed Black." Sometimes color or at least non-whiteness could be inferred from the status indicated for particular individuals: "29 June 1727, . . . Cyprianna, daughter of Antonio Pereyra, freed slave, and of Thomacia, slave of Domingos Martins Pereyra." In most cases, it is reasonable to assume that unless contradicted by specific labels, an individual with both Christian and surname was White.

20. According to the *Ordenações filipinas*, the natural illegitimate children of commoners (as opposed to *cavalleiros*, gentlemen) could inherit from their fathers. *Ordenações do Senhor Rey D. Affonso V*, livro iv, título 98. In practice, however, illegitimate children were much more likely to inherit if their fathers mentioned them as heirs in his will. On the rights of natural children to inherit, see Lewin, "Natural and Spurious Children," 351–96.

21. In the 1727 registration, 76.9 percent of girl slaves and 100 percent of boy slaves had free male godparents; in the 1731–32 registration, 83.3 percent of girl slaves and 80 percent of boy slaves had free male godparents. In 1727, 20 percent of the nonslave and illegitimate children had an enslaved godmother (number of slaves was 10). In 1731–32, 20 percent of the nonslave and illegitimate children had either an enslaved godmother or a godmother who was a freed slave (number of slaves was 15).

sign that both his race and his illegitimacy marked him as a person belonging to the less prestigious ranks of free society in Sabará.

On the other hand, the fact that enslaved women in colonial Sabará could serve as godmothers for free children illustrates one way in which the divisions between slave and free individuals in this slave society remained fluid. At least in the religious realm, it was possible for slaves to achieve an important position of status and to have free individuals placed in a ritual position of subordination to them. That the Church allowed such role reversals to take place may in part explain the appeal of baptism for some adult slaves, who may otherwise have felt little attraction to being converted. The exclusive association of enslaved godmothers with illegitimate children may indicate that this practice was typical among lower-class people in the *comarca*, but not among members of the privileged and married elite.

Gonçallo's baptismal registration, and numerous others that resemble it, illustrate that there could be both material and symbolic outcomes to baptism and godparentage not directly related to the religious implications of becoming a Christian. Records like Gonçallo's suggest that the legal and economic barriers that separated freeborn individuals, freed slaves, and slaves could not always be rigorously maintained in relationships of godparentage. If both a free man and a slave woman could act as godparents to the same freeborn child, then the social (in this case defined by religious) position of these two individuals was at odds with their economic and legal status in the community. Indeed, as a godparent, the religious status of Joanna, the Black slave woman, appears to have been identical to that of her fellow godparent, a free and probably White male. It was most certainly not the case, however, that Joanna's legal or economic status approached that of João de Olanda Porto. As a slave woman, it was therefore possible for her to assume an important religious role in the community and in so doing to transcend, albeit to a limited degree, the legal and societal bonds of slavery.

If the baptism of freed children could lead to godparent relationships that apparently inverted the legal and social hierarchies of a slave regime, the potential for the baptisms of slaves to subvert those hierarchies also existed and was even more significant. For Christians, the rite of baptism signified the cleansing of original sin. It also meant membership in the Catholic Church and equality as a Christian among others. To baptize an individual and to stand as witness and supporter of that baptism as a godparent signaled recognition of the baptized person's humanity and freedom from sin.[22]

Humanity, equality, and freedom were, of course, exactly what masters sought to obscure and diminish, if not altogether erase from their relationships with slaves. The incompatibility of baptism's essential qualities with those of master-slave relationships may underlie the early resistance of Brazil's slaveholders to Church and crown directives to extend to slaves both the privilege of church membership and the freedom to be active, practicing Catholics. As colonial documents from Sabará and elsewhere reveal, this resistance ultimately gave way to some degree of accommodation as colonizers in Minas Gerais and throughout Brazil did come around to supporting the conversion of slaves to Catholicism. Their acceptance of the Church in the lives of their slaves was no doubt aided by the Church's clear support for the institution of slavery and its own participation in the colonial slave economy.[23]

The acceptance among slaveholders of church membership for slaves did not, however, eliminate the potential conflicts between the role of masters and that of godparents. Godparenthood called for spiritual protection and in practice often entailed providing material aid to godchildren. To assume the role of godparent for one's own slave, a slave owner would either have to violate the spiritual responsibility to aid a sponsored Christian or to limit his or her own exploitative behavior. In the *comarca* of Sabará, masters avoided this dilemma not by declining to serve in the role of godparents, but by *never* serving as sponsors to their own slaves.[24] Stuart Schwartz has made the same observation for Bahia in the eighteenth century and quotes Henry Koster, an Englishman, who administered an estate in Brazil and recorded his travels there in the early nineteenth century: "I have never heard of the master in Brazil being likewise the god-father; nor do I think that this ever happens; for such is the connection which this is

22. Stephen Gudeman and Stuart Schwartz, "Cleansing Original Sin: Godparenthood and the Baptism of Slaves in Eighteenth-Century Bahia," in Raymond T. Smith, ed., *Kinship Ideology and Practice in Latin America* (Chapel Hill: University of North Carolina Press, 1984), 41–42.

23. See selections from the sermons of Antônio Vieira, a Jesuit defender of slavery in seventeenth-century Brazil, in Conrad, ed., *Children of God's Fire*, 163–74.

24. The baptismal registers analyzed in this chapter indicated the name of the slave baptized and the name of the slave's owner. In addition, the names of the godparents selected were listed so that it was possible to know whether the godparent and the master of the slave were the same person.

supposed to produce, that the master would never think of ordering the slave to be chastised."[25] The evidence that masters never sponsored their own slaves in godparent relationships provides strong support for the idea that slave owners were quite conscious of the material and symbolic outcomes to baptismal arrangements and carefully weighed their worldly concerns for adequate slave control against their roles as religious sponsors and protectors.

If slave owners were indeed conscious of the need to evaluate their worldly interests with regard to slave baptisms and their own roles as godparents in a slave society, it is also likely that slaves were similarly conscious and engaged in similar evaluations. Scholars are divided in their interpretations of how much control owners exercised over the process of slaves becoming Christians and of how much credence should be given to the notion of slave agency when discussing godparent choices.[26] In colonial Sabará, it seems probable that both masters and slaves sought baptism for captives, albeit for very different reasons. Masters, as a class, sought paternalistic ties with the slave population through baptism, but they were much more successful in doing so with women and children than with adult males. Adult male slaves, if they did not strongly resist being converted altogether, were more likely to seek godparent relations from among their own peers for the purpose of establishing meaningful social and ritual connections to one another.

The ritual ties of spiritual kinship that resulted from baptism could serve the needs of slaveholders when these ties fostered patron-client relationships. Godparents assumed a status of *co-parents* with the biological kin of

---

25. Koster, *Travels in Brazil*, 199, quoted in Gudeman and Schwartz," Cleansing Original Sin," 42.

26. Those scholars who stress the authority of masters have argued that godparentage reinforced patron-client relationships in society and that owners supported the creation of spiritual ties between masters and slaves. Sidney W. Mintz and Eric R. Wolf, "An Analysis of Ritual Co-Parenthood (Compadrazgo)," *Southwestern Journal of Anthropology* 6:4 (1950): 341–65; M. Bloch and S. Gugenheim, "Compadrazgo, Baptism, and the Symbolism of a Second Birth," *Man* 16 (Spring 1981): 376–86; Joseph H. Lynch, *Godparents and Kinship in Early Medieval Europe* (Princeton: Princeton University Press, 1986); Gudeman and Schwartz, "Cleansing Original Sin," 40. In the opposing analysis, Mattoso has argued that the ties created between individual slaves and masters through godparentage were less important than those created among the slaves who chose godparents from their own ranks. Mattoso, *Ser escravo no Brasil*, 113–34. Both Schwartz and Mattoso have observed that slaves used baptism and choice of godparents instrumentally as a way of improving either their own lives or those of their children. Schwartz, *Sugar Plantations in the Formation of Brazilian Society*, 408; Mattoso, *Ser escravo no Brasil*, 133–34.

their godchildren.[27] When masters served in the role of godparents of enslaved children in Brazil, they also immediately became co-parents with
adult relatives of the slave child. To this day in Brazil and in Spanish America, this relationship of co-parentage (*compadrio* in Portuguese, *compadrazgo* in Spanish) has provided an important social mechanism for creating kinship networks and for mediating relations between households of
widely differing socioeconomic status.[28] In Latin America as well as in Europe, parents of the baptized (*afilhado* is the Portuguese word for godchild) often sought individuals of higher economic or social status as godparents for their children.[29] In such cases, the ritual *compadrio* relationship
expresses mutual obligations and reciprocity, but the exchange is between
patron and client, not between equals. The anthropologists Sidney Mintz
and Eric Wolf have argued that in modern Latin America this *compadrazgo*-patron-client relationship has far outweighed the one between
godparent and godchild and that the former has a sociological function
that has transcended any original religious purpose.[30]

In environments such as those that characterized colonial Spanish America and colonial Brazil where central authority was often too weak to provide security and administer justice at the local level, the *compadrazgo*
system may have been particularly appropriate.[31] In the absence of strong
police or military institutions, the difficulties faced by a small elite attempting to control a much larger population could be ameliorated by
creating social linkages between the dominant classes and those being
dominated. In those Latin American colonies where African slavery was
important, it was clearly a considerable challenge for slave owners to con-

27. Mintz and Wolf, "An Analysis of Ritual Co-Parenthood," 341–65; Bloch and Gugenheim, "Compadrazgo," 376–86; Lynch, *Godparents and Kinship*.
28. See Mintz and Wolf, "An Analysis of Ritual Co-Parenthood"; Stephanie Blank, "Pa-
trons, Clients, and Kin in Seventeenth-Century Caracas: A Methodological Essay in Colonial
Spanish American History," *HAHR* 54 (May 1974): 260–83; Hugo G. Nutini and Betty Bell,
*Ritual Kinship: The Structure and Historical Development of the Compadrazgo System in
Rural Tlaxcala*, 2 vols. (Princeton: Princeton University Press, 1980 and 1984); Schwartz,
Sugar Plantations in the Formation of Brazilian Society, 60–64, 406–12. In present-day
Spanish America, the ties of co-parentage remain strong and operant in modern society; in
Brazil today, such relationships seem much less significant, at least in urban areas.
29. In the colonial slave societies of Brazil, this search for higher-status godparents also
took place. Stuart Schwartz describes the usefulness of such powerful sponsors for slaves in
colonial Bahía in *Sugar Plantations in the Formation of Brazilian Society*, 408–9. Mattoso
also mentions slaves' making use of more powerful sponsors in *Ser escravo no Brasil*, 132–
33.
30. Mintz and Wolf, "An Analysis of Ritual Co-Parenthood," 355.
31. Blank, "Patrons, Clients, and Kin," 262.

trol a massive enslaved population. It is not surprising then that godparentage and co-parentage systems gained the support of slave owners.

From an anthropological perspective, some of the nonegalitarian, symbolic content of the baptismal ritual may also have served the interests of
slave owners. Baptism signifies a second birth, spiritual in character, and
superior to the earlier natural birth. The ritual of baptism cleanses the
polluted essence of the natural birth and allows an initiate to enter into a
superior state of being free from original sin. Baptism thus symbolizes
gaining membership into an alternative community, one that is superior to
the community in which an individual originated.[32] Through the acquisition of godparents, the *afilhado* acquires access to the larger society and at
the same time is instructed that such spiritual linkages to this larger society
are more powerful and meaningful than linkages to one's family, biological
kin, or natural origins.[33]

In this anthropological analysis of baptism, a slave who is baptized benefits from linkages to nonslaves in society, linkages that are created
through godparentage and co-parentage. At the same time, the slave is
now tied, not so much to his or her original community of family and
biological kin, but much more appropriately, to the larger colonial community, which is controlled by a small group of slaveholders. Through the
ritual of the second, superior birth, a slave can "join" society; the power to
"create" these new members of society is allocated to those who control
the larger community, the slaveholders.[34] Both the message of baptism and
the process of enacting the ritual could therefore have served to reinforce
the authority of slaveholders.[35]

Paradoxically, the offer of entrance into an alternative community
through the process of becoming a Christian could have another and quite
different appeal for the slaves themselves. Dislocated slaves, living in an
unfamiliar world, could actually acquire a spiritual family through baptism, one that might well serve as a substitute for the original that was
forever lost through their uprooting. Membership in the spiritual community in fact raised the status of a slave from a pagan to a Christian and, in

32. Bloch and Guggenheim, "Compadrazgo."
33. Bloch and Guggenheim, "Compadrazgo."
34. Bloch and Guggenheim, "Compadrazgo," 385.
35. Schwartz appears to categorically disagree with this conclusion, but his objections are
to the older, more traditional argument that masters derived additional authority over their
own particular slaves *by serving as godparents to them.* See Schwartz, *Sugar Plantations in
the Formation of Brazilian Society,* 407.

theory, made the slave an equal among other Christians. Slave parents could and did seek free people to serve as godparents and provided a potentially significant connection not only for their children but also for themselves. Through baptism, adult slaves created extended kinship networks for themselves by selecting godparents from among their peers. Baptism, godparentage, and co-parentage could work for the slaves as much as it might ultimately work *against* them.

From two perspectives, then, must one must examine the phenomenon of slave baptisms in colonial Sabará. On the one hand, the data available express the desires, goals, and actions of the slaves themselves who were seeking baptism for their children or for one another. On the other hand, the data also reflect the calculations of masters who encouraged or impeded baptisms in accordance with their own objectives. What emerges from the available evidence is a portrait of baptismal decisions that reflect preferences for men slaves very different from those for women and enslaved children. The different preferences of enslaved men met with considerable opposition from slave owners and crown officials and this opposition may in part explain the relative absence of adult male baptisms in the *comarca*.

Most children baptized in 1727 and in 1731–32 were slaves.[36] Even with the unbalanced sex ratio among adult slaves, the slave population was so much larger than the population of free persons that it was able to surpass the free population in producing children. Over the course of the eighteenth century, as the free population slowly increased in size, this situation ultimately reversed itself, and free children outnumbered the enslaved children.[37] Among the slave children, more girls than boys were baptized.[38] (See Tables 4.1 and 4.2.)

36. In 1727, twenty-seven of forty-six children were born as slaves (58 percent). In 1731–32, fifty-nine of ninety-one children were born as slaves (65 percent). The baptisms of children were distinct from those of adults in their registration because (with the exception of *expostos*) the name of at least one parent was provided. For example, Vicencia, baptized in January 1727, is identified as the daughter of Domingas, a slave belonging to Izabel Pinheira. Two days later, a slave named José is baptized, and he is identified only as belonging to the master, José de Crasto. People who are identified as *filhos, expostos*, or *inocentes* in these documents were definitely children and probably infants, whereas those identified as slaves with no parents were adults or youths who were not born in Sabará.

37. By the 1770s, free persons outnumbered slaves, although White free persons remained a minority in Sabará throughout the eighteenth century. See Chapter 2.

38. In the figures for 1731–32, freeborn girls also outnumbered freeborn boys. These numbers may simply reflect the fact that infant mortality tends to be higher among boys, particularly in stressful environments.

Had enslaved children and enslaved adults been baptized in numbers that accorded with their proportions in the slave community, baptisms of adult slaves would have vastly outnumbered the baptisms of children.[39] As recorded, these adult baptisms outnumbered those of child slaves only by a margin of less than two to one.[40] This ratio could simply reflect the fact that the pool of unbaptized adult slaves was not equivalent to the entire adult slave population: slaves like Luiza Pereira do Lago arrived in Sabará already baptized. It could also mean that not all adult slaves arriving in Sabará chose to be baptized or had masters who thought baptism for slaves was important.

Some masters in Sabará were, in fact, indifferent to the religious beliefs of their slaves and did little to oppose celebrations of African religious rituals. In 1734, Gaspar Pimentel Velho, a resident of Rossa Grande, was called before the Visitor, Doctor Lourenço José de Queiroz Coimbra, precisely for allowing his slaves or the slaves of other masters to participate in "superstitious dances." According to Dr. Coimbra, the slaves participating in these dances believed that the rituals frightened away demons.[41] The visiting cleric also admonished the slaves themselves who participated in these dances. He warned Catherina, an Angolan slave woman, about dancing in such rituals as a way of invoking demons.[42] The commitment of slaves to their own African religious rituals, in combination with the indifference of masters to their celebration, could have reduced the numbers of African slaves baptized in Sabará.

If both the attitudes of some masters (either indifference or opposition) and the resistance of adult slaves to the prospect of conversion did have a negative effect on the numbers of baptisms recorded in Sabará, it is important to observe the gendered nature of the results of such influences. The baptismal data from 1731–32 suggest that the baptism of women slaves in

39. The inventories from 1725 to 1759 suggest that on average there were more than five times the number of adult slaves as compared with child slaves. See Table 2.9.

40. In 1727, twenty-seven children were born as slaves, but five were freed at the time of their baptism. The adult-child slave ratio was 1.8. In 1731–32, fifty-nine children were born as slaves; four were freed at birth. The adult-child slave ratio was also 1.8.

41. "Gaspar Pimentel Velho . . . que de nenhum modo consinta em sua casa os seus escravos ou escravas fação as supersticiosas danças . . . por haver presunção de que nas dittas danças asustem os demonios," Cúria Municipal de Belo Horizonte, *Livro segundo dos termos*, fol. 72.

42. "Catherina preta Angola escrava de Domingos Coelho . . . que de todo se aparte de dançar as supersticiosas danças . . . pela grande presumpção de que com as dittas danças invocão os demonios," in Cúria Municipal de Belo Horizonte, *Livro segundo dos termos*, fol. 52v.

Sabará was more likely than that of enslaved men. In these data, the proportion of women among baptized adults substantially exceeds the proportion of women in the adult slave population. Two women were baptized for every three men, whereas in the adult slave population there was one woman for every four men.[43] Although we do not know what proportion of adults arriving in Minas Gerais were already baptized, there is little reason to suspect that such a disproportionate number of these would have been men.

The 1731–32 baptismal registrations suggest that in Sabará more men than women chose not to convert to Catholicism. It is possible that women slaves sought baptism more often than did men because their concentration in urban settlements and greater contacts with free colonists allowed them to more readily perceive and make use of the practical benefits of becoming a christianized slave. Masters may also have felt more strongly that female slaves should become Christians. The occupations of women in the mining region were more likely to ensure their contact with the religious practices of the Luso-Brazilian colonists. As domestic servants, concubines, and venders of various local products, women slaves had more day-to-day contact with town life and the religious milieu of the Portuguese and Brazilian settlers than did enslaved men who were more likely to be simple laborers. Because of such day-to-day contact, and perhaps because such women served as their concubines, masters and other free males may have concluded that the christianization of these women contributed to the moral atmosphere and maturity of the growing mining communities.

Women slaves who occupied positions closer to the dominant culture of slave owners than did male slaves may have responded favorably to the expectations of masters (that they be baptized) because they had carefully evaluated the worldly benefits that would accrue to them in doing so. In particular, they may have understood that in the eyes of the masters, the status of a child born to a Christian slave woman may have been higher than the status of child born to a pagan mother. Because higher status meant better treatment for that slave child, slave mothers would be encouraged to be baptized and to have their children christened.

On the other hand, slave owners may also have been both more tolerant toward and more controlling of the conversion rituals of female slaves. Masters in Sabará may have been more tolerant of enslaved women's be-

43. See Table 2.7.

coming baptized because these women were much more likely than were enslaved men to seek or agree to accept godparents (*padrinhos*) who were free males. The baptism of women slaves was therefore much more likely to produce godparent ties of a patron-client nature than ties promoting solidarity among fellow slaves.

The social and political implications of godparent selection for converted slaves were of interest not only to individual slave owners, but also to crown administrators in the mining region. In 1719, Dom Pedro de Almeida, the governor of Minas Gerais, who had ordered local clergy to seek out unbaptized slaves and christen them, also declared that only White men could serve as godparents for slaves. He argued that having any slave in a subordinate position to another slave was an affront to the desired social order in the mining region. Moreover, he saw the prohibition against non-White godfathers as a means of "weakening the power that Blacks are acquiring against Whites."[44] In this respect, the governor saw the nomination of non-Whites to the position of godparents as further evidence of the erosion of the color line as the most significant marker of status in the slave society.

For those slaves in Sabará who were baptized in 1727 and 1731–32, the governor's order was frequently honored in the breach. For their children and for themselves, slaves acquired godparents in a multitude of combinations. The distribution of various combinations of godparents among the baptized slaves in Sabará in the years examined do not entirely support the argument that slave baptisms in Brazil were more significant for the ties that they established among fellow slaves than for the ties between slaves and their masters.[45] Two-thirds of the baptized women and over three-quarters of the baptized children had sponsors who were free men. Over 30 percent of the baptized men had free male sponsors as well. For example, in June 1727, João, an adult slave belonging to Captain Gaspar Rodrigués Barboza, was baptized with two free individuals serving as godparents: Joseph Fernandes Rodrigués and Anna de Oliveira Barboza.[46] Godparents who were free women such as Anna de Oliveira Barboza were

---

44. "[S]ó acceitarem homens brancos para padrinhos de baptismo e casamentos dos negros, para evitar a subordinação de uns a outros . . . e . . . enfraquecer o poder que os negros iam adquirindo contra os brancos," D. Pedro de Almeida, Conde de Assumar to os vigarios da vara das minas, 26 November 1719, APMSC, Códice 11, fol. 171v.

45. See note 26 above.

46. Cúria Municipal de Belo Horizonte, *Registo de batizados*, vol. 2, n. p.

much less numerous in these slave baptisms, a fact reflecting the relative scarcity of women in the free population..[47] (See Tables 4.3 and 4.4.)

If one of the goals of slaves seeking baptism in colonial Sabará was to acquire godparents who in colonial society could serve as influential benefactors for their children or for themselves, then it was most preferable to have godfathers who were male, freeborn, and White. Godmothers who were White and free were undoubtedly also preferable to non-White or nonfree godmothers, even if White women had much less power in Sabará than did White men. Having godparents who were not White and were slaves or ex-slaves best served the goal of helping the baptized slave build a social network among peers or near-peers.

That free men did serve as godparents for so many slave children has made it tempting for scholars to speculate as to whether these men were their biological fathers. The temptation increases when one finds children with a lone free male godparent or with two free godfathers. It was not, however, only slave children who had lone free male godparents. In fact, in

Table 4.3.   Godparent combinations in Sabará, 1 January–29 June 1727

Types of Godparents	Boy Slaves	Girl Slaves	Men Slaves	Women Slaves
Free male/				
free female	2	6	4	4
Free male	1	1	7	0
Two free males	1	0	0	1
Free male/				
freed Black woman	2	1	0	0
Free male/				
female slave	3	2	3	0
Male slave/				
free female	0	0	2	1
Male slave	0	0	6	0
Male slave/				
female slave	0	2	17	0
Male slave/				
freed Black woman	0	1	1	1
Two male slaves	0	0	4	0
Totals	9	13	44	7

47. In 1727, 16 of 73 slaves had free godmothers (21.9 percent); in 1731–32, 22 of 162 slaves (13.6 percent).

Table 4.4. Godparent combinations in Sabará,
4 October 1731–29 September 1732

Types of Godparents	Boy Slaves	Girl Slaves	Men Slaves	Women Slaves
Free married couple	0	1	0	0
Free male/				
free female	7	5	3	6
Free male	2	6	3	5
Two free males	0	1	0	0
Free male/				
freed black woman	9	6	10	11
Free male/				
female slave	2	6	9	8
Freed married couple	1	0	0	0
Freed male/				
freed female	1	2	0	0
Freed male/				
female slave	1	1	0	0
Male slave	0	1	14	3
Male slave/				
female slave	2	0	16	6
Male slave/				
freed black woman	0	1	9	3
Two male slaves	0	0	1	0
Totals	25	30	65	42

Sabará in 1727, only two slave children had just one godparent who was a free male, whereas nine free children were in this situation. Six of these nine free children were legitimate. Of those free children sponsored by two male godparents, three out of four were also legitimate. In these cases, it is obvious that the godfathers and biological fathers were not the same. In 1731–32 as well, of those children with just one free male godparent, the free outnumbered the enslaved. Among these free children, more were legitimate than illegitimate. Therefore, for a slave child to have just one godparent (a free male) did not set him or her apart from other more privileged children in Sabará, and it cannot lead automatically to the conclusion that in such cases the godfather and the biological father were the same.

Because free males served as godparents for both the enslaved and the free, the distribution of free male godparents, who held the power in Sabará's slave society, apparently did not neatly correlate with the social status of the baptized. It was, of course, true that not all free males were equally powerful in colonial Sabará. Some were far richer than others, and some were White and others were Black or of mixed racial descent — factors shaping their social status in the community.[48] Still, the presence of those with nonfree and ex-slave godmothers emerges as a useful indicator in assessing the relative social status of people being baptized.

Although the nomination of free males as godparents was not necessarily significant in determining the social status of women and child slaves, the relative absence of free male sponsors among adult male slaves is an important indication that for some slaves baptism did not result in further ties of a paternalistic nature with the free male population in Sabará. Fewer than one-third of the slave men had free male godparents in 1727; fewer than 40 percent did in 1731–32. These data indicate that enslaved men acquired the least prestigious combinations of godparents among all the initiates. If slaves chose godfathers in part to protect themselves from harsh masters or to acquire material benefits, enslaved men in Sabará should be seen as disadvantaged in comparison with other baptized slaves. On the other hand, if slaves chose sponsors from among their own peers to promote a sense of collective identity and solidarity among slaves, then enslaved men were the most successful group of all. It remains unclear whether male slaves began to use baptism as a means of building a social network from the very start or as a consequence of the fact that free men initially had declined to serve as sponsors for these individuals. The pattern of free godfather distribution among the enslaved could still reflect the biases of Sabará's master class even as it reveals how slaves turned such biases to their own benefit.

The lack of free male godparents for adult male slaves does not indicate that the process of naming godparents lay entirely outside the control of the slaves. Indeed, the combinations of godparents named for many slaves suggest that they had considerable say in choosing their sponsors. If masters actually had supervised the choosing of the godparents for their own slaves and they had not objected to appointing nonfree sponsors, then such appointments would have been done at the master's convenience. Masters probably would have selected the nonfree sponsors from among their other slaves. In fact, the most common pattern of sponsorship does not confirm this suggestion. For example, on 17 February 1727, Antonio, a

---

48. As the children of Manoel de Crasto Porto would indicate, however, nonwhiteness did not automatically exclude one from elite status in Sabará; they became heirs to one of the largest fortunes in the captaincy.

slave belonging to Antonio de Sousa, was baptized. His godfather was Joaquim, a slave belonging to a second master, Joze Tavares, and his godmother was Quiteria, a slave belonging to yet another master, Andre Alves. Another example was the case of Rita, a slave woman belonging to Domingos Coelho. She was baptized on 22 June 1732, and her godfather was Caetano, a slave belonging to another master, Pedro Teixeira. Her godmother, Antônia, also a slave, belonged to yet a third master, Helena Martins Sam Payo. In both these cases, the selected godparents for the initiates did not share the same master as the baptized individual. Although it may not have been too difficult for masters to arrange for "outsider slaves" to serve as sponsors, it does seem an unnecessary complication for both the godfather and the godmother to be captives of separate masters. Thus the naming of godparents in these cases was not particularly convenient to the owners of the slaves being baptized.

The examples of Antonio and Rita were not at all uncommon among adult slaves in colonial Sabará. In 1727, of the enslaved sponsors to adult initiates, over 70 percent did not answer to the master of the individual being baptized. In the nine cases where baptized adults did have enslaved godparents who belonged to their own masters, six of these initiates also had another godparent who did not belong to their master. Thus in more than nine out of ten cases involving enslaved sponsors, adult initiates had at least one godparent who was not subject to his or her own master's will. These combinations of godparents suggest that adult slaves, and not their masters, chose their own godparents.

The data from the 1731–32 period also support this suggestion. In this year, 86 percent of the enslaved godparents did not answer to the master of the individual whom they were sponsoring. In all but one case involving enslaved sponsors, adult initiates had at least one godparent who did not belong to their own masters. The cases of Antonio and Rita were also typical; each of their two enslaved godparents belonged to a different master. In 1731–32, more than four out of five adults baptized had two enslaved godparents belonging to a different master. Thus for the majority of adult baptisms, the slaves of three different masters were required for the christening to take place.

In acquiring enslaved godparents, most enslaved men did not acquire patron-benefactors. Instead, these men strengthened or reinforced social connections to fellow slaves living outside their immediate environment. For these new Catholics, the bonds of co-parentage were not those of a patron-client nature but were bonds between equals. Such bonds must surely have served to ameliorate the isolation and alienation of men who were both rejected and feared by their masters. The capacity of baptism to facilitate important social linkages in the male slave population helps to explain the governor's 1719 demand that only Whites should serve as godparents in Minas Gerais. If some masters in Sabará agreed with the governor's directive and refused to countenance a baptismal ritual requiring the presence of captives owned by three different slaveholders, such refusals may have been matched by an unwillingness among enslaved men to be baptized at all. The desire of slave men to use baptism instrumentally to create a community of peers and the resistance among masters to such goals may help to explain why in the baptismal registers examined here relatively fewer enslaved men were baptized in comparison with the numbers of enslaved women.

Conclusion

To explain the fact that slaves in colonial Sabará and elsewhere in Brazil became Christians at all, one must observe that masters did not systematically oppose their conversion and indeed benefited from that process. The benefits presented here include drawing slaves further into the established social order through spiritual ties of kinship. The provisions of Luiza Pereira do Lago's last will and testament exemplify this process of acculturation: they detail both her transformation from slave to slaveholder and her transformation into patron and supporter of Catholic organizations and sacred art. Luiza's story and that of others like her demonstrate that conversion of slaves to Catholicism served the interests of all masters in Sabará.

Ironically, baptisms could serve slaves as well, although it is clear that different groups of slaves in Sabará evaluated the benefits of baptisms in different ways. By seeking free male godparents, women slaves used baptisms instrumentally for themselves and for their children to acquire material benefits. Enslaved men, when they did not resist the idea of baptism altogether, also used baptisms instrumentally — but primarily as a vehicle to foster connections among fellow captives. Although masters could easily endorse the strategies of women slaves in their approach to baptism, the strategies elected by male captives were, without question, much more problematic for both masters and crown authorities.

If the baptism of slaves represented an unassailable good for the slaves themselves, then one would have expected many more slaves in Sabará, even the mostly African male adults, to have wholeheartedly endorsed this ritual and their conversion. The fact that they did not is testimony to the slaves' assessment that the benefits of baptism did not come without cost. The fact that only a minority of slaves in the baptismal registers that were examined were baptized completely on their own terms (with no free sponsors) suggests that masters saw the dangers of slave solidarity in the making and limited the means of fostering it. The phenomenon of slave baptisms in Sabará therefore reflects the struggle between slaves and masters for control over their own lives in the slave society of this *comarca*.

This evidence enlarges the portrait of slave society in Sabará to one in which slaves enjoyed a fair degree of physical mobility and personal autonomy. Slaves knew slaves belonging to other masters. Slaves had personal contact with captives with whom they did not share living quarters. Slaves could and did create ritual ties of kinship with fellow captives (belonging to other masters), ties that could enrich their lives and strengthen their ability to endure their own situations. As a result, masters did not entirely control the world in which the slaves of colonial Sabará lived.

5

Manumissions in Sabará

On 9 December 1735, Manoel da Costa Braga declared before the notary of Sabará, Minas Gerais, his decision to free from slavery his own children, Joseph, Marianna, and Maria, and to recognize them as heirs to his estate. In this declaration, Manoel da Costa Braga did not, however, choose to free the children's mother, Magdalena, who presumably remained enslaved.[1]

Fifty-five years later, on 10 February 1790, Senhora Maria Rodrigues Pereyra freed a child named Faustino in exchange for forty drams of gold paid to her by the father, Sebastião Angola. The records do not show whether Faustino's mother was ever set free.[2]

These two manumissions, each typical of the time in which they were granted, reflect the transformations in Sabará precipitated by the fluctua-

1. Carta de liberdade, 9 December 1735, *Livro de notas* (2 de August de 1735), MOSMG, fols. 86–88.

2. Carta de liberdade, 10 February 1790, *Livro de notas* (12 de October de 1789), MOSMG, fol. 39v. Given his appellation (i.e., Angola), it is very likely that Faustino's father Sebastião was still a slave himself at the time of his son's manumission. It is clear from the evidence examined that Sebastião Angola was not owned by Senhora Pereyra at the time of his son's manumission.

tions in the gold-mining economy. Manoel da Costa Braga owned slaves in the first half of the eighteenth century when gold production was booming, slave prices were extraordinarily high, and the colonizers of Sabará were largely White men rarely accompanied by White women. In contrast, when Maria Rodrigues Pereyra owned slaves in Minas Gerais, the gold rush had long been over, and the importance of gold production to the overall economy had diminished significantly. The populations of both slave and free in Sabará were, nonetheless, much larger in Maria Rodrigues Pereyra's day, and although White women were still outnumbered by White men,[3] women slaveholders were by no means a novelty. Furthermore, by the end of the eighteenth century, Whites had long since ceased to be in the majority in the free population. In this slave society, manumission decisions ultimately led to a population of free people (and slaveholders) both racially mixed and racially diverse. (See Table 2.1.)

The decline of gold mining and changes in the slaveholding population had major impacts on the manumission of slaves. Through a quantitative analysis of manumission records for 1,133 individuals, I examine evolving patterns of manumissions in the *comarca* of Sabará in the years from 1710 through 1809. Manumission decisions were linked to the advancement of slaveholders' familial and economic interests. Both the likelihood that slaves would be freed and the specific terms of manumission varied with the times as those interests were redefined by successive generations of masters. The generational differences among Sabará's slaveholders were, in part, due to the fact that in the last five decades of this study, increasing numbers of women granted a significant number of the manumissions. As attentive to the advancement of their familial and economic interests as men slaveholders, the manumission decisions of women slaveholders nonetheless differed from those of men. Women made their own distinctive choices as to whom to free and under what conditions.

The manumissions that Manoel da Costa Braga and Maria Rodrigues Pereyra granted in 1735 and 1790 illustrate only a few of the critical choices that masters in eighteenth-century Sabará made when deciding to free one of their slaves. Both chose to free children rather than adults; Braga chose to free relatives rather than strangers; and Pereyra chose to demand a large payment rather than bestow freedom as a gift. Other owners in this *comarca* made numerous other choices when manumitting

---

3. "População da provincia de Minas Gerais, *RAPM* 4 (1899): 294. In 1786, the sex ratio among Whites in Minas Gerais was 1.2 (i.e., 120 males per 100 females).

slaves: to emancipate Africans,[4] *crioulos* (Brazilian-born slaves), *mulatos*, adults, children, males, or females. Moreover, all those who freed slaves had to set the terms of manumission: the amount (if any) of a cash payment; the number (if any) of additional years of labor; and whether the manumission would be realized only after the owner's death.

These choices were not random. Previous studies analyzing manumissions in Brazil and elsewhere in the New World have noted owners' preferences for manumitting certain groups of slaves under certain terms of manumission.[5] This analysis of the manumission decisions made in colonial Sabará is indebted to the methodologies established by these previous researchers. Extending the investigation of slaveholders' preferences to yet another major slave society of the New World reveals distinctive patterns of owner behavior, which suggest particular attitudes on the part of slaveholders toward their slaves. In this analysis, I illustrate how decisions to manumit New World slaves were linked to specific historical and demographic contexts that could and did change over time.[6] The manumission

4. Among the Africans, owners had to choose from among various ethnic groups and evaluate the skills that (they thought) certain ethnic groups brought to the mines and the cooperativeness (and lack thereof) that (they thought) characterized particular ethnic groups. For a more thorough treatment of ethnicity and manumission, see Mieko Nishida, "Manumission and Ethnicity in Urban Slavery: Salvador, Brazil, 1808–1888," *HAHR* 73 (August 1993): 361–91.

5. For quantitative studies of manumission. like my own, which have relied on analyses of records of manumission, see David W. Cohen and Jack Greene, eds., *Neither Slave nor Free: The Freedmen of African Descent in the Slave Societies of the New World* (Baltimore: Johns Hopkins University Press, 1972); Mattoso, "A próposito de cartas de alforria na Bahia, 1779–1850," *Anais de história* 4 (1972): 23–25; Frederick Bowser, "The Free Person of Color in Lima and Mexico City: Manumission and Opportunity, 1580–1650," in Stanley L. Engermen and Eugene D. Genovese, eds., *Race and Slavery in the Western Hemisphere: Quantitative Studies* (Princeton: Princeton University Press, 1975); Schwartz, "The Manumission of Slaves in Colonial Brazil: Bahia, 1684–1745," *HAHR* 54 (November 1974): 603–35; James Patrick Kiernan, "The Manumission of Slaves in Paraty, Brazil, 1789–1822" (Ph.D. diss., New York University, 1976); Lyman L. Johnson, "Manumission in Colonial Buenos Aires," *HAHR* 59 (May 1979): 258–79; Jerome S. Handler and John T. Pohlman, "Slave Manumissions and Freemen in Seventeenth-Century Barbados," *William and Mary Quarterly* 41: 3 (1984): 390–408; Rosemary Brana-Shute, "The Manumission of Slaves In Suriname, 1760–1828" (Ph.D. diss., University of Florida, 1985) Kathleen J. Higgins, "Manumissions in Colonial Sabará," in "The Slave Society in Eighteenth-Century Sabará: A Community Study in Colonial Brazil" (Ph.D. diss., Yale University, 1987), chap. 4; Mary C. Karasch, "The Letter of Liberty," in *Slave Life in Rio de Janeiro, 1808–1850* (Princeton: Princeton University Press, 1987), chap. 11; "Special Issue: Perspectives on Manumission," *Slavery and Abolition: A Journal of Comparative Studies* 10 (December 1989); Nishida, "Manumission," 361–91.

6. For a study that carefully observes demographic changes among the manumitters and the

records of Sabará thus indicate one way in which the fortunes and misfortunes of slaves could vary as the slave society there evolved.

As the eighteenth century progressed, one significant change recorded in manumission letters[7] was a gradual increase in the number of women manumitters. This change illustrates an important characteristic of colonial Brazil's property and inheritance law. According to the Portuguese system of inheritance, female children were entitled to inherit from their parents' estates, could not be disinherited, and received a share of the wealth (including slaves) equal to that of any male children.[8] Consequently, the numbers of women who became slaveholders in Sabará increased in the second half of the eighteenth century.

Women made different manumission choices than did men. In part, this difference reflected the fact that by law and custom in colonial Brazil, women could own and control property in some but *not in all* of the same circumstances as men could.[9] Men could be manumitters at times when women could not. Although married women owned property (including

---

impact of these on manumissions, see Brana-Shute, "Approaching Freedom: The Manumission of Slaves In Suriname, 1760–1808," *Slavery and Abolition* 10 (December 1989): 40–63.

7. Letters of manumission contained information about both the master and the slave or slaves being freed. Owners identified themselves and their slaves. If the owner had once been a slave, then he or she was identified as a *forro*, a freed slave. Priests, military officers, town officials, and other notables were identified by their occupations. Information about the slaves commonly included name, sex, race, place of origin, a rough indication of age, and only occasionally occupation or marital status. Letters indicated some reason for the award of freedom and stipulated any conditions or limitations on that freedom. Manumissions requiring payment from the slave to the owner often, but not always, stated the price of freedom in the letter. In these letters, slaveholders asked crown officials to endorse the new status of their slaves: "[P]esso as justiças de sua magestade que Deos goarde lhe dem inteiro vigor para que possa andar por onde lhe paresser," Carta de alforria, 19 February 1773, *Livro de notas* (15 junho 1772), MOSMG, fol. 83v. A letter of manumission could be kept in the possession of the freed slave, but for safekeeping was copied into a *Livro de notas* at the notary's office alongside many other documents such as contracts or sales. The 1,133 letters of manumission examined quantitatively in this study were found in Sabará's *Livros de notas*. Another way of preserving the record of a manumission was for an owner to state so in a provision of his or her will. It is evident from testamentary manumissions that owners expected their slaves to receive actual letters of manumission from executors. It is *not* evident (from my own extensive examinations of Sabará's *Livros de registo de testamento*) that all slaves then had their letters copied into *Livros de notas*. In other words, quantitative analyses of letters of manumissions (as duplicated in *Livro de notas*) may very well underestimate the significance of testamentary manumissions.

8. Lewin, "Natural and Spurious Children," 351–96. Female children in colonial Brazil could and did receive greater inheritances than did male children through dowries. See Metcalf, *Family and Frontier*, and Nazzari, *The Disappearance of the Dowry*.

9. For a concise discussion of the authority of women over property in colonial Brazil, see Metcalf, "Women and Means," 277–98.

slaves), they, unlike widows or the never-married, had limited control over it. Portuguese law made husbands the heads of household and the managers of household property, the so-called *bens do casal.* Through marriage, then, men controlled the enslaved property of women.[10] One consequence of the constraints placed on women's ability to hold, control, and dispose of slaves as property was the *gendering* of the pattern of manumissions granted in Sabará during the period 1710–1809. These constraints effectively transformed the sex of the owner into an important variable that influenced both the selection of slaves for manumission and the terms of those grants.

Portuguese law contributed in another important way to the gendering of manumissions in colonial Sabará. Along with all other slave codes utilized by Europeans in the New World, Portuguese law declared that the children of enslaved women were slaves, regardless of the status of their fathers.[11] Manoel da Costa Braga, in freeing his own children, thus made a manumission decision in 1735 that woman owners in Brazil (or elsewhere in the New World) did not, as a rule, have to make, for women owners did not free their own biological offspring from slavery.[12] As free women,

10. By law, men did not have the right to alienate any real estate without the consent of their wives; because slaves were not real estate (*bens immoveis*) but rather moveable goods (*bens moveis*) and often referred to in inventories as self-moving goods (*bens se moventes*), husbands could legally and undoubtedly did manumit slaves without their wives' consent. *Ordenações filipinas* (first codified in 1603), liv. iv, tít. 48. On the other hand, there is some scattered evidence that couples sometimes regarded their slaves as property that the husband could not alienate without his wife's consent, as if the slave *were* real estate. On 16 April 1790, Maria Moreira da Assumpção freed her *half* of a *mulata* slave named Francisca. The letter of manumission stated that her husband had already freed his half of the *mulata,* who made up part of the couple's *bens do casal,* but that as he could not free his wife's half and then he had died, she was fulfilling his request to relinquish her ownership as well. Carta de liberdade, 16 April 1790, *Livro de notas* (12 October 1789), MOSMG, fol. 55v. The extent to which couples in eighteenth-century Minas Gerais regarded slaves as real estate and acted on that view is not known. In the inventories I examined in Sabará, Minas Gerais, for the years 1725–1808, slaves were not listed as real estate but as *bens moveis* or more often, *bens se moventes* (alongside the cattle, pigs, and horses). Of the 1,133 letters of manumission that I read, in only one (cited here) was it explicitly stated that the husband could not free a jointly owned slave without his wife's consent. Manumission cases in which couples were listed as the owners numbered 130 of the total examined.

11. All the New World slave codes adopted the principle of Roman law, *partus sequitur ventrem* (the child follows the mother), whereby the child of a slave mother inherited her status and not that of the father. David Brion Davis, *The Problem of Slavery in Western Culture* (Ithaca: Cornell University Press, 1966), 277.

12. A woman who had been freed from slavery could be in the position of owning her own children if she had purchased them for the purpose of then legally manumitting them. In a 1785 letter of manumission, Thereza Gonçalves is described as the "may e patrona" or mother and owner of Hipolito *crioulo.* She had bought him from his master and was then

their children were always and automatically born free. Men who fathered children born of enslaved women did, however, face the choice of freeing their own sons and daughters or condemning them to live and die as slaves.

As discussed in previous chapters, the men who came to Sabará to enrich themselves as miners through enslaved labor exploited the presence of women slaves by establishing numerous situations of concubinage as well as by imposing innumerable temporary sexual unions. Consequently, the biological relationship of the master to the slave had its influence on manumission decisions. With its incorporation of the Roman law principle of *partus sequitur ventrem* ("the child follows the mother"), Portuguese law made the sex of the master relevant to manumission decisions. This principle excluded free women from the right to procreate enslaved laborers and reserved for men the motivation to free their own offspring from slavery.

The significance of paternity-related manumissions such as those of Manoel da Costa Braga must be weighed against the fact that women slaveholders like Maria Rodrigues Pereyra did, in fact, free children. In her case, the child was not a *mulato*, but a *crioulo*, and in exchange for Faustino's freedom, she demanded and received a large quantity of gold. To assess the significance of either Braga's or Pereyra's manumission decisions, it is necessary to know whether Faustino's terms of manumission were more typically chosen by women than by men owners. Did these particular cases of manumissions simply represent behavior that was typical for owners in two very different moments in an evolving colonial slave society?

To answer this question, the following discussion of manumission choices made in the *comarca* of Sabará compares the most prevalent or typical manumission choices made by slaveholders during the years 1710–59 with those made during the years 1760–1809. As noted in Chapter 2, the first period is associated with a highly productive gold-mining economy and populations, both slave and free, overwhelmingly dominated by men. The second period coincides with a decline in gold mining and the diversification of the region's economy into agriculture and livestock raising. Although the region's export values and relative wealth diminished considerably in this second period, the populations of both slave and free did not. (See Table 2.1; see also Table 5.1.) Free women were far more

---

freeing him with this letter. Carta de liberdade, 16 June 1785, *Livro de notas* (12 mayo de 1784), MOSMG, fols. 102–102v.

Table 5.1.   Origin/color, age, and sex of the manumitted,
Sabará, Minas Gerais, 1710–1809 (N = 1,011)

Origin/Color	0–13		14–45		46–		Total	
	M	F	M	F	M	F	M	F
Africa	1	0	141	246	3	5	145	251
								(396)
Brazil								
Crioulo	50	58	41	117	0	1	91	176
								(267)
Mulato	81	101	16	49	0	1	97	151
								(248)
Cabra	7	20	5	13	0	0	12	33
								(45)
Pardo	9	6	15	16	0	0	24	22
								(46)
Mestiço	0	0	0	3	0	0	0	3
								(3)
Indian	0	0	1	1	0	0	1	1
								(2)
Total	148	185	219	445	3	7	374	637
								(1,011)

numerous than earlier, although still greatly outnumbered by men. This
comparison of manumission choices made in two different economically
and demographically defined contexts focuses on the fact that certain types
of manumission decisions made before 1759 became much less common
after that date; others that had been much less common before 1759 became more so thereafter. The experiences of both adult and child slaves
were dramatically affected by the changing climate for manumissions in
the evolving slave society of colonial Sabará.

Phase I (1710–1759)

Part I: Adult Manumissions

It should be noted at the outset that the colonists in Sabará who chose to
manumit their slaves did so in spite of complaints from crown authorities
that freeing slaves would have dire consequences for the colony. Governor

Dom Pedro de Almeida regarded the numbers of ex-slaves in the captaincy to be excessive. He observed in 1719 that masters issued letters of manumission to slaves without approval of the king or his colonial officials and ordered this practice to be stopped. Governor Almeida saw the mining region as a "land being populated by freed blacks, who like brutes, do not maintain the good order of the community. In a short time this land could fall into the hands of these blacks."[13] There is no evidence to suggest that masters in Sabará cut back on the practice of freeing slaves because of the governor's objections, nor is it possible to determine what percentage of the slaves freed did not have letters approved by colonial authorities.

In colonial Sabará, the sex ratio among those who manumitted slaves reflected the pattern of slave ownership in the *comarca*. When male colonists were the majority of the free inhabitants, they were also the majority of the slaveholders and therefore the majority of the manumitters.[14] During the years 1710–59, women slaveholders appeared in only approximately 6 percent of the recorded cases of manumissions. Male slaveholders who chose to manumit slaves freed women in numbers vastly out of proportion to those of men and despite the relatively low percentage of women slaves in the *comarca*.[15] Figure 5.1 illustrates that not only did the most prosperous decades of the mining century coincide with an unprecedented[16] bias in favor of adult female manumissions, but also that this tendency did not continue in succeeding generations. As the gold boom subsided, men slaveholders freed fewer and fewer women until

13. Bando do Governador D. Pedro de Almeida, Conde de Assumar, 21 November 1719, APMSC, Códice 11, fol. 283, cited and translated by Ramos in "A Social History of Ouro Preto," 229.

14. Luna and Costa found, for example, that in the years 1743–45 only 3.95 percent of slaveholders listed in *Livros de assento de óbitos* were women. Their data come from both the *comarca* of Sabará and the capital of Minas Gerais, Vila Rica. "A presença do elemento forro," 838.

15. See above, Chapter 2, note 92.

16. Where manumissions were granted to individuals by individuals and not by governments, historians have repeatedly noted that more often than not the slave freed was female. Aggregate analyses have suggested that in much of Latin America and the Caribbean twice as many female slaves as male slaves were manumitted. Herbert S. Klein's survey, *African Slavery in Latin America and the Caribbean* (New York: Oxford University Press, 1986), 277, states that "all recent studies have found that approximately two-thirds of the manumitted were women (from 60–67%)." Klein should have used the word *females* instead of *women*. For a useful table that provides comparative statistics on gender in manumission cases in Latin America, see Johnson, "Manumission," 262. See also Mattoso, "A próposito," 23–25; Mary C. Karasch, "The Letter of Liberty," in *Slave Life in Rio de Janeiro, 1808–1850*, chap. 11; Brana-Shute, "The Manumission of Slaves."

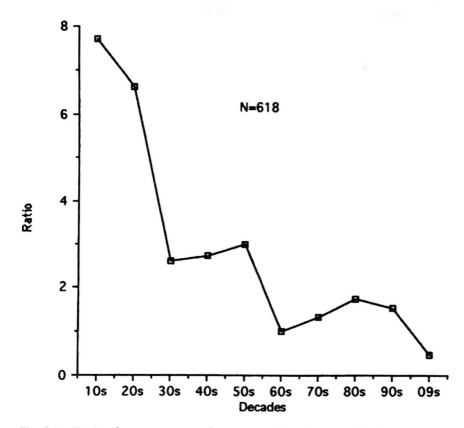

Fig. 5.1.   Ratio of women to men slaves manumitted by men, Sabará, Minas Gerais, 1710–1809. *Note:* These cases of manumission represent only those involving individual ownership of the slaves freed; the manumitters did not jointly own the slave freed. For graphic purposes only, I have consciously chosen to use a ratio of women to men rather than the customary demographic ratio of men to women. (Manumission letters, *Livros de nota*, 1718–1809, MOSMG)

such women no longer made up even a majority of the adults whom they freed in the *comarca*.

That a population of mostly single male slaveholders so often chose to free women[17] might suggest, at first glance at least, that the motivations of these early manumitters were entirely personal, if not wholly sexual in nature. There is, indeed, something to be said for the argument that per-

17. Among slaves manumitted by men in the years 1710–59, 68.3 percent of those freed were adults; the rest were children.

sonal relationships were behind many manumission decisions. After all, slaves in colonial Brazil had no legal right to demand manumission for themselves or their children.[18] An owner could very likely have been more willing to respond to a request to free a slave well known to him or her than to free a more or less faceless petitioner. The manumitters in Sabará denied freedom to the vast majority of their slaves, but were nonetheless motivated by affection, persuasion, self-recognition of their needs, and self-interest to manumit some of their current and potential labor force. The terms under which both adult and child slaves became freed, considered separately and in comparison with one another, provide substantial evidence that the actions of manumitting owners were self-interested in the vast majority of cases. These terms expose the limits of owners' affection even for those slaves best known to them as they detail the careful attention slave owners paid to protecting their own economic and social positions.

The terms of manumission for slaves in colonial Sabará determined whether slaves received conditional or unconditional grants of freedom. Unconditional terms were those stating that no further demands were to be placed on a slave and that freedom was to be achieved immediately. The owner could still demand an initial payment. For example, on 10 September 1730, a local slaveholder by the name of Joseph Pereira de Lemos presented to his slave woman, Marianna, a letter of manumission that from that day forward freed her from all captivity.[19] In the typical words of such a letter of manumission, she was now as free "to go wherever she might choose as if she had been born free of her mother's womb."[20] Although Marianna's master may have felt a certain degree of gratitude for the services that his slave had long offered to him, his account books could not have suffered from the liberation of this woman. In exchange for her

18. Sidney Chaloub, "Slaves, Freemen, and the Politics of Freedom in Brazil: The Experience of Blacks in the City of Rio," *Slavery and Abolition* 10 (December 1989):65; Manuela Carneiro da Cunha, in her brief article, " 'On the Amelioration of Slavery' by Henry Koster," *Slavery and Abolition* 10 (December 1989): 368–76, discusses the ties that Henry Koster (*Travels in Brazil*) had to the British abolitionist movements and posits this connection as an explanation for Koster's now famous misinformation on the legal right to a *peculium* and paid manumission in Brazil.

19. Carta de alforria, 10 September 1730, *Livro de notas* (25 de junho de 1729), MOSMG, fol. 152v.

20. "[P]ossa andar por onde lhe paresser como que forra nascesse de ventre de sua may," Carta de alforria, 19 February 1773, *Livro de notas* (15 junho 1772), MOSMG, fol. 83v.

freedom, Marianna, an African woman of the Mina nation, paid to Senhor Lemos the hefty sum of two pounds of gold.[21]

In the years 1710–59, 65 percent of the men who were freed and 70 percent of the women who were freed did, in fact, pay for their letters of manumission.[22] The prices paid by women were at least as high as those paid by men and clearly reflected market prices for slaves bought in the region.[23] For the slaves in early eighteenth-century Minas Gerais, accumulating the savings needed for self-purchase may not have been as unlikely an achievement as in other slave societies of the New World. Alluvial mining and marketing provided significant opportunities for both men and women slaves to earn a cash income that could be hoarded for purposes of buying one's own freedom.[24] The fact that self-purchasing accounted for so large a majority of the cases of adult manumissions suggests that the motivations of most masters in this period were assuredly not charitable and probably depended on the knowledge that new slaves could be purchased with the funds provided by those manumitted.[25]

21. Carta de alforria, 10 September 1730, *Livro de notas* (25 de junho de 1729), MOSMG, fol. 152v.

22. The number of adult slaves in these years (1710–59) is 239.

23. Values for slaves appear in inventories, wills, and accounts of dowries paid by parents to their daughters. In his will of 30 March 1722, for example, Manoel de Oliveira Dias explained his investments in a trading partnership and listed the prices for slaves sold in Minas Gerais. One woman (*negra*) sold for 240 drams of gold; two men (*negros*) for 230 and 220 drams respectively. Somewhat younger slaves (*molleques*) sold for 135 to 180 drams. A younger girl slave (*negrinha*) sold for 150 drams of gold. In contrast, a horse was sold for 32 drams. Testamento de Manoel de Oliveira Dias, 30 March 1722, *Livro de registo de testamento* (14 de agosto de 1719), MOSMG, fols. 183v.–184. Also, in the 1766 will of Luis Carvalho de Figueyro, he explained the terms of his oldest daughter's dowry, noting that it had included three *negras*, then valued at 730 drams of gold. Testamento de Luis Carvalho de Figueyro, 10 July 1766, *Livro de registo de testamento* (4 de julho de 1766), MOSMG, fol. 143.

24. Padre Martinho de Barros, who advised the Portuguese king on methods of tax collection in the mines in 1724, observed that slaves engaged in mining paid to their masters the sum of one-half an *oitava* (i.e., dram) per day and could keep the rest. "Voto do Padre Martinho de Barros sobre o quinto do ouro das Minas Gerais," 6 February 1724, AHU, Minas Gerais, Documentos avulsos, unpaged document found in the uncatalogued collection on Minas Gerais. Boxer documents the high prices of food that colonists (through women slaves) sold in towns at a good profit. *The Golden Age*, 187. Women slaves kept a portion of these profits for themselves.

25. It may also have been the case that masters manumitted women for high prices to buy even more men. Studies of the eighteenth-century slave trade indicate an increasing preference among slave purchasers for male slaves; in the earlier part of the century, women slaves may have been more available than desirable. Paul E. Lovejoy, "The Impact of the Atlantic Slave

For the remainder of the adult manumissions granted in the years 1710–59, where cash payments did not precede a grant of freedom, the letter of manumission was either provided as an outright gift to the slave, or it included conditional terms that could be more or less burdensome to the slave. As an example of the former, on 14 July 1738, Manoel Machado freed his slave Maria Angolla as a reward for the "good services" she had provided to him. No payments were required.[26] On the other hand, conditional terms required that the slave, or perhaps a relative of the slave, perform some additional service before the manumission would in fact be realized. Often, this entailed years of additional service before the slave's freedom was recognized. For example, in December 1718, João Gomes da Sylva freed his slave Maria on the condition that she continue to serve him as long as he remained in the mining region. Her letter stated that only when he decided to return to live in his native Portugal would Maria actually be freed.[27]

In some cases of conditional manumission, complete autonomy would never be offered to the slave; the freed slave could risk re-enslavement if he or she failed to meet the former owner's needs or whims. In November 1735, Joseph de Siqueira Aranha freed his slave woman named Rita. She, however, remained obliged to obey her former master and to be civil to him as well.[28] Manoel Sarayva Amaral freed his slave Francisca in 1756 for the price of eighty drams of gold.[29] Nonetheless, she remained obliged to keep him company "whenever she could."[30] For these two women, their freedom was not absolute despite their possession of a letter of manumission.

Trade on Africa: A Review of the Literature," *Journal of African History* 30 (1989): 365–94; Joseph Miller, "Slave Prices in the Portuguese Southern Atlantic, 1600–1830," in Paul E. Lovejoy, ed., *Africans in Bondage: Studies in Slavery and the Slave Trade* (University of Wisconsin Press, 1986), 43–78; Miller, *Way of Death,* 159–64.

26. Carta de liberdade, 14 July 1738, *Livro de notas* (11 mayo 1738), MOSMG, fol. 36v. In the years 1710–59, it was more likely that women who did not pay for their manumissions received them as outright gifts (as in Maria Angolla's case) rather than having to comply with conditional terms. For women, conditional manumissions in this period represented only 9.4 percent of the total. For men, however, conditional manumissions were much more common and represented 19.7 percent of the total. See Higgins, "The Slave Society," 249–52.

27. Carta de alforria, 14 December 1718, *Livro de notas* (12 fevereiro 1718), MOSMG, fol. 214.

28. Carta de liberdade, 15 November 1735, *Livro de notas* (2 agosto de 1735), MOSMG, fol. 71v.

29. This price was not high for the period and perhaps was discounted because of additional demands.

30. "[C]om condição que assiste em minha companhia em quanto pudesse," Carta de alforria, 25 August 1756, *Livro de notas* (3 julho de 1756), MOSMG, fol. 127.

In view of both the specific demands and the undetermined duration of the conditions sometimes stated in letters of manumission, self-purchase without further obligation was undoubtedly a preferred means of acquiring freedom in colonial Sabará. Although perhaps originating in very personal relationships with their masters, self-purchasing agreements at least offered slaves the possibility of ending or attenuating those personal ties to their owners in a way that conditional manumissions did not. It is possible that in the cases of Rita and Francisca, both remained in situations where their owners' conditions implied a continuing sexual relationship that these women were not free to end. The records do not suggest that Rita and Francisca were simply being required to attend their "former" masters as they became old and infirm.

One possible explanation for the higher rate of female self-purchase may relate to the sexual division of labor in colonial Sabará. Because the colonists who came to Sabará bought men for work in mines and used their women slaves in marketing activities in the urban centers, women may have been more likely than men to accumulate the savings necessary for self-purchase. Unless mining slaves were very lucky and discovered a particularly rich alluvial deposit for which their owners rewarded them, the task of saving enough gold for self-purchase was routinely impeded by the difficulty of surviving long enough to amass the price of freedom. As discussed in Chapter 2, debilitating illness and deaths among slaves working as miners were common. As the women slaves in Sabará did not usually work as miners, they also did not face the same risks to health and longevity. Their more favorable opportunities to accumulate some savings may help to explain why owners in Sabará during the years 1710–59 freed so many more women than men through self-purchasing agreements.

On the other hand, the dearth of adult male manumissions during the height of the gold rush in Sabará may have had little to do with the ability of enslaved miners to amass sufficient quantities of the gold dust that so regularly passed through their hands. The routine arrangements between owners and their laborers allowing these men to keep a portion of the gold produced daily suggest that masters in Sabará simply preferred incentives other than manumission to promote productivity among male workers. Their reasons quite possibly related to the competition among colonists for the best mining claims. According to the Portuguese crown's regulation of mining lands, colonists had to register their claims to particular deposits, after which they received royal grants of land based on the number of slaves owned.[31] Legal title to a royal grant of land did not, however, offer much security to colonists located in a forested and difficult terrain remote from Portuguese crown authorities. Consequently, slaves not only worked the mining claims but also defended them against encroachers. For this reason, among others, enslaved men in eighteenth-century Minas Gerais were often provided with weapons to defend themselves and their owners.[32]

The practice of arming enslaved men naturally complicated the master-slave relationship, but it apparently did not entirely eradicate the slave owners' authority, even as it made the recapture of runaway slaves particularly problematic.[33] The likelihood exists, however, that slave owners perceived a considerable danger to themselves in freeing those workers familiar with mining sites who had also served as henchmen and personal bodyguards. The frustrations experienced by colonists in attempting to counter the activities of runaways undoubtedly illustrated that once freed, ex-slaves could become formidable competitors for and possibly usurpers of previously unreported gold deposits. As freedmen, former slaves had both the right to register land claims and the right to own mining slaves themselves.[34] Sabará's colonists may have sought to limit the immediate competition that experienced mining slaves could mount against them by severely restricting their access to the degree of freedom that only a grant of manumission provided.

Like freedmen, freed women acquired and exercised the right to own land and slaves, but they did not generally do so in the arena of the economy perceived to be most lucrative by the colonists. The available evidence also does not suggest that enslaved women participated in the violent competition for the best land claims. The slave owners who manumitted in the

31. "Regimento das minas do ouro de 1702," article 5, 330–32.
32. Bando do Governador D. Pedro de Almeida, Conde de Assumar, 30 December 1717, APMSC, Códice 11, fol. 270.
33. There is considerable evidence that runaway slaves were a continuing problem for owners and royal officials throughout the eighteenth century: Letter of the *câmara* of Villa Real to the king, 18 July 1727, AHU, Minas Gerais, Documentos avulsos, caixa 4; letter of the *câmara* of Vila Rica to the king, 14 May 1735, AHU, Minas Gerais, Documentos avulsos, caixa 112; bando do governador e capitão general desta capitania, Luis Diogo Lobo da Sylva, 8 April 1764, APMCMS, Códice 35, fols. 79v–87v; circular do Governador Dom Rodrigo José de Menezes aõs nove capitães-mores da capitania, 23 February 1780, APMSC, Códice 226, fol. 1v. For more information on runaway slave communities in Minas Gerais, see Carlos Magno Guimarães, *Uma negação da ordem escravista: Quilombos em Minas Gerais no século XVIII* (Icone, 1988); João José Reis and Flávio dos Santos Gomes, *Liberdade por um fio: História dos quilombos no Brasil* (São Paulo: Companhia das Letras, 1996).
34. As early as 1720, half the ex-slaves registered in tax rolls in Sabará, Minas Gerais, were currently owners of their own slaves. "Lista dos escravos . . . para pagarem os reaes quintos de 1720 athé o de 1721," APMSC, Códice 2.

boom decades of gold mining quite probably opposed seeing formerly enslaved men acting as freedmen in lucrative mining zones. These same men would have had less to fear from the manumission of nonmining slave women.

Although the numbers of enslaved women manumitted in Sabará from 1710 to 1759 exceeded the numbers of enslaved men who were freed by large margins, it is important to recall that these figures represent only a very small fraction of the total slave population in the region. I have calculated that for the *comarca* of Sabará in the 1730s, the crude rate of manumission was less than one-third of a percent per annum.[35] The numbers of manumitted women were never so high as to make it especially problematic to replace them with new slaves acquired through the international traffic, even though women represented a minority of the Africans imported to Brazil. Similarly, replacing the even smaller number of manumitted men with new African arrivals was not compromised by limited supply in the slave market. Contemporary observations on the slave trade to Minas Gerais, as well as recent historical analyses of the international slave traffic in the eighteenth century, both suggest that as long as the mines thrived it was not difficult to buy new slaves for gold.[36] A shortage of available substitute workers therefore was not likely to have figured among those reasons that bolstered the slaveholders' opposition to more frequent manumissions in early eighteenth-century Sabará. Thwarting competition for what White men thought they had an exclusive right to, gold and slaves, was undoubtedly a much greater concern for slave owners and served to maintain low rates of manumission even during the most prosperous decades of the gold mining era.

Part II: Child Manumissions

> Say I Manoel de Seitas Velho that among the moveable goods that I possess there is a women of the Mina nation named Joanna . . .

35. In colonial Brazil, rates of manumission have been calculated as falling between 0.33 and 1 percent per year. In early nineteenth-century Argentina, a somewhat higher rate of 1.3 percent per year was found. Schwartz, "The Manumission of Slaves," 606; Kiernan, "The Manumission of Slaves," 83; Higgins, "Manumissions in Colonial Sabará," in "The Slave Society," chap. 4, 198; Johnson, "Manumission," 277. These low rates of manumission should be contrasted with textbook literature statements that "[m]anumission was common" in Latin America. See Leslie Bethell, ed., *Colonial Spanish America* (Cambridge: Cambridge University Press, 1987), 332.

36. Miller, "Slave Prices in the Portuguese Southern Atlantic, 1600–1830," in Lovejoy, *Africans in Bondage;* Miller, *Way of Death,* chap. 12.

who has two children, a *mulatinho* named João and a *mulatinha* named Ignes whom I free because they are my children, and I free their mother from this day forward and they are free of all servitude as if they had been born free of their mothers' wombs, the children as well as the mother, and a *crioulinho* named Antonio who is the son of said woman I give as alms to his mother and to his siblings to accompany them and to serve them while they live and by their death he shall be free.

— Letter of manumission, 23 June 1718[37]

Not only did the White male colonists of Sabará, Minas Gerais, act decisively to secure exclusive rights to the labor of slaves and the gold produced by them, they also often acted as powerful arbiters of their slaves' personal lives and the lives of their slaves' children. Manoel de Seitas Velho's choice of whom to set free and whom to leave enslaved provides both a poignant illustration of the master's authority over his slaves' lives and a telling demonstration of a pattern of manumission decisions in which the mixed-race offspring of slaves were more likely to be freed than the *crioulo* children. During the boom decades of gold production, mulatto children were very much over-represented in the population of manumitted children;[38] their owners were much more likely to free them unconditionally and without payment required,[39] and male owners did, in a significant number of cases, acknowledge that they were the biological fathers of the slaves freed. In those cases where the manumitter was a European male and the mulatto children *were male* and were freed unconditionally, almost one-half (47.8 percent) of the owners acknowledged that they were the manumitted boys' fathers. Where the same terms of manu-

---

37. "Digo eu Manoel de Seitas Velho que entre os mais bens movens que possuo bem asim he hua negra de gentio da Mina por nome Joanna . . . a qual tem dois filhos hum mulatinho por nome João e hum mulatinha por nome Ignes que por serem meus filhos os forro e a may de hoje para todo sempre e os hey por livres de toda a servidão como se de ventre de suas mays sahiraõ livres asim os filhos como a may, e hum crioulinho por nome Antonio filho da dita negra dou de esmolla a sua may e irmaons para os acompanhar e servir en quantos vivos e por morte delles sera forro," Carta de alforria, 23 June 1718, *Livro de notas* (12 fevereiro de 1718), MOSMG, fol. 93–95.

38. Mulatto girls represented 82 percent of all freed female children and mulatto boys 68 percent of all freed male children in this period. In the years 1710–59, the number of child slaves for whom race is identified is 114. In contrast, the available inventories of slave-owning households in the years 1725–59 indicate that the vast majority of slave children were *crioulos*, entirely of African descent. Only 12.8 percent of the children listed were identified as mulattos. The number of children in these inventories for these years is 83.

39. Eighty percent of the mulatto girls manumitted were freed by means of outright gifts; almost seventy percent of the mulatto boys were freed by means of gifts.

mission applied (the grant of manumission was an outright gift) and the mulatto children were female, over one-fourth (28.6 percent) of the owners acknowledged that they were the manumitted girls' fathers. In sum, among the cases examined in the years 1710–59 in which male owners granted manumissions as gifts to mulatto children, over one-third (36.2 percent) of these children received those grants from their self-proclaimed fathers.[40]

This evidence of favorable treatment toward enslaved progeny during the most prosperous decades of the gold-mining era should not be viewed uncritically and certainly is not a useful measure of the behavior of masters toward the vast majority of slaves.[41] The behavior of Sabará's slaveholders as manumitters of their own children, in fact, serves best as evidence of their individual desires and their immediate concerns, both of which were short term in outlook. As noted in Chapter 2, one important concern of the early slaveholders in Sabará was the lack of heirs. For those unmarried men who had made fortunes that they wished to pass on, the mulatto children whom they fathered were the only potential recipients of their estates.[42] In the face of their own mortality, and with no White children to admit preference for, manumission of enslaved offspring and acknowledgment of their paternity became a reasonable alternative. So it was for Antonio Vieyra Porto, a Portuguese immigrant to the mining region with no legitimate children. Porto did, however, have a son, Joseph, who was the child of his slave woman Maria Mina (i.e., a native of the Costa da Mina in Africa). In his will of 17 August 1740, Antonio Vieyra Porto freed Joseph from slavery and named him as his heir.[43]

Although masters in this period acknowledged their sons more often

40. In the years 1710–59, the number of child slaves for whom race and terms of manumission could be identified is 111.

41. The long-term ideological consequences of manumission practices on slave societies were of central concern to Frank Tannenbaum, *Slave and Citizen: The Negro Citizen in the Americas* (New York: Vintage Books, 1946), 69. For a more modern treatment of this important subject, see Chaloub, "Slaves, Freemen," 64–84.

42. Lewin, "Natural and Spurious Children," 366.

43. Testamento de Antonio Vieyra Porto, 17 August 1740, *Livro de registo de testamento* (17 de dezembro de 1739), MOSMG, fol. 133. Porto also stated in his will (fol. 135v) that the other mulatto slave children owned by him could be freed if their fathers or other *senhores* agreed to pay his estate for their letters of manumission. Antonio Vieyra Porto happened to be a widower. As the records on concubinage and numerous wills document, most of these men were *solteiros* or bachelors. See, for example, Testamento de Joseph Mendes de Carvalho, 26 December 1740, *Livro de registo de testamento* (17 de dezembro de 1739), MOSMG, fol. 151.

than their daughters, they freed (without acknowledging any biological connection) more mulatto girls than mulatto boys, and they were much less likely to require payments for the freedom of the girls than of the boys.[44] In the short term, such decisions limited the phenomenon of freedmen competing with free men for the region's resources.[45] Masters may also have reasoned that it was potentially more lucrative to leave enslaved more of those male youngsters whom they did not intend to acknowledge as sons and heirs. Those unacknowledged Brazilian-born boy slaves would, after all, mature into the extremely valued, acculturated, adult male captives whom owners seemed most reluctant to free.[46] Boy slaves not needed as heirs seemed more likely to evoke fear and greed in their owners than beneficence.

Phase II (1760–1809)

The mining sites of Sabará, along with those throughout Minas Gerais, did not flourish indefinitely. As the century progressed, the mining economy declined steadily. In the years 1760–1809, the slaveholders made manumission decisions in a very different economy as well as in a fundamentally transformed social and demographic context. Under these changed circumstances, the rates of manumission decreased for *all* groups of slaves. Although the slave population in the *comarca* of Sabará experienced continual growth throughout the colonial period, registrations of letters of manumission did not keep pace with this growth, and by the first decade of the nineteenth century registered letters of manumission numbered only twenty-five per year. Thus I have argued for a decline in the rate of manumission in the second half of the eighteenth century.[47]

44. Before 1760, for mulatto boys there were twenty-five gifts versus eleven paid manumissions. Before 1760, for mulatto girls gift manumissions outnumbered the paid by five to one (forty gifts versus eight paid).

45. In the long term, of course, freeing more girls than boys led to an increase (natural) in the free population of mixed racial descent.

46. Adult *crioulos*, men born in Brazil, did not outnumber African men in Sabará's manumission figures in any decade of the eighteenth century and even in the first decade of the nineteenth century. Adult *crioulas*, women born in Brazil, began to outnumber freed African women in the manumission letters as early as 1760. See Higgins, "The Slave Society," 222.

47. See Higgins, "The Slave Society," 198. This view of a decline in rates of manumission consequent to reduced levels of gold production contradicts earlier arguments by Wilson

Even though the price of new slaves was much lower than it had been in the early decades of the century, José João Teixeira Coelho wrote in 1779 that the price of slaves in Minas Gerais remained relatively high in comparison with their potential productivity. A resident of Minas Gerais for eleven years who served in the administrations of three colonial governors, he observed that since the easiest mining sites had been exhausted, more slaves were needed to extract the same amounts of gold that had been produced by fewer slaves in earlier decades. Even at lower prices for slaves, masters earned profits insufficient for the purchase of new labor.[48] Slaves owners who could ill-afford to buy a new slave may have become more reluctant to part with those that they already owned, even if their relative productivity was declining. Slaves who earned incomes in the mining economy would also be poorer in a depressed economy and less able to accumulate sums for self-purchase.

Enslaved women were among the most adversely affected by the changing climate for manumissions. The ability of women to save profits from their marketing activities diminished in the course of the widespread economic decline. The likelihood that owners would foresee a continually bright economic future with ready access to slaves from the international market was undoubtedly reduced as well. These circumstances clearly restricted the opportunities for enslaved women to transact a self-purchasing agreement with their owners. Consequently, women were much more likely to spend their entire lives as slaves or to await freedom consequent to their owner's death.[49] Thus, for example, on 21 November 1785, Man-

---

Cano, "Economía do ouro em Minas Gerais (século XVIII)," *Contexto* 3 (1977): 91–109. Gorender echoed Cano's views in *O escravismo colonial*, 347: "Uma depressão econômica profunda podia provocar alforrias em avultada quantidade, pois havia senhores que perdiam as condições para sequer sustentar seus escravos e não tinham a possibilidade de vendê-los. Foi o que ocorreu ao menos uma vez, quando se verificou o declinio vertical da produção aurifera em Minas Gerais, no final do século XVIII."

48. "Não ha dúvida em que . . . são os Negros mais baratos, do que forão em outro tempo; mas assim mesmo são caros; porq. as utilidades das lavras das Minas, no estado presente, são muito menores do que erão por causa de se ter tirado o Ouro dos lugares mais faceis de se lavrarem e se trabalhar agora nos sitios dificultozos." José João Teixeira Coelho, "Instrucção para o governo da capitania de Minas Gerais," 1780, reprinted in *RAPM* 8 (1903): 501.

49. In the years 1760–1810, adult female manumissions to be realized after the owners were dead made up almost one-fourth of the total granted and five times more than in the years 1710–59 (24.7 versus 5 percent). Also among adult females, conditional manumissions nearly doubled in comparison with the first five decades of this study (rising from 9.4 to 18.1 percent of total). Higgins, "The Slave Society," 251–52. The number of adult slaves in the years 1760–1810 is 442 (180 males, 262 females).

oel Pereira Silverio freed Maria Angolla and her mulatto son Pedro on the condition that they both serve him until his death.[50]

The economic standing of miners and the relative purchasing power of captives were not, however, the only factors influencing slaveholders' decisions to manumit slaves, nor were they the only factors subject to important changes as the mining society in Sabará evolved during the course of the eighteenth century. Colonial Brazil's property and inheritance law eventually transformed the sex ratio among slave owners in Minas Gerais.[51] From the first generations of early mining men who made fortunes by accumulating wealth, land, slaves, and sexual partners with whom they had children, new generations of slaveholders emerged, among whom were more and more women.[52]

Despite the legal and customarily defined restrictions that reduced the opportunities and moments during a woman's lifetime when she could act on her own authority to manumit a slave,[53] women manumitters were exceptionally numerous in Sabará in the period 1760–1809. In these decades, women listed as individual (as opposed to joint) owners of slaves accounted for over one-fourth, and eventually one-third, of the cases of manumission.[54] Figure 5.2 illustrates how much more numerous women manumitters had become in the second half of the eighteenth century.

The available evidence suggests that women who owned slaves as individuals and not as joint owners (i.e., with spouses or siblings) were indeed over-represented among the manumitters of Sabará. Inventories of slaveholders in the years 1760–1808 indicate that such women represented

50. Carta de liberdade, 21 November 1785, *Livro de notas* (12 mayo de 1784), MOSMG, fol. 151.

51. It was not necessary for children to be legitimate to inherit. According to Portuguese law, among commoners, natural children — "offspring of individuals who might have married because law imposed no impediments to their marriage" — had the right to inherit, and in Minas Gerais they assuredly did. On the distinction between natural and spurious children, see Lewin, "Natural and Spurious Children," 363, 366.

52. *All* the freed female children of slaves, whether they were acknowledged as heirs or not, contributed to the transformation of the sex ratio among slaveholders. Freed slaves and the children of freed slaves became slave owners in colonial Sabará, often solely as a result of their own hard work as miners or marketers. The available documentary record does not show that former slaves eschewed the institution of slavery in Sabará. Numerous documents do, however, portray former slaves as owners of others.

53. It was particularly difficult for women to exercise control over property although they were married. See notes 9 and 10 above.

54. Women mentioned in manumission documents who were not named as sole owners were named as members of a married couple. In the period 1760–1809, couples represented between 13.3 and 15 percent of the cases of manumission in each decade considered here.

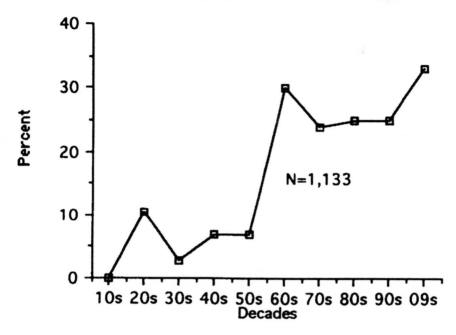

Fig. 5.2.   Slaves manumitted by women, Sabará, Minas Gerais, 1710–1809.
Note: Only cases of manumission by women who owned their slaves individually
(not jointly) are represented. (Manumission letters, *Livros de nota*, 1718–1809,
MOSMG)

only 18.9 percent of the slaveholders and owned only 16.2 percent of the
slaves. Of these women slaveholders, one-half were widows.[55] Manumission records did not always record the marital status of manumitters, and
therefore we cannot know precisely what proportion of those women had
never married. It is likely, however, that a large number of the women
slaveholders who manumitted were indeed widows.

The manumission decisions of women in Sabará did not duplicate those
of men in the years 1760–1809. As the gold boom subsided, the tendency
of male slaveholders to free so many more women than men gradually
abated. By the final decade of this study, women no longer made up even a
majority of the adults whom male slaveholders freed in the *comarca* (See
Fig. 5.1.) In contrast, during the second half of the eighteenth century, the

55. In the inventories examined for 1760–1808, the number of slaveholders is 58 (16 men,
10 women, 32 couples); the number of slaves is 774 (500 men, 132 women, 142 children).
Five of the ten women owners were widows.

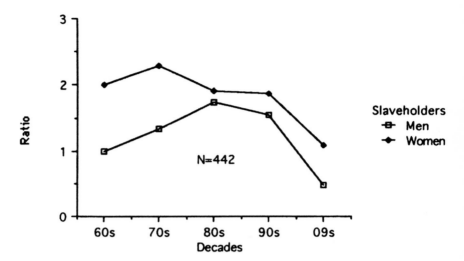

Fig. 5.3. Sex ratio among adults manumitted, female/male, Sabará, Minas Gerais, 1760–1809. These cases of manumission represent only those involving individual ownership of the slaves freed; the manumitters did not jointly own the slave(s) freed. For graphic purposes only, and to parallel the choice made in Figure 5.1, I have consciously chosen to use a ratio of women to men rather than the customary demographic ratio of men to women. (Manumission letters, *Livros de nota*, 1760–1809, MOSMG)

preference for freeing more women than men was more pronounced among female slaveholders. In every decade from 1750 forward, women freed adult females more readily than did men.[56] (See Fig. 5.3.)

The sex ratios illustrated in Figure 5.3 do not match the distribution of male and female adult slaves among slave-owning households in the years 1760–1808. Inventories of slaveholders in these years indicate that adult male slaves outnumbered adult female slaves by a large majority. Male slaveholders, however, owned more men (relative to women) than did female slaveholders.[57] With the patterns of slaveholding indicated by the in-

56. The couples who manumitted in these years also freed adult female slaves more readily than did the manumitters who were men named as sole owners.

57. In these years, men owned nearly three times as many adult males as adult females, and women owned twice as many adult males as adult females. Among slaveholders who were couples, the sex ratios were the highest. In slaveholdings headed by couples (accounting for 53.4 percent of the slave-owning households and 62.9 percent of the slaves), the sex ratio was four to nine (male: female). The number of slaveholders is 58; the number of adult slaves is 632.

ventory records, it is safe to conclude that all manumitters continued to prefer freeing women (rather than men) in the years 1760–99. This preference was, however, much less marked than in the first half of the eighteenth century, and it actually disappears in the first decade of the nineteenth century. Male slaveholders, in particular, demonstrated a more marked decline in their preference for freeing women than did female slaveholders.[58]

The evidence about the terms of manumission for slaves in the years 1760–1809 suggests that men who freed slaves also offered less desirable terms of manumission than did women who freed slaves. Slave owners who, during the booming decades of gold mining, had made unconditional grants of freedom via self-purchasing agreements with captives gave way to owners such as Manoel Pereira Silverio who, in the much less prosperous year of 1785, postponed the freedom of Maria Angolla and her son Pedro until Silverio's death.[59] From the slaves' point of view, the most desirable terms of manumission, in which freedom was granted as an outright gift with no further service required, became less likely. In the second half of Sabará's gold-mining century, the owners who did manumit their slaves outright were more likely to be women.[60] (See Fig. 5.4.)

The cases of manumission accounted for in Figure 5.4 include those of children, but men and women slave owners were not equally likely to free children rather than adults. In the years 1760–1809, men consistently freed three adult slaves for every child slave. In contrast, women manumitted, on average, three adults for every two children. Both these ratios (3:1 and 3:2) represent a change from the manumission choices made by slave owners during the years 1710–59. In those years, male slaveholders, representing the vast majority of all manumitters, freed fewer than two adults for every child.[61] The manumission choices of male slaveholders in the

58. The inventories analyzed for the years 1760–1808 indicate that men and women slaveholders owned similar proportions of the total population of enslaved women. Men owned 24.2 percent of all enslaved women. Women owned 22.7 percent of all enslaved women. The remainder belonged to households headed by couples. Male slaveholders were, however, more numerous than female slaveholders (27.5 versus 18.3 percent). From the adult female slaves' perspective, nearly as many were owned by women as by men. The number of slaves is 774 (500 men, 132 women, 142 children).

59. See note 50 above.

60. Slaveholders manumitting as couples were also more likely than were men acting as sole owners to free slaves outright.

61. Among male slaveholders in the years 1710–59, the ratio of adult to child manumission was 1.92:1. The number of cases in these years was 354 (84 percent with male owners, 6.2 percent with female owners, 9.6 percent with couples as owners).

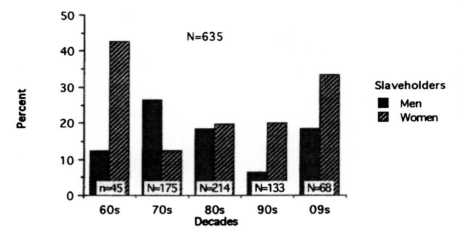

Fig. 5.4. Manumissions granted as outright gifts, Sabará, Minas Gerais, 1760–1809. These cases of manumission represent only those involving individual ownership of the slaves freed; the manumitters did not jointly own the slave(s) freed. (Manumission letters, *Livros de nota*, 1760–1809, MOSMG)

years 1760–1809 differed not only from those of women slaveholder contemporaries, but also from those of previous generations of male slave owners.[62]

The noticeably distinct behavior of men and women manumitters in Sabará, Minas Gerais, during the years 1760–1809 suggests that different motivations informed the manumission decisions of these owners. Male slaveholders clearly had arrived at the decision that it made little sense to free many more women than men slaves, as they had done in the first half of the eighteenth century. By the first decade of the nineteenth century, they actually freed twice as many adult men as they did adult women. On average, during the second half century of this study, male slaveholders freed fewer children than did women slaveholders, and they were the least likely of any group of manumitters to free a slave as an outright gift.[63] These manumission decisions, combined with the fact that enslaved men

62. The inventories analyzed for the years 1760–1808 indicate that men and women slaveholders owned similar proportions of the total population of enslaved children (each owned 24.6 percent). The remainder belonged to households headed by couples. Male slaveholders were, however, more numerous than were female slaveholders (27.5 versus 18.9 percent). From the enslaved child's perspective, just as many were owned by women as by men. The number of enslaved children is 142.

63. Couples who manumitted were also more likely to free slaves through outright gifts than were men acting as sole owners.

were the most likely to be manumitted conditionally (owing additional years of service to owners) or only after the owner had died, suggest that male slaveholders may have been attempting to preserve as much as possible a current workforce and possibly to encourage the reproduction of future laborers.[64] Captain André da Silva Cardozo's 1772 letter of manumission for Anna *crioulinha* is also suggestive of such a strategy. He had kept his captive Joanna enslaved long enough for her to become a grandmother, had not freed her daughter Maria, and had only parted with the granddaughter, Anna, in exchange for a hefty payment in gold. Cardozo had already benefited from years of this slave family's labor, and yet he expressed (through the terms of manumission chosen for Anna) considerable reluctance to reward their labors at his own expense.[65]

As the previously mentioned 1785 terms of manumission for the *mulato* child Pedro suggest, manumitters like Manoel Pereira Silverio no longer privileged mixed-race children in grants of freedom as much as had the male slaveholders in the years 1710–59. Although in these earlier decades three-quarters of the mulattos manumitted were freed by means of outright gifts, fewer than one-half of those manumitted after 1760 received their "freedom" unconditionally and without payment.[66] Among those who were freed by means of an outright gift after 1760, a somewhat smaller percentage of male slaveholders acknowledged that they were the biological fathers of the children being freed — 31 percent versus 36.2 percent earlier.[67] Moreover, although the overall statistics indicate that during

64. In the years 1760–1809, the terms of manumission for adult males indicate that in over one-third of the cases (approximately 35 percent), the slaves received conditional manumissions or manumissions postponed until the owner's death. For this calculation, the number of adult men is 194.

65. Carta de alforria, October 17, 1772, *Livro de notas* (15 junho de 1772), MOSMG, fol. 48.

66. Among mulatto boys freed from 1760 to 1809, distribution of terms was as follows: 18 grants were outright gifts; 23 grants required payments. Among mulatto girls freed from 1760 to 1809, distribution of terms was as follows: 23 grants were outright gifts; 20 grants required payments. Among nonmulatto boys (*crioulos, cabras,* and *pardos* — whom I lumped together because I could not be sure the *cabras* and *pardos* were really half White) freed from 1760 to 1809, distribution of terms was as follows: 17 grants were outright gifts; 21 grants required payments; 16 were conditional and/or death related. Among nonmulatto girls freed from 1760–1809, distribution of terms was as follows: 27 grants were outright gifts; 31 grants required payments; 21 were conditional, death related, or both. See also Higgins, "The Slave Society," fig. 4.7, for evidence of conditional manumissions among mulattos (boys and girls).

67. The gender gap disappears. The same percentages of girls and boys are acknowledged by fathers, unlike earlier.

the boom decades of Sabara's mining era nearly one out of four manumitted mulatto children benefited from explicit recognition by their free White fathers, in the less prosperous decades of the mining economy's decline, such recognition was bestowed in only one of every ten cases of mulatto child manumissions.[68]

Demographic changes in the slaveholding population itself provide an important explanation for increasing denials of paternal recognition of enslaved children. In the years 1760–1809, male slaveholders freed somewhat more than half of all the mulatto children manumitted (57 percent). The rest, however, were freed by female slaveholders or by couples. Widowed slaveholders may have realized that some of the enslaved mulattos in these households were their husbands' progeny, but these women, with children of their own, had little or no incentive to recognize their spouses' other offspring. Likewise, couples rarely were motivated to recognize the husband's enslaved offspring; to do so could compromise the inheritances of their own legitimate children. Consequently, enslaved mulatto children encountered the best chance of being freed by means of an outright gift, and virtually their only opportunity to be declared offspring of the master, if their owners were unmarried men who did not expect to marry. As the prospects for marriage to a White woman increased for White male slaveholders over the course of the eighteenth century in Sabará and as widows became more prominent among manumitters, enslaved mulatto children became a less privileged group among the manumitted slave children, even if they became no less common in the slave population as a whole.[69]

Among the male slaveholders like Cardozo and Silverio, there were fewer widowers and more younger individuals in comparison with the population of female slaveholders.[70] Such men were more likely to have

68. One obvious consideration is the fact that by the second half of the eighteenth century in Sabará, Minas Gerais, not all mulatto children born as slaves were fathered by free White men. The child of two enslaved mulatto parents was also a mulatto, but such families were not commonplace enough to account for the reduction in the proportion of mulatto slaves recognized by free fathers.

69. Whereas female slaveholders represented, on average, 27.4 percent of the owners in manumission cases in the years 1760–1809, they accounted for only 21.5 percent of the cases of mulatto child manumissions. These women also freed far fewer mulatto boys by means of outright gifts than did men (25.7 percent versus 48 percent). One could still argue that, in general, mulatto children remained over-represented among manumitted children (40 percent of total). In the inventories examined for the years 1760–1808, 16.6 percent of the enslaved children were mulattos. The number of children is 142.

70. In the inventories examined for 1760–1808, only 18.7 percent of the men owners were

been in the midst of developing their economic position in the region. Despite the emergence of women as slave owners and as manumitters in late-eighteenth century Sabará, Minas Gerais, the men described as individual (and not joint) owners still represented the *majority* of all manumitters. Their decisions to manumit reflected a deep interest in the preservation of slavery and in securing a profitable way of life.

It is difficult to imagine that women slaveholders in eighteenth-century Sabará were less committed than men to preserving slavery or to developing their own economic status in the community. Manumission, or the promise of manumission, may reflect, however, more indirect efforts by women to control slaves' behavior. For example, Victoria Bernarda de Oliveira's 1790 grant of manumission to the one-year old son of her slave Francisca was described as a reward for the "good services of the mother." Such a reward may well have been bought with years of extremely cooperative behavior from Francisca, both in the past and the future. There are no records indicating that Senhora Oliveira ever freed Francisca.[71]

Women in colonial Sabará who assumed the role of slave ownership did so without the same degree of authority held by free men in an institutionalized patriarchy. If these women owners manumitted more children than did men owners to attain cooperation from able-bodied enslaved parents, perhaps they did so for lack of alternative methods (such as physical or sexual violence) of eliciting such cooperation. Manumitters like Victoria Bernarda de Oliveira may also have weighed the loss of a child's future labor against the cost of raising a youngster who had a good chance of succumbing to disease and an unhealthy environment before becoming a productive asset. Child slaves were a risky investment and one not always worth making, especially if the freedom of that child could elicit an adult slave's productivity and cooperation that might otherwise not be forthcoming.

Because women slaveholders so often waited until widowhood to be able to manage their own assets, as a group, their manumission decisions were more likely those of older owners freeing men and women slaves of an advanced age. For example, the 1808 letter of Feliciana Maria de Conceição freeing Caetano Angolla after forty years of toil indicates that both

widowers; 50 percent of the women owners were widows. The number of slaveholders is fifty-eight (sixteen men, ten women, thirty-two couples).

71. "[P]elo bons serviços da mae," Carta de liberdade, 24 April 1790, *Livro de notas* (12 October de 1789), MOSMG, fol. 61v.

owner and slave were elderly.[72] Her motivations for freeing Caetano Angolla are therefore not entirely clear because one effect of freeing an older slave was to relieve the owner or the heirs of the financial burden of caring for a nonproductive laborer. Feliciana's manumission decision could well have been callously made to free herself or her family of the burden of caring for an old man. Even if her award of freedom to Caetano had been welcomed by him, Feliciana's letter demonstrates that she benefited from decades of another human being's involuntary labor. Her willingness to profit for so long from that labor surely speaks to a deep commitment to a slave society.

Slaveholders may, of course, have found that the tactics of ransoming an enslaved child's future or delaying until old age a promise of freedom were not always wholly effective in achieving cooperation and productivity from able-bodied slaves. For women owners who lacked community or familial support for their role as authoritarian masters, perhaps it was sometimes practical for them to resolve the issue of relentless slave resistance by dissolving the bonds of captivity and thereby eliminating the problem. This possibility could be the reason that, in the second half century of this study, women were more likely than men to free slaves outright and unconditionally, regardless of age or productivity.

Although the varying motivations are not in all cases verifiable, they are certainly plausible and offer an explanation for the distinctive behavior of women manumitters without suggesting that women slaveholders were any more likely than men slaveholders to act generously toward slaves or to do so without purpose. As women in eighteenth-century Sabará came to inherit slaves, they also faced legal and customary restrictions on their rights to dispose of property, restrictions that limited their ability to manumit slaves to those periods of their adult lives when men did not control women's assets. For adult women who never married, this period might have been a relatively long time, but only if they lived outside parental or familial control. For married women, it would have been a relatively short time, essentially confined to the period of widowhood.[73] Thus, the actions of women manumitters must be interpreted in terms of the age-specific and life-status-specific characteristics of property-controlling women slaveholders. Because these characteristics were defined by gender and legally

---

72. "[C]on que me tem servido a quarenta annos," Carta de liberdade, 31 August 1808, *Livro de notas* (18 abril de 1807), MOSMG, fol. 79v.
73. Metcalf, "Women and Means," 285–86.

constructed gender roles, it follows that manumission decisions in eighteenth-century Sabará were *gendered* phenomena.

Conclusion

As they were described at the opening of this chapter, the 1735 manumissions granted by Manoel da Costa Braga and the 1790 manumission
granted by Maria Rodrigues Pereyra were typical for the dates in which
they occurred in the *comarca* of Sabará, Minas Gerais. By the end of the
eighteenth century, Manoel da Costa Braga's decision to recognize his mulatto heirs would not have been impossible to make, but it would have
been much more unusual. Had he lived in Maria Rodrigues Pereyra's day,
he might have had a wife and the fortunes of legitimate children to protect
from such decisions. The freeing of Faustino *crioulo* by a woman owner
was very much in keeping with the pattern of manumissions granted at
that time. Female sole owners in the years 1760–1809 freed over two and
one-half times as many nonmulatto children as mulatto ones. Among the
non-mixed-race boys like Faustino, less than one-third were freed outright
by women like Maria Rodrigues Pereyra. Most had to pay for freedom as
he did or wait years for that freedom to be realized. Had his master in
1790 been a man, Faustino might still have been granted his freedom, but
such a decision by a male owner would have been less typical of the time
period.

   Both the presence of slave women and the initial absence of free women
appear to be central to the story of Sabará's development as a slave society.
Through the earliest manumission decisions of single male slaveholders,
the male and (to a lesser extent) female offspring of slaves became the
masters of their fathers' laborers. In addition, although the annual rates
of manumission in the *comarca* were very low, the cumulative impact of
manumitting women and female children over the course of an entire century can be seen in population statistics for the beginning of the nineteenth
century. By 1805, two-thirds of the free population in Minas Gerais were
non-White.[74] Manumission decisions that had originated as efforts to ad-

74. Free people were 46 percent of the total population. "População da provincia de
Minas Gerais," 294. In letters of manumission, owners were not often identified according to
race, and so it can not be determined whether non-White owners more commonly freed their

vance the individual slave owner's familial and economic interests had led, in the long run, to a society-wide transformation of the free and slaveholding populations in Sabará. This transformation did not diminish the importance of race and social stratification among Sabará's free people, but it did seriously challenge the automatic identification of a non-White as a slave in this part of the New World.

The male and female slaveholders of Sabará's second half century manumitted their slaves in ways that both differed from the mostly male owners of earlier decades and from one another. For the slaves in colonial Sabará, the odds of becoming freed in the years 1760–1809 continued to vary according to their age, sex, race, and place of origin; how these odds varied for each subgroup of the slave population also depended considerably on whether the owner was a man or a woman.

In this examination of manumissions in the *comarca* of Sabará, I have tried to link the decisions to free slaves to the social, economic, and demographic contexts in which such decisions were made. Because these contexts clearly changed over time, in the gold-mining world of colonial Minas Gerais, the phenomenon of manumission was not static. When viewed collectively, the manumission decisions recorded in Sabará help to document the evolution of slave ownership patterns in the *comarca* and provide evidence identifying the behavior of slave owners according to their sex, life status, and relative authority in the slave regime. The manumission choices of slave-owning women and the generational differences in the decisions of slave-owning men both suggest that manumission records can reflect larger changes taking place in a slave society and are a relatively untapped source for exploring the evolving circumstances of those who were enslaved.

---

slaves than did White owners. Among the 1,133 manumission cases examined, thirty-three of the owners were identified as former slaves. In some of these cases, the freed owners were acting to free relatives whom they had just purchased, but in most cases they were freeing slaves of no relation to them for the same variety of terms described for the rest of Sabará's manumitters.

6

Slave Resistance and Autonomy in Sabará and Minas Gerais

In his letter of 21 November 1719 to the Chief Magistrate of Sabará,[1] the governor of Minas Gerais, Dom Pedro de Almeida, Count of Assumar, declared: "Without severe discipline against the blacks, it could happen one day that this captaincy shall become a pitiable stage for their evil deeds and that which occurred at Palmares in Pernambuco will be repeated; or even worse for the freedom which the blacks of this captaincy have [is] unlike that in other parts of America, certainly it is not true slavery the manner in which they live today as it more appropriately can be called licentious liberty."[2]

1. The chief magistrate (*ouvidor geral*) was a crown-appointed official with judicial authority in the *comarca* of Sabará. Such officials, along with magistrates, judges, and justices of lower rank and more limited jurisdiction, represented one layer of administration in the colonial period subordinate to that of the (also appointed) governor of the captaincy. A different layer of colonial administration was represented by the municipal councils of towns like Sabará (also technically subordinate to the governor), but the authority or autonomy of such indirectly elected councils (presided over by a local magistrate) could be greater or lesser depending on their proximity to centralized forms of authority. See Boxer, *The Golden Age*, 148–50.

2. "Sem uma severidade mui recta contra os negros, poderá suceder q' hum dia seja este governo theatro lastimozo dos seus maleficios e q' suceda o mesmo que nos Palmares de

The governor's assessment of local conditions led him to fear that substantial runaway slave communities could form and flourish in the mining region. Dom Pedro worried that such communities, known as *quilombos*, would be even larger and more dangerous than the famed *quilombo* of Palmares in northeastern Brazil, against which the Portuguese had fought protracted campaigns in the seventeenth century.[3] Along with such populous *quilombos*, the governor foresaw crimes against the colonists of Minas Gerais far worse than the transgressions committed by the runaways of Palmares. To forestall such crimes by discouraging slaves from fleeing, Dom Pedro proposed that one foot of fugitive slaves be cut, thereby permanently limiting their mobility and their liberty.[4]

Such liberties as slaves in Minas Gerais possessed were, of course, insufficient to quell their desire for complete freedom from supervision and for absolute personal autonomy. Slaves in Sabará and elsewhere in the mining region consistently tested the bonds of their captivity and resisted constraints placed on them. Such resistance was most obvious to slave owners when it took the form of flight, and the apparent ease with which slaves could escape to the densely forested hills of the mining region concerned the Count of Assumar.

The issue of runaway slaves was, in fact, very serious during Assumar's rule in Minas Gerais (1717–21), and his efforts and those of his successors did not eliminate the problem. Throughout the eighteenth century, escaped slaves banded together into numerous *quilombos*.[5] These were defined as four or more slaves living together, perhaps in a hut, or perhaps just having tools for subsistence.[6] Such *quilombos* could range in size from a few

---

Pernambuco; ou muito peyor pella differente liberdade q' os negros tem neste governo, âs demais partes da America, sendo certo q'não he verdadeira escravidão a forma em q' hoje vivem quando com mais propriedade se lhe pode chamar liberdade licencioza," Dom Pedro de Almeida, Count of Assumar, governor of the captaincy of Minas Gerais, to the *ouvidor geral* of the *comarca* of Rio das Velhas, 21 November 1719, APMSC, Códice 11, fol. 170.

3. Palmares was a large-scale runaway slave community located in the captaincy of Pernambuco in the northeast of Brazil. When it was finally destroyed in 1694, a force of 6,000 troops was required to defeat the slaves. Dom Pedro de Almeida had served as governor of Pernambuco during some of the campaigns against this early and powerful runaway slave community. R. K. Kent, "Palmares: An African State in Brazil," in Richard Price, ed., *Maroon Societies: Rebel Slave Communities in the Americas* (Baltimore: Johns Hopkins University Press, 1979), 170–90. For more recent discussions of Palmares, see the chapters by Pedro Paulo de Abreu Funari, Richard Price, and Ronaldo Vainfas in Reis and Gomes, *Liberdade*.

4. Letter to *ouvidor geral*, 21 November 1719, APMSC, Códice 11, fol. 170.

5. Guimarães, "Uma negação."

6. Carta régia, 6 March 1741, APMSC, Códice 68, fols. 45–46, cited in Guimarães, "Uma negação," 54.

individuals to dozens and could vary enormously in duration. In one community discovered in the captaincy and destroyed in 1759, children born to runaway slave women while living in the *quilombo* were twelve years old.[7] Thus at least some *quilombos* achieved considerable stability and longevity.

Despite the intentions of Dom Pedro de Almeida and succeeding governors to reduce the likelihood of slave flight, the problem of controlling slaves to prevent their fleeing continued to trouble colonial officials and slave owners long after the boom period of mining had subsided. At least 160 runaway slave communities formed in the captaincy of Minas Gerais from 1710 through 1798. More than half of these *quilombos* were discovered in the second half of the century.[8] This fact suggests that as the urban mining towns became larger and more established, the ability of masters and colonial officials to prevent slave flight did not substantially improve. The opportunities for slaves to flee and hide far from the colonial towns may have been nearly as good in the 1770s as in the 1720s.[9] The motivations for slaves to leave were likely to have been just as strong.

Runaway slaves represented a serious threat to the social order in Sabará as well as in other *comarcas* of the captaincy. In November 1719, Dom Pedro de Almeida had heard from the chief magistrate of Sabará that three men had been found dead, presumably killed by the inhabitants of the recently discovered *quilombo* of Serra do Caraça, located close to the town of Sabará.[10] In July 1727, officials of the municipal council of Sabará writing to the king of Portugal described fugitive slaves as murderous thieves

7. Governador José Antonio Freire de Andrade to Thomé Joaquim da Costa, 14 November 1759, APMSC, Códice 110, fol. 135, cited in Guimarães, "Uma negação," 47.

8. Guimarães, "Mineração, quilombos, e Palmares," in Reis and Gomes, *Liberdade,* 141. See also Guimarães, "Uma negação," anexo 2, 181–86. Guimarães's sources are the codices of the Arquivo Público Mineiro, Secção colonial, which represent a vast compilation of official correspondence, mostly of the governors of Minas Gerais to their superiors and subordinates. This figure represents the minimum; it is not possible to know the total number of runaway communities, only the total number of communities reported in the available documents.

9. The slave population in the 1770s was more than four times larger than it was in 1720, but the number of reported *quilombos* was only three times greater in the 1770s than it was in the 1720s. See Table 2.1. *Quilombos* may have become somewhat less of a problem relative to the total number of slaves. Although the necessary data are not available to confirm this, it is also possible that fewer *quilombos* had much larger numbers of inhabitants than in the earlier period. From the point of view of colonial officials monitoring the problem, runaways and *quilombos* remained difficult issues throughout the eighteenth century.

10. Dom Pedro de Almeida to Dr. Jeronimo Correa do Amaral, 22 November 1719, APMSC, Códice 11, fol. 169v.

who menaced the travelers along public roads. The escaped captives enjoyed safety in numbers as they banded together into gangs of forty, fifty, or even sixty individuals. After their crimes were committed, the runaways retreated into the dense forest, where it was difficult to pursue them.[11]

The situation in Sabará mirrored that in other *comarcas* of Minas Gerais. In May 1735, the officials of the municipal council of Vila Rica, capital of the captaincy, wrote to the king about the "great and continuous insults, robberies, and murders" committed by the runaway slaves who lived in their midst.[12] For the members of this local council, the crimes committed by fugitives were chronic and unrelenting.

Such depredations remained endemic to the mining region as a whole, and the problems of inhibiting the criminals defied simple solutions. More than forty years after the Count of Assumar had written on the issue, another governor of the captaincy, Luis Diogo Lobo da Sylva, was again decrying the murders committed in Minas Gerais by runaways living in the region's unruly *quilombos*. In 1764, he observed that fugitives went out onto the roadways robbing, wounding, mistreating, and even killing those whom they encountered.[13] By robbing individuals along the roads, escaped slaves also interfered with the steady transit of goods in the captaincy. They stole food as well as other needed supplies.[14] Worse than attacking travelers and supply trains, runaways were also known to attack houses in outlying parishes and even those in the vicinity of the towns themselves. In such cases, the well-armed escapees were known to kidnap White women and bring them back to their hideaways, along with Black women and slaves whose numbers served to strengthen the *quilombo* as a whole.[15]

Even in the later decades of the eighteenth century, escaped slaves continued to present serious problems to colonial officials. In February 1780, Governor Dom Rodrigo José de Menezes wrote of the "continuous disor-

---

11. Letter of the *câmara* of Villa Real to the king, 18 July 1727, AHU, Minas Gerais, Documentos avulsos, caixa 4. These are boxes of loose, uncatalogued, unordered documents.
12. Letter of the *câmara* of Vila Rica to the king, 14 May 1735, AHU, Minas Gerais, Documentos avulsos, caixa 112.
13. Bando do governador e capitão general desta capitania, Luis Diogo Lobo da Sylva, 8 April 1764, APMCMS, Códice 35, fols. 79v–87v. "[O]s escandallozos factos de sahirem as estradas, roubarem, ferirem, maltratarem e matarem," first paragraph.
14. Bando do governador e capitão general desta capitania, Luis Diogo Lobo da Sylva, 8 April 1764, APMCMS, Códice 35, fols. 79v–87v.
15. Bando do governador e capitão general desta capitania, Luis Diogo Lobo da Sylva, 8 April 1764, APMCMS, Códice 35, fols. 79v–87v. "[D]esta escandalloza liberdade tem nam poucas vezes resultado nam so violentamente de mao armado tirarem mulheres brancas dos mesmos povoados, mas levarem igualmente pretas e escravas com que reforssam as tropas."

ders and crimes" committed by runaways who "infest the public roads and assault the travelers."[16] As the century was coming to a close in January 1798, Governor Bernardo José de Lorena urged the local law enforcers throughout the region to take all possible measures to rid the captaincy of the "scourge" of fugitive slaves who plagued the colonists.[17]

Colonial officials in Minas Gerais initially responded to the phenomenon of slave flight with decrees intended to restrict the opportunities for slaves to run away. In March 1714, Governor Dom Braz Balthezar decreed that slave owners must provide passes for any captives who traveled more than half a league (approximately two miles) from their living quarters or from their work site and supervisors. Those slaves found farther from supervision without passes would be arrested and brought to the nearest town jail and could be retrieved by their owners only after a fine was paid. By this measure, officials hoped to identify those slaves who were away from their owners without authorization and at the same time force the slave owners to comply with the act by imposing a fine.[18]

The men who were to seek, capture, and return runaway slaves in colonial Brazil were known as *capitães do mato* or bush captains.[19] These bush captains were already operating in the mining region early in the eighteenth century, although the crown did not formally endorse the use of such men in Minas Gerais until January 1719.[20] Bush captains, to be recognized by colonial officials, required a Letter of Patent issued by the governor. Still, at least in the early years of the eighteenth century, one could seek runaways, capture them, and apply for a Letter of Patent afterward.[21]

16. Circular do Governador Dom Rodrigo José de Menezes aõs nove capitães-mores da capitania, 23 February 1780, APMSC, Códice 226, fol. 1v., cited in Guimarães, "Uma negação," 105.

17. "[A] todos os capitães-mores que façam todas as diligencias possíveis para procurar extinguir o mais que for possível o flagelo em que se acha esta capitania com o excessivo número de negros fugidos," Bando do Governador Bernardo José de Lorena, 26 January 1798, APMSC, Códice 277, fol. 13, cited in Guimarães, "Uma negação," 105.

18. Bando de Dom Braz Balthezar, 22 March 1714, APMSC, Códice 9, fols. 16–16v, cited in Guimarães, "Uma negação," 37.

19. *Capitão do mato* was considered by higher colonial officials to be the commonly used name for all who hunted for fugitive slaves; even though some of these individuals had specific ranks such as captain, sergeant, and corporal, others had no position of rank whatsoever. Another term was *homem do mato*, which meant simply "man of the bush." Letter of the *câmara* of Vila Real to the king, 18 July 1727, AHU, Minas Gerais, Documentos avulsos, caixa 4.

20. Carta régia to Governador Dom Pedro de Almeida, 12 January 1719, AHU, Minas Gerais, Documentos avulsos, caixa 1.

21. "Regimento dos capitães do matto, 17 December 1722," *RAPM* 2 (1897): 389–91.

The incentive for becoming a bush captain was largely economic. Individuals who captured fugitive slaves received payments in gold on a sliding scale, dependent on the distance traveled in pursuit of the captive. The bounties owed to these bush captains for their efforts could be substantial. Slaves found less than one league (four miles) away from their expected place of work or residence brought a reward of four *oitavas* of gold. Slaves found more than one league and two days of travel distant brought eight *oitavas*. As the number of days of travel increased, so did the reward until a maximum of twenty-five *oitavas* was reached. For slaves living in *quilombos* — defined for these purposes as more than four slaves living together and in a site with clear signs of prolonged residence — bush captains could claim a bounty of twenty *oitavas* of gold. In such cases, masters might pay a reward for the return of their slaves representing 5 or perhaps even 10 percent of the slave's purchase price.[22]

According to the earliest available regulations governing the actions of the bush captains in Minas Gerais, which were promulgated in February of 1715, these slave catchers were instructed to return the recaptured slaves directly to the slave owners who would then pay the required bounty.[23] Later, in 1722, this instruction was amended, and bush captains were to deliver their recaptured slaves to the nearest town jail or local law enforcer. Masters could then retrieve their recovered workers only after paying the bush captain's reward and fees to the jailer for maintenance.[24] Town jails were financed by the municipal councils, and often, as in Sabará, the jail was located in the basement of the council house.

Bush captains obviously incurred expenses in their searches for runaways, and the rewards they received had to be sufficiently high to cover expenses and still provide incentive for individuals to take on the task. Seeking slaves who lived in *quilombos* or who traveled in large bands required assistants who needed some form of remuneration themselves. Such

22. "Regimento dos capitães do matto, 17 December 1722," *RAPM* 2 (1897): 389–91. If the price of a slave was two pounds of gold or 256 *oitavas*, then a twenty-*oitava* fine represented 8 percent of the purchase price. A young adult male slave, who would have been a good candidate to be a runaway, could easily have cost 256 *oitavas* in 1722 when the regulations were first promulgated.

23. "Regimento para os capitães do mato," 4 February 1715, APMSC, Códice 6, fols. 46–46v., reprinted in Guimarães, "Uma negação," 173–74. This set of regulations did, of course, contradict the 1714 order (mentioned earlier) about passes; the earlier order indicated that slaves without passes were to be brought to town officials first.

24. "Regimento dos capitães do matto," 17 December 1722, *RAPM* 2 (1897): 389.

assistants would form a squad of foot soldiers whom the bush captain would lead into the fray. When, in 1727, the municipal council of Sabará was facing the task of combating large gangs of fugitive slaves marauding the travelers on local roads, the local "squad" of hunters had twenty-five men.[25] Whoever assisted the bush captains (these persons were referred as *pedestres*) did not require a Letter of Patent, but did require the references of local officials. Their participation in a slave hunt had to be recorded beforehand for them to share in the bounty fees collected by the bush captains.[26]

Because an encounter with runaway slaves could be violent, it was inevitable that some slaves would be killed in the effort to recapture them. To further encourage bush captains to attack and destroy *quilombos* even if it meant the death of some runaways, a royal decree of 1741 amended the rewards provided to slave hunters. For delivery of the heads of slaves killed while resisting capture, slave hunters could receive a bounty of six *oitavas* of gold.[27] This policy remained in effect for the duration of the eighteenth century. Thus it occurred that in December 1796 Francisco Mariano, corporal of the squad of slave hunters in Rossa Grande, a parish of Sabará, encountered a runaway named Caetano who resisted capture. After a long struggle with the slave, the slave hunter, Francisco, was finally able "to separate" the slave's head from his shoulders, whereon he brought the trophy to the local judge and was later awarded six *oitavas* of gold.[28] Similarly in that same year, the municipal council of Sabará paid the bush captain Antonio Lourenço da Rocha six *oitavas* for each of the two heads of runaway slaves.[29] In these as in other cases where the fugitive slave died while resisting capture, the local municipal councils paid the slave hunters, not the masters of the slaves themselves.

Bush captains were numerous in Minas Gerais throughout the eigh-

25. Letter of the câmara of Villa Real to to the king, 18 July 1727, UHU, Minas Gerais, Documentos avulsos, caixa 4.

26. Bando do governador e capitão general desta capitania, Luis Diogo Lobo da Sylva, 8 April 1764, APMCMS, Códice 35, fols. 79v–87v. See fifth paragraph.

27. Bando do governador e capitão general desta capitania, Luis Diogo Lobo da Sylva, 8 April 1764, APMCMS, Códice 35, fols. 79v–87v. This royal decree is referred to in paragraph 1.

28. Document without title, beginning "Diz Francisco Mariano Cabo de Esquadra do Mato do distrito de Rossa Grande," 14 December 1796, APMCMS, Códice 63.

29. Document without title, beginning "O Procurador actual da Câmara desta villa pagará ao capitão do Matto Antonio Lourenco da Rocha," 22 December 1796, APMCMS, Códice 63, pages without numbers.

teenth century. Although the exact number of these slave catchers remains unclear, the available records indicate that during the years from 1710 through 1798 more than 450 individuals received from the colonial governors of Minas Gerais Letters of Patent that permitted them to operate as bounty hunters in the captaincy.[30] Because these bush captains often worked as leaders of squads of unlicensed foot soldiers, several thousand men could easily have been involved in the pursuit of runaway slaves over the course of the century. The task of controlling slave flight and recapture in eighteenth-century Minas Gerais had clearly elicited a considerable commitment of manpower from the local population. Nonetheless, the labors of all these pursuers of runaways were apparently insufficient to discourage captives from escaping.

The licensing of men to pursue runaway slaves produced a corps of crown-sanctioned bounty hunters who added a new layer of law enforcement to the existing vehicles of local self-defense and social control in the mining region. In the *comarca* of Sabará, the free male population of both the principal population centers and the outlying parishes was already organized into *companhias de ordenança*, reserve militia companies. The superior officers of the militia companies were the captains-major and sergeants-major, who were regarded as important town officials.[31] Where the outlying parishes and thus the companies were three or more days' travel from the centers, additional captains-major or sergeants-major oversaw the reserve groups. These militia companies were intended to serve as auxiliary troops to the regular foot soldiers and cavalry (of both European and local origin) garrisoned in the captaincy.[32]

In 1738, reserve troops of the nineteen militia companies in the *comarca* of Sabará numbered 1,642. In the captaincy of Minas Gerais as a whole, there were over 7,000 men available for service. These figures do not represent all the free men potentially capable of defending the colonists from

---

30. Guimarães, "Uma negação," anexo 3, 188–210. His sources are again the codices of the Arquivo Público Mineiro, Secção colonial. I consider the exact figure that Guimarães provides (467) to represent the minimum number of Letters of Patent issued. These were found in various locations interspersed with other official documents. There was apparently no master list of bush captains available in the codices.

31. Mappa das ordenanças das minas, 25 January 1738, AHU, Minas Gerais, Documentos avulsos, caixa 20. In 1738, the principal centers of population were the *vilas* of Sabará, Caeté, Pitanguí, and the parish of Santa Barbara.

32. Mappa das ordenanças das minas, 25 January 1738, AHU, Minas Gerais, Documentos avulsos, caixa 20. Royal troops were never permanently stationed in the *comarca* of Sabará, but remained close to the capital of Vila Rica.

attack; in some outlying areas, only one adult male from each household was registered, even when more men were residing there.[33] In comparison with the potentially available troops of the reserve militia companies, the number of bush captains and their auxiliaries operating in Minas Gerais at this time seems less impressive and perhaps even unnecessary. These reserve militias could have served instead of the bush captains to combat the *quilombos* in the captaincy, and with their much larger numbers they might also have been more successful in their efforts to destroy runaway slave communities.[34]

Slave hunters remained, in theory, subordinate to the local officers of existing militia companies, but the companies themselves were apparently not systematically put to the task of recovering runaways or repelling their assaults. Controlled by local wealthy men who usually occupied the highest ranks in them, the militia companies did not set out into the forests to attack and destroy *quilombos*. Instead, these tasks were assigned to profit-seeking mercenaries licensed by the colonial governor.

The reasons that the bush captain system was employed rather than the companies of reserve militia were probably financial. It was in the interest of the free males of the *companhias de ordenança* to favor the destruction of *quilombos* and the end to assaults committed by the fugitive population. Most of these men were undoubtedly slave owners themselves; it would not have been a lack of enthusiasm for the goal that would have kept these individuals out of the fight against escaped captives. Employing the militia companies to establish greater control over slaves in the mining region would, however, have required considerable funding, which, if not forthcoming from the royal authorities in Lisbon, would have had to come through the levying of more taxes on the local population. Apparently, the royal government was unwilling to provide funds for slave owners to control their own property. Colonists were unlikely to have tolerated any additional taxes; they could scarcely be persuaded to pay the Royal Fifth.[35]

33. Mappa das ordenanças das minas, 25 January 1738, AHU, Minas Gerais, Documentos avulsos, caixa 20. At this time, the slave population in the *comarca* of Sabará was 24,284; for Minas Gerais as a whole, it was 96,541. See Table 2.1.

34. In the decade 1730–1739, at least 79 Letters of Patent were issued to individuals in Minas Gerais. In the previous decade (1720–29), at least 118 were issued, and in the following decade (1740–49), the number was at least 68. These figures were compiled from data collected by Guimarães, "Uma negação," 137–40.

35. In 1733, for example, the crown collected less than one-third of the fifths owed in that year, Cardoso, "The History of Mining in Colonial Brazil," 431; see also chaps. 25 and 26 passim.

In contrast, the bush captain system placed no systematic burdens on the Royal Treasury, despite appeals from local municipal councils to contribute to their expenses.[36] In fact, the colonial government collected fees for the Letters of Patent that it issued to the bounty hunters.[37] The bush captain system did not require the levying of a community-wide tax on the local populations. The expenses incurred and the profits earned by the mercenary slave catchers came, for the most part, from the pockets of individual slave owners whose captives had been recovered. Using bush captains rather than militia companies was undoubtedly preferable to the free colonists of Minas Gerais, who disliked taxation at least as much as they worried about the runaway slave population.[38]

The use of bush captains, albeit preferable to a more expensive alternative, still produced varying degrees of dissatisfaction among both the slaveholders of Minas Gerais and the crown-appointed colonial officials. For slaveholders, the immediate complaint against the bush captains was that they captured slaves who had not been reported as runaways, apparently in areas near work sites and sleeping quarters of the slaves or close to the towns. Unscrupulous bush captains thought it a good deal easier to capture a nearby slave, who in fact had never run off to begin with, rather than to venture into the densely forested and remote areas of the *comarcas*. The bush captain then turned that slave over to his or her master for the established reward. By these actions, bush captains ceased to be the protectors of the interests of slaveholders and transformed themselves into crown-sanctioned extortionists, blackmailing the property holders in the captaincy.[39]

The colonial governors of Minas Gerais attempted to respond to the complaints of slave owners about the activities of the bush captains. In

36. Letter of the *câmara* of Villa Real to the king, 18 July 1727, AHU, Minas Gerais, Documentos avulsos, caixa 4. In this letter, the municipal council of Sabará petitioned the king for funds to pay for the expenses of a gang of twenty-five bushmen who were combating gangs of runaway slaves.

37. Guimarães, "Uma negação," 106. The fee was 750 *réis*.

38. The volume of official correspondence about the difficulties of successfully taxing the colonists of Minas Gerais easily measures up to and undoubtedly exceeds the numbers of documents referring to the colonists' problems of controlling the slave population. See the codices of the Arquivo Público Mineiro, Colonial Section.

39. Regimento para os capitães do mato, 4 February 1715, APMSC, Códice 6, fols. 46–46v., reprinted in Guimarães, "Uma negação," 173–74; "Regimento dos capitães," 389–91; Bando do Governador Luis Diogo Lobo da Sylva, 8 April 1764, APMCMS, Códice 35, fols. 79v–87v.

1715, Governor Braz Balthezar da Silveira declared that slave catchers could not capture slaves within the borders of the captaincy's towns and they could not capture slaves from the *senzalas* (sleeping quarters or barracks) where slaves resided. The only exception was if a master specifically stated that one of his or her slaves was missing and requested that the bush captain search for that slave within a town's borders.[40] In 1722, Governor Lourenço de Almeyda declared that those slave catchers who customarily captured slaves who were not fugitives should be prohibited by the local justice or law enforcement official from continuing as bush captains. To renew their positions, such individuals would require permission from the governor, and until that was given, no bounties would be awarded for their capturing any slaves.[41] Dom Lourenço also extended the zone in which bush captains were prohibited from operating to within one league (four miles) of the towns or outlying settlements, unless a master had requested the bush captain to act.[42] The intent of both of these governors' modifications of previous laws was to prevent bush captains from making numerous easy arrests of slaves relatively close to home. In making these modifications, the governors were also acquiescing to the demands of the slave owners for fewer restrictions on the mobility of their laborers.

Another complaint of the slaveholders against the bush captains was that these slave catchers were not content to receive the bounty for capturing the runaway, but also wished to make use of the runaway's labor. Bush captains retained the slaves they recaptured for indefinite periods before bringing them to the master or to local authorities. In 1715, Governor Braz Balthezar warned the bush captains that they were obligated to return captured slaves immediately and could not use their labor for personal

---

40. Regimento para os capitães do mato, 4 February 1715, APMSC, Códice 6, fols. 46–46v., reprinted in Guimarães, "Uma negação," 173–74.

41. "Sendo q.e alguns Cap. es do matto sejam uzeiros e vezeiros a prender negros q.e nam sejam fogidos, sendo notorio este seo mao procedimento, se me dará logo te a proceder contra elles, e o Juis ordinario e na sua falta o cabo do districto lhes prohibira q.e na, continuem no exercicio dos d.os postos athé nova ordem minha, e prendendo alguns negros lhes nam pagarão tomadias." "Regimento dos capitães do matto," 17 December 1722, *RAPM* 2 (1897): 390.

42. "Regimento dos capitães do matto," 17 December 1722, *RAPM* 2 (1897): 389. This effectively overthrew the previous decree of 1714, which had demanded traveling passes for slaves more than a half-league from their work site and supervisors. Bando de Dom Braz Balthezar, 22 March 1714, APMSC, Códice 9, fols.16–16v, cited in Guimarães, "Uma negação," 37.

gain. Bounty hunters who retained captured slaves would be considered guilty of theft and subject to the penalties for that crime.[43] In 1722, Governor Lourenço de Almeyda observed that recaptured runaways worked on the agricultural lands of the bush captains or at other tasks in their service, a practice harmful to the common good of the community. He declared that any slave catcher who retained a captured runaway in his power for more than fifteen days would not receive a bounty from the owner.[44]

More than forty years after these governors condemned bush captains for capturing slaves who were not runaways and for retaining captives rather than returning them to the authorities, these practices were still common in the mining region. In April 1764, Governor Luis Diogo Lobo da Sylva observed that the foot soldiers of the bush captains maliciously imagined that slaves who were diligently working for their masters were fugitives and therefore arrested them.[45] In the new regulations of bush captains, which Dom Luis Diogo Lobo da Sylva issued at this time, the governor declared that the local military officials, as the superior officers of the bush captains, were responsible for the abuses committed by these slave catchers. These captains-major were to take immediate measures to stop the bush captains and their assistants from retaining slaves rather than delivering them to the local jails. Thus, in his efforts to remedy the abuses of the bush captains, the governor emphasized the subordination of the bounty hunters to the regular law enforcement agents in each *comarca*.[46] This effort may have served to remind slaveholders of who, at the local level, was accountable for the abuses of the bush captains.

In the eyes of the slaveholders, the bounty hunters' action that represented the most serious challenge to their property rights was the killing of runaways. Masters in Sabará, as well as in the rest of the captaincy of Minas Gerais, therefore protested against the practice of killing runaways and in some cases actively discouraged bush captains from doing so. On this particular issue, however, neither the royal governors of Minas Gerais

43. "Regimento para os capitães do mato," 4 February 1715, APMSC, Códice 6, fols. 46–46v, reprinted in Guimarães, "Uma negação," 174.

44. "[J]ustificando os senhores dos negros q.e o Cam os teve em seo poder ou em sua caza maes de quinze dias dipois da sua prizao, lhes não pagarão tomadias algu'as." "Regimento dos capitães do matto," 17 December 1722 *RAPM* 2 (1897): 391.

45. Bando do Governador Luis Diogo Lobo da Sylva, 8 April 1764, APMCMS, Códice 35, fols. 79v–87v; see paragraph 20.

46. Bando do Governador Luis Diogo Lobo da Sylva, 8 April 1764, APMCMS, Códice 35, fols. 79v–87v; see paragraphs 6 and 9.

nor the Portuguese crown supported the position of the slaveholders, but instead stood clearly behind the actions of the bounty hunters. To encourage slave hunters to continue to seek out *quilombos* and destroy them and to protect such individuals from recrimination by masters, the king of Portugal declared in March 1741 that bush captains and any other person who pursued runaways could not be prosecuted for killing a slave.[47] More than twenty years later, however, in 1764, Governor Luis Diogo Lobo da Sylva observed that the fear of blame still caused some bush captains not to pursue *quilombos* as they should.[48] In response to this reluctance on the part of slave hunters to pursue their prey more aggressively, Dom Luis, in his new regulations, ordered that the king's decree of 1741 be entirely respected, and he reaffirmed that bush captains and all other slave hunters could not be punished for the death of a slave killed while resisting capture.[49]

Although it was not always the case that bush captains needed to be persuaded to pursue fugitive slaves more aggressively,[50] the governors of Minas Gerais did criticize the bounty hunters in their jurisdiction for being complacent about their duties, if not downright lazy at times. In 1722, Dom Lourenço de Almeyda observed that bush captains, having received their Letters of Patent, were content to stay at home and let others (possibly slaves) do their work for them. He ordered the local justices to force the bush captains to leave their towns or settlements and to strike out into the forests to seek the fugitives. If necessary, the justices could do this by arresting the stay-at-home bounty hunters.[51] With the similar intention of

47. Bando do Governador Luis Diogo Lobo da Sylva, 8 April 1764, APMCMS, Códice 35, fols.79v–87v; see paragraphs 1 and 3.

48. "E como me consta que o receyo das culpas que em algumas partes deste governo tem formado contra os officiaes militares e capitoens de mato . . . tem sido causa de os [i.e. os negros] nam procurarem." In Bando do Governador Luis Diogo Lobo da Sylva, 8 April 1764, APMCMS, Códice 35, fols.79–87v, paragraph 3.

49. "[O]rdeno que enteyramente se observe a este respeyto o que sua magestade fidellissimo dispoem na ordem de seis de mayo de mil sete centos e sessenta e hum em que positivamente manda nam sejam culpados os officaes militares, capitoens de mato e mais pessoas que matarem os referidos negros em acto de resistencia." In Bando do Governador Luis Diogo Lobo da Sylva, 8 April 1764, APMCMS, Códice 35, fols. 79–87v; paragraph 3.

50. "Encomendo aos dittos Cap. es que nas investidas de quilombos, se nam hajam com a crueldade com q.e alguns se havião antecedentemente." Paraphrased: Dom Lourenco de Almeyda, governor of Minas Gerais, urged the bush captains not to carry out their future assaults against *quilombos,* "Regimento dos capitães do matto, 17 December 1722," *RAPM* 2 (1897): 390.

51. "[E] nam sahindo ao exercicio dos seos postos, o do Juiz ordro e na sua falta os offes sobredittos os [capitaes de matto] poderam prender para deste sorte os obrigar a sahir de suas

keeping the slave catchers committed to the task of capturing fugitives, Dom Luis Diogo Lobo da Sylva declared in 1764 that the bush captains and their troops should remain in the woods continuously and leave only for the purpose of acquiring additional food and other necessary supplies. He ordered that only one-half of a squad of slave hunters should leave the woods at any time and stated that these men were permitted to remain in the towns or settlements only for three days. Even while they were outside the woods, the bush captain and his men were not considered to be on vacation, but were still obligated to seek and arrest runaway slaves.[52] It seems clear from the official responses of these governors to the actions of bush captains that aggressive pursuit of fugitive slaves was not constant in eighteenth-century Minas Gerais. Moreover, the ambition and commitment of the men employed to capture fugitives were insufficient to ensure that they would strive as hard as possible to end the problem of runaway slaves and *quilombos* in the captaincy.

There is perhaps little wonder in the observation that mercenary slave trackers lacked sufficient interest in, and commitment to, the ultimate goal of their activities, discouraging slaves from fleeing to begin with. The fulfillment of that goal, after all, eliminated the need for their positions. In the eyes of the colonial governors, however, it was not simply the actions of slave trackers that stymied efforts to properly control the captive population in Minas Gerais. For these provincial-level, crown-appointed officials, the problem of slave control also entailed the actions, and inactions, of the *comarcas'* district military officers and local justices, as well as those of the slave owners themselves.

The regulations of the bush men's activities issued by the governor of Minas Gerais in 1764 revealed considerable criticism of the district military officers who served in each of the captaincy's *comarcas*. In these regulations, Dom Luis Diogo Lobo da Sylva repeatedly exhorted the captains-major to properly oversee the actions of the bush captains and to enforce the provisions of earlier royal decrees and provincial regulations.[53] His ex-

---

casas e a entrar nos mattos a prender os d.os negros." "Regimento dos capitães do matto, 17 December 1722," *RAPM* 2 (1897): 390.

52. "[T]endo bem entendido que de nenhuma sorte lhe será permitida mayor demora que o dos tres dias e que nelles nao ficarem desobrigados de procurarem prender os ditos negros de que tiverem noticia andam nella." Bando do Governador Luis Diogo Lobo da Sylva, 8 April 1764, APMCMS, Códice 35, fols. 79v–87v, paragraph 7.

53. Bando do Governador Luis Diogo Lobo da Sylva, 8 April 1764, APMCMS, Códice 35, fols. 79v–87v, paragraph 7. One example of this can be found in paragraph 8 of the regulations, which states that district captains should bring recaptured fugitives directly to the

hortations and delineations of the responsibilities of these captains took on the character of threats, as he warned that failure to comply with his orders could mean the loss of their jobs and other punishments.[54] Because these regulations were intended to serve as reforms of current practices, they indicate that up to this time the district captains had not been carrying out their expected duties.

The governor was also critical of the actions taken by the *comarcas'* local justices who were responsible for releasing recaptured fugitives to their masters after the bounties were paid to the bush captains. He observed that many of these judges, in complete violation of the existing legislation, were adjusting the amounts of the bounties paid by slave owners. The powerful and well-known masters paid less than the required sums for their own slaves in exchange for contributing to the fines of less well-to-do masters.[55] The governor ordered these judges to stop reducing the fines owed by the powerful slave owners and to make no exceptions for the difficult economic circumstances of less well-to-do masters.[56] Apparently local justices were enmeshed in the power structure of the small towns of the mining region and preferred to compromise royal directives rather than be alienated from the local elite. The governor of the captaincy was, however, more concerned with the diminution of royal authority that such compromises wrought as well as with the lax behavior of slave owners resulting from knowing that the fines for recovering a runaway could be negotiated.

Slave owners in Minas Gerais should have felt, and at least some did feel, enormous concern for the problem of runaway slaves and the difficulties of recovering them. Nonetheless, their actions and methods of con-

---

judicial authorities and not to slave owners. This procedure had been required since 1722. See "Regimento dos capitães do matto, 17 December 1722," *RAPM* 2 (1897): 389.

54. "[F]icando os capitoens dos distritos na intelligencia de que abuzando desta minha ordem serem privados dos postos alem do mais castigo que reconhecer merecerem pella gravidade de seus delictos." Bando do Governador Luis Diogo Lobo da Sylva, 8 April 1764, APMCMS, Códice 35, fols. 79v–87v, paragraph 2; see also paragraph 17.

55. "E porque me he presente que muitos juizes nam so arbitram aos capitoens de mato e pessoas particullares que prendem negros quillombados e fugidos menos quantia pellas tomadias do que as Reaes Ordens e Regimento determinam, mas por empenhos lhe tiram as que lhes tocam dos ditos negros pertencentes as pessoas poderosas e conhecidas fazendose nesta parte contribuir aos que os nam tem para serem rellevados do que justamente devem dar em premio de tam ariscado e util trabalho." Bando do Governador Luis Diogo Lobo da Sylva, 8 April 1764, APMCMS, Códice 35, fols. 79v–87v, paragraph 4.

56. Bando do Governador Luis Diogo Lobo da Sylva, 8 April 1764, APMCMS, Códice 35, fols. 79v–87v, paragraph 4.

trolling slaves frequently contradicted the efforts of royal officials to eliminate or reduce the "licentious liberty" of the region's captive population.
The individual interests of slave owners could also conflict with the collective or class interests of masters as a whole. The most obvious way in
which masters increased the dangers of slaves revolting, committing crimes,
or simply fleeing was by providing their slaves with arms. Sebastião
Pereira de Aguilar was one such slave owner who thought arming his
slaves was in his interests. In 1716, he owned a large tract of land in the
comarca of Sabará and forty-nine slaves, only nine of whom were women.
Among his other possessions, he listed a pair of pistols for his own use, but
he also claimed to own a additional twenty firearms for use by his slaves.
As discussed in Chapter 2, Pereira de Aguilar was also a slave owner who
made contractual arrangements to split the profits of his slaves' labors
with them. Through such contractual arrangements, he must have been
able to convince his armed slaves to defend his land claims against other
encroachers.[57]

As noted earlier, slaves in eighteenth-century Minas Gerais carried a
wide variety of weapons, including firearms (muskets and pistols), swords,
small axes, daggers, cudgels, and clubs.[58] Owners like Sebastião Pereira de
Aquilar armed their slaves to protect their claims to gold-bearing lands
and possibly to serve as bodyguards.[59] They also made use of armed slaves
to launch protests against the plans of colonial governors to increase taxes
in the region.[60] Slave owners were known to use their armed slaves to rob

57. Testamento de Sebastião Pereira de Aguilar, 27 October 1716 (*Livro de registo de
testamento*, 1, 1716–23), fol. 13. See above, Chapter 2, note 74.
58. Bando do Governador D. Pedro de Almeida, Conde de Assumar, 30 December 1717,
APMSC, Códice 11, fol. 270. "[P]rohibindo . . . o uso de armas pelos negros, mulatos,
bastardos ou carijós, inclusive bastões ou páos guarnecidas de castões de metal, ou paós
agudos, porretes e machadinhas." See also Bando do Governador D. Pedro de Almeida,
Conde de Assumar, 24 March 1719, APMSC, Códice 11, fol. 279. "[P]rohibindo o uso de
armas de fogo curtas e compridas, facas, punhaes, espadas, porretes, páos ferrados ou encastoados, aos negros e mulatos escravos."
59. I believe that slaves may have served as bodyguards because the laws prohibiting the
use of arms by slaves consistently made exceptions for times that the slaves were in the
presence of their masters. I do not think that such exceptions were made solely to bolster the
prestige of miners who could then parade through town with their armed entourage. Armed
slaves may have protected mining claims simply by guarding the lives of the claims' owners.
Bando do Governador D. Pedro de Almeida, Conde de Assumar, 30 December 1717,
APMSC, Códice 11, fol. 270; Bando do Governador D. Pedro de Almeida, Conde de Assumar, 24 March 1719, APMSC, Códice 11, fol. 279.
60. The most famous uprising against the crown's tax policy took place in the capital of
Minas Gerais, Vila Rica, in 1720. Part of the plot entailed using bands of slaves to seal off the

and otherwise intimidate other free people in the mining region. In 1732, for example, Governor Lourenço de Almeida ordered the arrest of slave owner Antônio Barrabas for allowing his slaves to wander about armed, permitting them and perhaps ordering them to rob other people.[61]

The phenomenon of armed slaves naturally contributed to the fact that so many runaways were also armed and exacerbated the dangers such fugitives posed to the free colonists and their pursuers. The free colonists of Minas Gerais, were not, however, united in their opposition to runaway slaves or even to the larger runaway slave communities (*quilombos*). Fugitive slaves who acquired goods through thefts and who had access to gold by panning in rivers and streams could participate in clandestine sales with local traders. Governor Luis Diogo Lobo da Sylva observed in 1764 that vendors and tavern keepers in Minas Gerais actually aided runaways and other slaves by allowing them to do business after hours when darkness protected them from discovery. Tavern keepers and vendors sold the slaves whatever they required, even if they requested powder and shot. They also purchased from these slaves whatever stolen goods they had to offer.[62]

For fugitive slaves, the willingness of free colonists to sell them ammunition and other needed supplies was probably essential to their survival. For the vendors and traders, the behind-the-scenes transactions made with runaways brought additional profits. Aside from the obvious consideration that providing runaways with supplies increased their ability to wreak havoc in and around local mining communities, the colonial authorities also condemned the participation of free colonists in commerce financed by untaxed gold. The gold panned by escaped slaves clearly was not declared, and the fifth part of it did not go to the Royal Treasury as it should have. The inability of the crown to tax this gold was one of the major reasons that it objected to the illicit trade.

---

streets of the town and incite a complete state of chaos. See Ramos, "A Social History of Ouro Preto," 413. In the same year and for the same reason, there was an uprising in the Pitangui region of the *comarca* of Sabará. Governador, Dom Pedro de Almeida, Conde de Assumar, to João de Souza Souto Mayor, et. al., 1 January 1720, "appellando para os seus sentimentos de bons vasallos de S. Magestade, pede a sua contribuição para o apasiguamento de Pitangui," APMSC, Códice 11, fol. 196v.

61. Portaria do governador, Dom Lourenço de Almeida, 11 November 1732, APMSC, Códice, fol. 101. Barrabas was a resident of Congonhas, Minas Gerais.

62. "E porque me consta que os vendeyros e taberneyros sam os que amparao os mesmos calhambolos e mais escravos de forma que ahoras de terem as mesmas tendas e tabernas fechadas os recolhem em suas cazas para lhes comprarem os furtos e lhes venderem o que querem os mesmos negros ainda que seja pólvora e xumbo," Bando do Governador Luis Diogo Lobo da Sylva, 8 April 1764, APMCMS, Códice 35, fols. 79v–87v, paragraph 12.

Free colonists and others who benefited from the phenomenon of runaways and the illegal commerce that could be conducted with them were, quite sensibly, reluctant to pass on knowledge about the whereabouts of runaways to bush captains or other military officers. The Count of Assumar's response to such treachery was severe. In 1717, he ordered that those Whites who failed to reveal the existence and whereabouts of *quilombos* they were familiar with should be whipped through the streets of the town they lived in and then exiled to Benguela, Africa. Slaves who failed to disclose such information would be executed.[63] Nonetheless, in spite of the severity of the punishment, protecting runaways from discovery by colonial authorities was a practice that continued throughout the eighteenth century.[64]

The Count of Assumar and his successors in the governorship of Minas Gerais strongly objected to the phenomenon of armed slaves in the captaincy, and they promulgated various decrees prohibiting the practice.[65] Such prohibitions were extended to include not only Black and mulatto slaves but also bastards[66] and Indians, and the list of weapons forbidden to these individuals was extensive. Aside from the obvious firearms and knives, slaves could not carry sharpened sticks that were sometimes encased in metal or that had metal heads. They were also forbidden to carry staffs.[67] On the other hand, despite their objections, the governors did not

63. Bando do Governador D. Pedro de Almeida, Conde de Assumar, 12 December 1717, APMSC, Códice 11, fol. 269. "Quem souber da existencia de quilombos e não os denunciar, sendo branco será açoitado pelas ruas e degredado para Banguela, sendo negro ou carijó terá pena de morte."

64. Registo de editais que o juiz ordinario e mais officiães de câmara mandarão publicar, 12 February 1754, APMCMS, Códice 27, fols. 143–45; Bando do Governador Luis Diogo Lobo da Sylva, 8 April 1764, APMCMS, Códice 35, fols. 79v–87v, paragraph 18.

65. Bando do Governador D. Pedro de Almeida, Conde de Assumar, 30 December 1717, APMSC, Códice 11, fol. 270. "[P]rohibindo . . . o uso de armas pelos negros, mulatos, bastardos ou carijós, inclusive bastões ou páos guarnecidas de castões de metal, ou paós agudos, porretes e machadinhas." See also: Bando do Governador D. Pedro de Almeida, Conde de Assumar, 24 March 1719, APMSC, Códice 11, fol. 279. "[P]rohibindo o uso de armas de fogo curtas e compridas, facas, punhaes, espadas, porretes, páos ferrados ou encastoados, aos negros e mulatos escravos"; Bando do Governador D. Lourenço de Almeida, 31 March 1730, APMSC, Códice 27, fol. 65; Bando do Governador Luis Diogo Lobo da Sylva, 8 April 1764, APMCMS, Códice 35, fols. 79v–87v, paragraph 16.

66. Bastards usually implied persons of mixed race and unless otherwise stated were free.

67. Bando do Governador D. Pedro de Almeida, Conde de Assumar, 30 December 1717, APMSC, Códice 11, fol. 270. "[P]rohibindo . . . o uso de armas pelos negros, mulatos, bastardos ou carijós, inclusive bastões ou páos guarnecidas de castões de metal, ou paós agudos, porretes e machadinhas." See also: Bando do Governador D. Pedro de Almeida, Conde de Assumar, 24 March 1719, APMSC, Códice 11, fol. 279. "[P]rohibindo o uso de

outlaw the arming of slaves altogether. A 1717 decree stated that as long as the slaves were accompanied by their masters they were free to carry such weapons as they owned or were given by their owners. Only when slaves were alone and armed would they be violating the law.[68] Later this provision was amended and stated that only a slave who was alone, armed, and did not carry written permission from the master was violating the law. In such cases, slaves were arrested and imprisoned for up to twenty days and could receive up to two hundred lashes of the whip. Masters could also be fined twenty *oitavas* of gold for their slave's transgression.[69]

Permitting slaves to remain armed while in the presence of their masters was undoubtedly a compromise forced on the colonial authorities rather than one reached by negotiation. It clearly would have been impossible for a limited number of royal officials to have successfully disarmed groups of slaves in the presence of their masters and without their consent. Colonial officials may also have recognized that they would have needed to disarm all slaves at exactly the same moment to avoid having the miners who still had armed forces attack and usurp the lands of the unfortified masters. Because the colonial authorities were incapable of rigorously policing the mining region and protecting miners from lawless slaves, as well as from one another, official policy became to outlaw arms for slaves *only* when their masters said they should not have them. Such a compromised policy of slave control implicitly recognized that the free colonists, not the royal authorities, controlled the laborers in Minas Gerais.

Even the colonial authorities did not hesitate to recruit slaves for their armies. Just as miners used armed slaves to protect land claims, so did the governors of the captaincy. When, in 1726, Dom Lourenço de Almeida sent out a party of free men to a newly discovered gold claim, he ordered them to bring slaves experienced in mining and armed with firearms and ammunition. Each free man was to bring two armed captives.[70] A few

---

armas de fogo curtas e compridas, facas, punhaes, espadas, porretes, páos ferrados ou encastoados, aos negros e mulatos escravos"; Bando do Governador D. Lourenço de Almeida, 31 March 1730, APMSC, Códice 27, fol. 65; Bando do Governador Luis Diogo Lobo da Sylva, 8 April 1764, APMCMS, Códice 35, fols. 79v–87v, paragraph 16.

68. Bando do Governador D. Pedro de Almeida, Conde de Assumar, 30 December 1717, APMSC, Códice 11, fol. 270. "Só permitte que, acompanhando seus senhores, possam negros conduzir armas lícitas e não prohibidas por lei."

69. Bando do Governador D. Lourenço de Almeyda, 4 April 1724, APMSC, Códice 27, fol. 4; Bando do Governador D. Lourenço de Almeida, 31 March 1730, APMSC, Códice 27, fol. 65. This latter *bando* mentions the penalty of 200 lashes.

70. "[E] precizo q. tambem vao negros mineiros que saibam fazer experiencias e vao ar-

years earlier, when the free residents of the *comarca* of Sabará, in the district of Pitangui, arose in revolt against royal plans to raise taxes in the region, the governor, Dom Pedro de Almeida, used armed slaves to put down their uprising. He requested that several major slaveholders in the *comarca* each contribute a dozen armed slaves to the military party sent to pacify the area. In total, he planned to send at least one hundred armed captives to Pitangui, along with their free supervisors.[71] When Dom Pedro was replaced as governor of the captaincy in 1721 by Dom Lourenço de Almeida, the latter chose to recognize those free citizens who had helped to put down the 1720 tax rebellions in Sabará and in the capital of Vila Rica and to request honors for these individuals from the king. Dom Lourenço wrote to the king of Portugal in September 1721 to suggest that Captain-Major Henrique Lopes of Vila Rica merited the honor of membership in a military order "for being always ready to serve Your Majesty, with fifty armed slaves."[72] The colonial governors had apparently decided that as much as armed slaves might be responsible for all manner of disorders and crimes in the mining region they could, at the same time, serve as the instruments of royal authority. They were even willing to use armed captives to fight against the free citizens of the captaincy.

If colonial officials were willing to use armed slaves against the outlaws of the free citizenry, then it should come as no surprise that they would also use slaves, ex-slaves, and free men of color in pursuit of runaway captives. In 1764, Governor Luis Diogo Lobo da Sylva demanded that free men of whatever status, including ex-slaves and free men of color, accompany bush captains in their slave hunts.[73] Freedmen, free Blacks, and free

---

mados de fogo, pólvora e ballas." Ordem do governador, D. Lourenço Almeida à Cam Mor Domingos da Rocha Ferreira, APMSC, Códice 27, fol. 25.

71. Ordem do governador, D. Pedro de Almeida, Conde de Assumar, ao ajudante de tenente Manoel da Costa Pinheiro, 12 December 1719, APMSC, Códice 11, fol. 194v.; Carta do governador, D. Pedro de Almeida, Conde de Assumar, a João de Souza Souto Mayor, Joseph Correa de Miranda, et. al., "appellando para os sentimentos de bons vasallos de S. Magestade, pede a sua contribuição para o apasiguamento de Pitanguy, . . . Essa contribuição era de 12 negros armados sobre o mando de um branco," 28 January 1720, APMSC, Códice 11, fol. 196v.

72. "[P]or estar sempre pronto para tudo o que for servir a Vossa Majestade com mais de cinqüenta negros armados," Carta do governador, Dom Lourenço de Almeida, ao Rey, September 17, 1721, APMSC, Códice 23, reprinted in *RAPM* 31(1980): 87–88.

73. "Ordeno que sucedendo em qualquer parte dos distritos deste governo cometerem os negros do Mato o que vulgarmente chamam calhambollas algum [insulto] os capitoens dos respetivos distritos *apennem* (emphasis mine) os seus moradores inclusive pardos e negros livres para que com os ditos capitoens de mato . . . ataquem e sigam os ditos negros athé os prenderem," Bando do Governador Luis Diogo Lobo da Sylva, April 8, 1764, APMCMS,

men of mixed race (*pardos*) also received Letters of Patent from the colonial governors to work as bush captains in their own right. Of those bush captains in Minas Gerais for whom records exist and who received Letters of Patent between the years 1710 and 1798, just over 8 percent were former slaves, and almost 13 percent were identified as non-Whites.[74] On infrequent occasions, individuals who were currently enslaved were issued letters of patent making them bush captains. In 1731, for example, Amaro de Queiroz, a Black slave of José de Queiroz, became a bush captain. Domingos Moreira de Azevedo, a *crioulo* slave, became a bush captain in 1760, as did José Ferreira, a *pardo* slave, in 1779. Slaves and ex-slaves were thought to make useful bush captains because of their familiarity with the territory in which they would seek runaways.[75]

There was another practical benefit of recruiting ex-slaves as trackers of fugitives. By demanding that free colonists serve in the squads of the bush captains and by including ex-slaves in that call for service, the colonial officials were more or less forcing the freed slaves to identify themselves with the free colonists of the captaincy rather than with the fugitives. Even if the message of social acceptance implied by shared participation in these community corvées did not appeal to all ex-captives in Minas Gerais, it undoubtedly produced in the community of freed people some allies for the ruling Whites in the captaincy. The position of bush captain, for which an individual applied and was not forcibly recruited, was in fact sought after by former slaves and free men of color. It was, no doubt, wise for the colonial governors to repeatedly assert through the mechanism of the bush

---

Códice 35, fols. 79v–87v, paragraph 2. *Apennem* comes from the verb *apenar*, which the 1858 (6th ed.) of Antonio de Moraes Silva, *Dicionario da lingua portugueza*, defines as "Notificar com comminação de pena para comparecimento ou apresentação em certo tempo, ou lugar, para dar, ou fazer alguma cousa, principalmente do serviço público." That is, *apenar* means "to order, with promise of punishment for failure to comply, the appearance of a person or persons to perform a public service." Joining the slave trackers was therefore not simply a matter of volunteering, but of being drafted, as in "apenou os officiaes para trabalharem na galé": "[he] ordered the officers to work in the galleys."

74. Guimarães, "Uma negação," anexo 3, 188–210. His sources are the codices of the Arquivo Público Mineiro, Secção colonial. There are 468 names of bush captains and bushmen listed in these pages. Thirty-nine (8.3 percent) are identified as *forros*, freed slaves. Twenty-one (4.5 percent) are identified not as *forros* but simply as men of color, either *pardos* or *pretos*. According to Guimarães, not all, although most, Letters of Patent indicated whether bush captains were White, Black, of mixed race, ex-slaves, or slaves. It is therefore possible that the percentage of ex-slaves and free men of color among the bush captains was somewhat higher than the figures provided in this text. See Guimarães, "Uma negação," 24.

75. Guimarães, "Uma negação," 118. These three individuals were the only slaves identified from 468 Letters of Patent. This represents .6 percent of the total.

captain system that the freed slaves and free people of color were on the side of the free Whites in the mining region rather than on the side of the runaway slaves. In this way, the institutional means of slave repression might serve to build and strengthen social ties between White miners and freed captives.

Those free and freed colonists recruited into the squads of the bush captains were accompanied by slaves, some of them their own and others not. Although a slave who had been named to the position of bush captain was permitted to bear arms,[76] all others who formed part of the slave-hunting crew were not. The only exception to this rule was for the *capineyros*, slaves who carried machetes with which to cut away the undergrowth in the forests. It seems likely, however, that such restrictions were honored only in the breach; regulations issued in the second half of the eighteenth century reaffirmed the general prohibition of arms for slaves and specified that weapons for captives who joined slave-hunting expeditions were also forbidden.[77] Thus, in addition to the difficulties they faced in influencing the behavior of slave owners who consistently armed their captive laborers, colonial officials had to police their own law enforcement agents who also illegally armed the slaves in their entourages. For much of the eighteenth century, armed slaves apparently remained the rule rather than the exception in the captaincy of Minas Gerais.

The slaves who accompanied squads into the forests were supposed to serve as guides who would lead them to *quilombos*. Not all such slaves, some of whom were recaptured fugitives, faithfully executed their duties, but instead purposefully deceived the slave hunters whom they led. Governor José Antonio Freire de Andrade wrote in 1759 that the *quilombo* of Sapucaí, "the largest, most populated, and oldest in this captaincy," had not yet been destroyed because "of the deception of slave guides" who prevented that *quilombo*'s discovery.[78] The dependence of the fugitive slave hunters on duplicitous servants (who may or may not have been armed)

76. Ordem do governandor, D. Pedro de Almeida, Conde de Assumar, 20 February 1719, "concedendo licença para que o preto Manoel Monjollo, morador em Cattas Altas, possa trazer armas necessarios para o officio de apanhar negros fugidos." APMSC, Códice 11, fol. 112.

77. Bando do Governador Luis Diogo Lobo da Sylva, 8 April 1764, APMCMS, Códice 35, fols. 79v–87v, paragraphs 15 and 16.

78. "[o quilombo do Sapucaí] que dizem ser o maior, digo, mais povoado, e antigo desta capitania e a causa de se não ter assaltado este quilombo tem sido o engano que os negros que servem de guias tem feito para que se não saiba do dito quilombo," Carta do governador, José Antonio Freire de Andrade, 14 November 1759, APMSC, Códice 110, fol. 135, cited in Guimaraes, "Una negação," 96.

certainly contributed to the difficulties faced by the colonial officials as they attempted to eradicate *quilombos* and to reduce the general lawlessness of slaves residing in the captaincy.

When the colonial governors and other local officials in Minas Gerais were not addressing the issue of runaways and their recapture, they focused instead on what they described as the *desordens*, disorders or turmoil, brought on by slave actions in or near the mining communities. One particular object of their attentions was the activity of female slaves, female ex-slaves, and free women of color in the captaincy. In Sabará, as in all other *comarcas* of Minas Gerais, many of these women worked as itinerant vendors selling food and drinks, which they carried with them on large planks of wood, or trays, wherever they walked. These *negras de taboleiro*[79] took their goods to the mining sites and sold them to the male slaves and freedmen working there. The Portuguese crown objected to these sales because such transactions were made with gold that had not yet been taxed and would not be. In addition, owners of those slaves working in the mining site objected to the presence of these women because the gold that the slaves used to pay for their food and drink belonged to their masters. On the other hand, the owners of the slave women who sold these goods, as well as the freed slave women who worked for themselves, profited by sales to prospecting captives at the mining sites and therefore ignored such objections.[80]

In September 1729, Governor Lourenço de Almeida responded to complaints against the *negras de taboleiro* made by the residents of a mining area in Congonhas, a parish located in the *comarca* of Sabará. These residents objected to the "repeated disorders and disgraces" occurring at the local mining site because of the numerous vendors present. These vendors sold food and alcoholic beverages to slaves and freedmen and made them drunk and caused them to fight and injure one another. Besides selling food and drink, the *negras de taboleiro* also "lead the men astray" and "with no fear of divine punishment" apparently exchanged sexual favors for quantities of the recently panned gold.[81] In his response to the resi-

79. *Taboleiro* is the Portuguese word for the wooden tray used to carry the food items being sold. Some of these trays had wooden drawers beneath them.

80. Bando do Governador D. Lourenço de Almeida, 28 June 1725, APMSC, Códice 27, fol. 17; Carta régia ao governador das Minas Gerais, 28 March 1732, APMSC Códice 36, fols. 29v–30; Bando do Governador Luis Diogo Lobo da Sylva, 8 April 1764, APMCMS, Códice 35, fols. 79v–87v, paragraphs 10 and 11.

81. "[O]s moradores asistentes no morro das Congonhas. . . .[queixam] . . . da oppressam q. continuadamente tem pellas repetidas desordens e disgraças soccedidas por causa das muitas vendas q. no ditto morro ha, as quaes estando abertas de dia o de noute consomem os

dents' complaints, Governor Almeida opined that the majority of the women working at the mining sites were not sellers of goods or panners of gold, but prostitutes.[82] He then banished these women vendors from the mining site and from the area within two hundred paces of it and imposed severe penalties for violators of the ban. Any woman, Black or mulatto, slave or free, discovered conducting business in the proscribed area could be imprisoned for three months, given 100 lashes of the whip, deprived of all of her goods, and fined twenty *oitavas* of gold.[83] In this way, the governor sought to restore order and perhaps grace to the working sites.

The owners of slaves working at mining sites undoubtedly welcomed Governor Almeida's directive, but the owners of the slave women who frequented such sites would have resisted the prohibition as an interference with their efforts to earn profits. Freed slave women and free women of color who worked as *negras de taboleiro* were also threatened as the ban was intended to deprive them of one of their most significant locations for sales and therefore to significantly reduce their means of earning a living. For the governor, order and grace could have happily come at the expense of economic survival for these women.

In fact, neither the economic survival of the *negras de taboleiro* nor the practice of prostitution in the *comarca* of Sabará was much affected by the governor's decree. In regard to the latter, just a few years later, in 1734, the Inquisition's Visitor to the *comarca* of Sabará discovered that several local residents were actively promoting prostitution. The Visitor, Doctor Lourenço José de Queiroz Coimbra, condemned Luiza Pereira, a freed *parda* woman, for having her living quarters serve as a house of prostitu-

---

jornaes aos negros, embebedando-se estes, de que tem resultado haver entres elles pendencias, e ferirem-se gravemente, concorrendo tambem para esta desordem a multidão de negras, escravas, e forras q. no ditto morro andão vendendo com taboleiros, e faiscando, a mayor parte das quaes procedem sem temor algum de Deos Nosso Senhor desencaminhando aos d.os negros, e servindo-lhes de occasião para cometerem infinitos insultos," Bando do Governador D. Lourenço de Almeida, 11 September 1729, APMSC, Códice 27, fols. 58–59; "Offenses against God," as in "lhes servia de igoal prejuizo as muitas negras forras que vão a o d.to morro a tirar os jornaes aos negros com offensas de Deos," was another cryptic reference by colonial governors to the practice of prostitution at mining sites in the captaincy. See Bando do Governador D. Lourenço de Almeida, 11 June 1728, APMSC, Códice 27, fol. 42; Bando do Governador Luis Diogo Lobo da Sylva, 8 April 1764, APMCMS, Códice 35, fols. 79v–87v, paragraph 10.

82. Bando do Governador D. Lourenço de Almeida, 11 September 1729, APMSC, Códice 27, fol. 58.

83. Bando do Governador D. Lourenço de Almeida, 11 September 1729, APMSC, Códice 27, fol. 58. If free, the woman had to pay the fine and the costs of the jail, and if a slave, the master would pay such costs.

tion for *"negras"* selling themselves to *"negros."*[84] Manoel Angola, a slave belonging to Manoel André Pinto, was also warned not to use his living quarters for illicit meetings of slave women and men or else suffer condemnation for operating as a pimp.[85] The visiting cleric also condemned Gracia da Fonseca, a freed Black woman, specifically for allowing her own female slaves to have sexual encounters with men in her house.[86] Thus, had the governor's decree been more successful than it actually was in forcing the slave women, ex-slave women, and free women of color to stop selling sexual favors at the mining sites, they could still have operated in other locations in the *comarca*.

Dom Lourenço de Almeida's decree restricting the sexual and nonsexual activities of the *negras de taboleiro* at mining sites in Sabará was repeated for other locations in the captaincy of Minas Gerais until the prohibition became general for the entire region.[87] These women continued, however, to sell goods, and themselves, in precisely the same locations as they had before the ban. More than thirty years later, in 1764, Governor Luis Diogo Lobo da Sylva observed that much commerce still took place at mining sites in the captaincy. *Negras de taboleiro* continued to sell food and drinks and all manner of goods. For Governor da Sylva, the major wrong that resulted from the presence of the women vendors at gold production sites was not so much "the notable scandal of public offense against the Lord" — the sales of sexual favors. What really contradicted the interests of the colonial government was that these women served as fences for goods stolen by runaways, who could come to the mining sites, remain undiscovered, and conduct their business. Slaves who were not fugitives also brought to the mining sites items stolen from the masters they still lived

---

84. "Luiza Pereira parda forra, . . . que de tudo se aparte e não consinta em casa negros e negras o qual vão o fim de se deshonestizarem servindolhe a mesma casa de alcouce," 20 January 1734, Cúria Municipal de Belo Horizonte, *Livro segundo dos termos*, fol. 19. The implication of the terms *negros e negras* is that the individuals involved were slaves, but freed persons of color may also have been involved here.

85. "Manoel preto angola escravo de Manoel André Pinto . . . que não consinta em sua caza ajuntamentos de negros com negras pela suspeita de que se deshonestão dando para o escandaloso fim casa de alcouce, com comminação de que tornando a admittir os referidos ajuntamentos em sua casa, se lhe haver por provado o crime de alcouceiro," 15 January 1734, Cúria Municipal de Belo Horizonte, *Segundo livro de termos*, fol. 7.

86. "Gracia da Fonseca, preta forra, . . . que não consinta que as suas escravas se deshonestem com negros que vem a sua casa," 15 January 1734, Cúria Municipal de Belo Horizonte, *Segundo livro de termos*, fol. 10.

87. Carta régia to governador of Minas Gerais, 28 March 1732, APMSC, Códice 36, fols. 29v–30.

with and traded them with the *negras de taboleiro*. These vendors could hide, in their trays or on their persons, goods and untaxed gold illegally brought to them; they therefore formed the link between legal commerce and the clandestine trade that was widespread in the captaincy. The governor observed that sales made by these women represented unfair competition to the established merchants "of good faith" who operated in the towns. Moreover, such sales deprived the treasury of its entitled revenues.[88]

As the governors of Minas Gerais and at least some of the miners openly opposed the illegal vending engaged in by the *negras de taboleiro*, it is difficult to understand how such powerless and vulnerable women, many of whom were enslaved, Black, and African born, managed to escape restraint and continued to exercise that "licentious liberty" so abhorrent to the Count of Assumar. These women worked without supervision, but the slaves among them must have answered to their masters at least by way of returning to them a proportion of their daily earnings. The penalties for engaging in the illegal commerce applied to the individual women involved (they could be imprisoned for twenty-five days), but in the case of enslaved vendors, the fines levied were to be paid by the owners of the transgressors.[89] Therefore, although the actions of the enslaved female vendors may have exceeded the desires of the colonial officials in Minas Gerais and indeed went beyond the limits of the law, these women doubtless still worked at the behest of their owners who were held accountable by the government for their crimes. *Negras de taboleiro* could not have defied both the colonial officials and the owners of mining sites without the urging and support of the masters for whom they labored.

The opposition of the colonial government and of the individual mine owners who had lodged complaints against them was insufficient to eliminate illegal sales at the mining sites at least well into the second half of the eighteenth century. Considerable support must have existed among the free colonists of Sabará and those living elsewhere in Minas Gerais for the

---

88. "[N]os arrayaes lavras e morros em que se minera se seguem as consequencias de serem as ditas negras referidas tratantes os receptacullos aonde vay parar nam somente parte dos furtos que fazem os calhambolas mas tudo o ouro e trastes que das lavras e cazas divertem os que nam andao fugidos a seus senhores alem das mais desordens de sam origen as ditas tendas vollantes e tabolleyros com notavel escandallo de publico offensa de Deos e prejuizo das logeas estabellecidas por negociantes de boa fe nos ditos arrayaes," Bando do Governador Luis Diogo Lobo da Sylva, 8 April 1764, APMCMS, Códice 35, fols. 79v–87v, paragraphs 10 and 11.

89. Bando do Governador Luis Diogo Lobo da Sylva, 8 April 1764, APMCMS, Códice 35, fols. 79v–87v, paragraph 10.

continuance of such illegal activities. Apparently, not all slave owners supported one another in every means of controlling the slave population that they collectively dominated. The free population of eighteenth-century Minas Gerais was diverse; it consisted of large and small slaveholders, those directly engaged in the production of gold, and those connected to the agricultural, pastoral, and commercial sectors of the economy. The interests of these free citizens, as evidenced by the means of employing their captive laborers, were at times contradictory. In addition, slave owners could readily put their individual interests ahead of the collective interests of their class.

On the other hand, had the slave owners been very seriously divided among themselves, the colonial authorities could and would have imposed themselves as the final arbiters or directors of events in the captaincy. Despite the fact that there were important moments in the history of the captaincy where provincial-level officials took advantage of divisions among slaveholders and assumed the upper hand,[90] the colonial governors of Minas Gerais never achieved absolute control over the free citizens of the captaincy. In spite of their differences and their often quite contradictory needs, slaveholders, who controlled the laboring population and therefore the production of gold and other significant commodities, remained sufficiently united to function as powerful agents of change and continuity in the mining region. One issue that certainly united the slaveholders, although it affected them all in different ways, was that of taxation, and from their opposition to it ensued many of the conflicts relating to the conduct of slaves.

The Portuguese crown demanded that one-fifth of all the gold produced in the mines of Brazil be collected and turned over to the Royal Treasury. As the experience in the mines of São Paulo had demonstrated to colonial officials in the seventeenth century, it was difficult to force prospectors and miners to declare all the gold they had discovered. Calculating the amounts of gold actually owed to the Royal Treasury was therefore problematic. Collecting a reasonable proportion of the estimated sums destined

---

90. The classic instance of this occurring was during the War of the Emboabas (1708–9) and the period of its resolution (June 1710–September 1711) when the miners divided into two camps: one of *paulistas* from São Paulo and the other of *emboabas* from Bahia. The colonial governors stepped in at this time and thereby established the first institutional structures of royal authority in the mining region. The authority established at this moment should not, however, be mistaken as either absolute or permanent, particularly because the colonial officials later had to contend with free settler and slave revolts. See Boxer, *The Golden Age,* 61–83. See also Ramos, "A Social History of Ouro Preto," chap. 26 passim.

for the crown's coffers was a task that challenged even the most astute and loyal officials. In São Paulo, tax collectors had great difficulty with contrabandists, and only a fraction of the Royal Fifths was collected.[91]

When the gold rush in Minas Gerais finally caught the attention of the Portuguese officials, they saw that the miners in this region were just as unwilling as those in São Paulo had been to bring all their gold to inspection stations or to foundry houses where they would be taxed. The Portuguese crown therefore proposed, in 1710, that the governor of Minas Gerais commute the payment of the Royal Fifths into an annual tax on each *bateia* or mining pan used in the goldfields. Thus the crown would levy a tax on each slave who mined for gold in the captaincy. The amount of the tax levied per capita was presumably high enough so that the total amount collected represented an increase over previous amounts collected by the earlier methods.[92]

The free colonists of Minas Gerais resisted the imposition of a crown-imposed capitation tax, and their threats to civil order in the captaincy forced the colonial governor to negotiate a compromise method of revenue collection.[93] In 1714, Governor Braz Balthezar da Silveira accepted the colonists' proposal to pay the crown thirty *arrobas*[94] of gold per year, an amount to be raised according to their own methods of collection. The colonists chose to levy taxes on merchandise, animals, and slaves entering the mining region. They also levied a tax on each mining pan, that is, on each slave working in the mining fields. What made the colonist-imposed head tax more acceptable than that proposed by the crown was that the amount requested per slave was only one and three-quarters *oitavas* per year, less than one-sixth of the crown's desired figure.[95]

Thus, from nearly the very beginning, the taxation of slaves served as an important means of collecting the Royal Fifth and other taxes in Minas Gerais and continued to do so for much of the eighteenth century. From 1714 through 1724, the colonists continued to pay a tax on slaves in lieu of one on gold production. By 1720, the tax had been extended to include

91. See Chapter 1.

92. "Minas e quintos do ouro," *RAPM* 6 (1901): 855–58; Cardoso, "The History of Mining in Colonial Brazil, " 384. Cardoso dates the crown proposal as coming in 1709.

93. The history of tax revolts in Minas Gerais is probably worthy of considerably more attention than I can give it here. Cardoso does provide a useful outline of the most famous incidents of tax revolts in his dissertation, "The History of Mining in Colonial Brazil," chap. 23.

94. Each *arroba* weighed between twenty-five and thirty-two pounds.

95. "Minas e quintos do ouro," *RAPM* 6 (1901): 858; Cardoso, "The History of Mining in Colonial Brazil," 388.

all slaves, whether they worked in mining or not.[96] The total amount of gold required as payments for the fifths increased in 1722, and the amount of tax per slave changed accordingly.[97] Between 1725 and 1732, the crown chose not to tax slaves for the Royal Fifth, but instead implemented a plan for a smelting house and mint in Vila Rica to increase the sums collected.[98] Still, during this time, the colonists raised a donation to pay for the marriage of the crown prince in Portugal by placing an added tax on all slaves in the captaincy.[99] From 1735 through 1750, the colonial authorities returned to the capitation tax on slaves as the principal means of collecting the Royal Fifth. After 1750, the colonists promised to pay an annual sum of 100 *arrobas* of gold, which was raised principally at locally placed smelting houses. If sufficient sums were not collected at the smelting houses, the colonists collected the remaining quota in the manner of their choice, by levying various taxes on the local population. In keeping with their previous choices, the colonists collected for this remaining quota and other royal taxes imposed in this post-1750 period through duties on commodities and slaves brought into the region and presumably on slaves already living there as well.[100]

Whether or not it was an alternative preferable to even more onerous forms of revenue collection, the taxation of slaves was a burdensome and unfair method of raising the Royal Fifth. Owners paid exactly the same impost on each of their slaves regardless of their productivity. The lucky owner with just a few captive laborers who happened to discover a rich source of gold deposits could pay fewer taxes than an unlucky owner with many captives who may have spent long, relatively fruitless days panning for gold. The capitation method did not tax gold production itself, and it could penalize those who owned many slaves producing very little.[101]

96. "Lista dos escravos . . . para pagarem os reaes quintos de 1720 athé o de 1721," APMCMS, Códice 2.

97. In 1722, the total amount due to the Royal Treasury rose to fifty-two *arrobas*. Cardoso, "The History of Mining in Colonial Brazil," 411.

98. Cardoso, "The History of Mining in Colonial Brazil," 408–30.

99. Cardoso, "The History of Mining in Colonial Brazil," 456.

100. The sum of 100 *arrobas* owed annually for the fifths remained fixed for the duration of the eighteenth century. "Minas e quintos do ouro," *RAPM* 6 (1901): 917–65. An impressive list of royal taxes imposed in addition to the fifth in the post-1750 period can be found in a letter of complaint to the king written by the *câmara* of Marianna on 20 June 1789, in *RAPM* 3 (1898): 68–70. At least one of these taxes, the *subsidio literario*, which lasted for more than twenty years, was a levy on incoming slaves to Minas Gerais. See José João Teixeira Coelho, "Instrucção para o governo da capitania de Minas Gerais," 1780, reprinted in *RAPM* 8 (1903): 501.

101. "A primeyra [dezigualdade] consiste em ser o Lansamento da dita taxa igual a todos

Those who did have many slaves had, however, a better chance of obscuring the exact number they owned from inquiring authorities.[102] Masters did hide their slaves and declared them as fugitives, precisely for the purpose of avoiding the capitation taxes. Bush captains were instructed to hunt both for slaves who had run away and those who were "concealed."[103] Masters whose slaves did not engage in gold extraction may have found it particularly tempting not to register all their slaves; by means of the capitation, they shared the burden of the Royal Fifths and did not profit from the gold. In addition, these masters paid the *dizimo* or 10 percent tithe on all their agricultural produce.[104] They were therefore taxed even more than those who actually extracted the gold.

If the capitation tax disadvantaged the free citizens of Minas Gerais, it also posed problems for treasury officials. In 1724, the Conego João da Motta, a cleric writing to advise the king on the advisability of the capitation system, observed that by this method, the masters engaged in mining in effect paid the fifth only on the gold turned over to them by their slaves. No fifth was then actually paid on the gold that the slaves kept for themselves. Motta asserted that the proportion of gold that the slaves kept to themselves was actually larger than that delivered to their owners and suggested that the Royal Treasury was sorely prejudiced by this arrangement.[105] Another contemporary source suggests that slaves engaged in mining paid to their masters one-half an *oitava* per day each and kept whatever extra gold remained for their own subsistence.[106] If Motta was correct in stating

---

não o sendo o lucro que os mineiros tirão do trabalho dos seus negros, que alguns em poucos dias, e com poucos negros, tirão grandes porções, quando outros com mayor numero de escravos e em muitos mezes ou não tirão couza algua, ou tão pouco, q' apenas lhes excede a despeza q. fizerão," "Sobre o quinto do ouro das Minas Geraes: Parecer do Conego João da Motta," 1724, AHU, Documentos avulsos.

102. "[O]s pobres se queixão de que pagão infalivelmente por todos os seus escravos, quando os ricos só pagão pellos que dão a Rol," "Sobre o quinto do ouro das Minas Geraes: Parecer do Conego João da Motta," 1724, AHU, Documentos avulsos.

103. Carta de patente de João de Barros Pereira, November 1710, APMSC, Códice 7, fol. 36v, cited in Guimarães, "Uma negação," 29; see also Bando do Governador Luis Diogo Lobo da Sylva, 8 April 1764, APMCMS, Códice 35, fols. 79v–87v, paragraph 18.

104. Sobre o quinto do ouro das Minas Geraes: Parecer do Conego João da Motta," 1724, AHU, Documentos avulsos.

105. "A quarta deziguáldade consiste em q. por este modo de Lansamento pagão os Senhores dos escravos do ouro, que lhes dão por convenção e o não cobra a fazenda real do ouro que os ditos escravos tirão por sy sendo q. esta parte comq. os escravos se utilizão se valia em muito maior do que a outra que entregão a seus senhores," Sobre o quinto do ouro das Minas Geraes: Parecer do Conego João da Motta," 1724, AHU, Documentos avulsos.

106. "[N]as ditas Minas se achão ao prezente mais de cincoenta mil negros que nellas

that the portion kept by the slaves exceeded that returned to the masters, then the quantities of gold escaping taxation in this manner were enormous.

The crown had already been aware of this problem, and its remedy, taken at the time the first capitation tax went into effect, was to place a flat tax on all shops and *vendas* (stands) operating in the mining region. The gold the slaves kept for themselves was spent in such places, and the crown was therefore collecting its fifth from the slaves as they made purchases. It is doubtful, however, that the quantities of gold collected by taxing these selling establishments could have approached what was owed to the treasury had the gold produced and kept by slaves been more properly accounted for. Of course, this system of taxing *vendas* and shops also meant that free miners, who were all paying some tax on their slaves, were being taxed yet a second time when they too made purchases at these locations.[107] This multiple form of taxation once again encouraged slave owners to reduce their tax burden by failing to report all the slaves they owned.

No matter what form the collection of the Royal Fifths took in Minas Gerais, the autonomous behavior of their slaves aided the slaveholders in their efforts to avoid paying all the taxes owed to the Portuguese treasury. When the capitation taxes were in force, masters hid their slaves so that they would not be entered onto the official rolls. After 1750, when capitation for the fifths ended and masters were required to bring all gold extracted to the foundry houses located in the capital of each *comarca,* they sent their women vendors to the mining sites to conduct a brisk business in gold that was never accounted for by the royal tax collectors.[108] Although some owners of mining lands clearly objected to the presence of these vendors, it is also possible, in view of the persistence of the problem in the region, that many others found the illegal transactions conducted near

---

trabalhão: cada hum dos quaes ao menos tira meya oitava de ouro cada dia, porque isso he o que pagão a seus senhores, alem do que lhes fica para seu sustento," "Sobre o quinto do ouro das Minas Geraes: Voto de Padre Martinho de Barros," 6 February 1724, AHU, Documentos avulsos.

107. "[N]as ditas logeas comprão pellos mesmos pressos, não só os negros, mas tãobem os senhores, e estes o fazem com o seu ouro já quintado, vem a pagar duas vezes, hua no lansamento dos escravos, outra o das logeas," "Sobre o quinto do ouro das Minas Geraes: Voto de Padre Martinho de Barros," 6 February 1724, AHU, Documentos avulsos.

108. Alvará de 3 de dezembro de 1750, *RAPM* 6(1901): 917–20; Bando do Governador Luis Diogo Lobo da Sylva, 8 April 1764, APMCMS, Códice 35, fols. 79v–87v, paragraphs 10 and 11.

their work sites a convenient outlet for their own undeclared and untaxed gold. Thus, in Minas Gerais, masters of slaves actually promoted and benefited from the "disorders" and "disgraces" committed by their captive laborers.

Conclusion

"Licentious liberty" was undoubtedly an apt description for the condition of slaves in the early decades of the eighteenth century in the captaincy of Minas Gerais and could even have continued to characterize some slaves at the century's close. The slaves of Minas Gerais were often armed and dangerous. They could not be taken for runaways unless they were farther than a league (four miles) from supervision. The slave catchers were prohibited from seeking their prey in the borders of the towns and settlements, so that the mobility of slaves was unhindered and unsupervised in the urban areas. Slaves engaged in mining routinely retained part of the gold they extracted at mining sites. They used it to participate in a widespread clandestine trade fostered and nurtured by slave owners through the employment of their female captives. Runaway slaves plagued the free colonists of the captaincy by committing thefts, kidnappings, and murders along the public roads and even in the settlements themselves. This slave society was clearly not one in which the autonomy and mobility of the captives were successfully repressed.

The efforts to control the slave population of the captaincy were sincere enough, but they were also compromised by conflicts between the free citizenry of Minas Gerais and the crown-appointed officials who governed them. Masters did not comply with decrees calling for them to disarm their slaves because of the simple need to defend themselves from one another and because of their wish to reduce the ability of colonial officials to impose royal authority on them. The actions of colonial governors also failed to serve the end of rigorously controlling the slave population, because they too used armed captives to fight against free citizens and to capture fugitive slaves.

The agents employed by the colonial officials to inhibit slave flights and to capture fugitives were self-interested mercenaries; through their abuses, they became the enemies of masters rather than their allies. Bush captains captured slaves who had not fled and retained them to make use of cost-free labor. With the blessing of the crown, they also destroyed the property of slaveholders by killing slaves who may or may not have resisted capture. Slaveholders responded to such actions by intimidating the bush captains who then became reluctant to pursue fugitives to their death.

The more powerful slaveholders in the captaincy seemed most able to resist the efforts of the colonial governors to regulate the actions of slaves and to reduce their personal mobility and autonomy. These slaveholders could seek and forge alliances with the local administrators of justice who agreed to "adjust" fines for recaptured runaways and release them from the local jails. They probably also induced the local military officials, captains, and sergeants-major to deal directly with them when a captured fugitive was brought in, rather then turning that fugitive over to an unfriendly justice.[109] Such officials, no doubt, looked the other way when taverns and shops remained open after dark to permit runaways and other slaves to sell their stolen goods to free merchants.[110] The degree of autonomy and mobility enjoyed by slaves can probably be directly correlated to the power and standing of their masters. As one group of miners put it in 1732: "Customarily, the slaves in these mines are as rebellious and as daring as their masters are powerful."[111]

The judges appointed to the individual *comarcas* of the captaincy also sometimes chose to protect fellow functionaries rather than punish slaves for crimes they had committed. In August 1750, João Gomes de Mesquita, a soldier stationed in the foundry house in the town of Sabará, sent his slave to work in some pastures where the slave was murdered by a slave belonging to a local justice official, Jozé da Silva Pessoa. At the hearing, the magistrate rejected testimony that placed the blame on Pessoa's slave, with the result that Mesquita received no compensation for his captive's death. To protect his colleague from the payment of this compensation, the judge allowed a slave whom witnesses had declared to be a murderer to go unpunished. Loyalty to friends, allies, and clients was not always compatible with enforcement of the laws intended to control slave actions and to inhibit violent crimes. This act prompted João Gomes de Mesquita to de-

109. Bando do Governador Luis Diogo Lobo da Sylva, 8 April 1764, APMCMS, Códice 35, fols. 79v–87v, paragraph 8.
110. Bando do Governador Luis Diogo Lobo da Sylva, 8 April 1764, APMCMS, Códice 35, fols. 79v–87v, paragraph 12.
111. "E sabido que costumão os escravos nestas minas serem tanto mais revoltozos e ouzados quanto são mais poderosos os seus senhores," Preposta q. fizerão os mineiros de diamantes da comarca do Serro Frio a câmara da mesma comarca, APMSC, Códice 27, fol. 122v.

clare that "in this comarca, in disgrace to Your Majesty and to the prejudice of its residents, justice is administered more in name than in reality."[112] The vulnerable free citizens of Sabará could not rely on any higher authority to protect them from the depredations of those slaves shielded by the influence of powerful masters.

112. "[N]aquelle comarca por desgraça de M. e perjuizo dos moradores se administra a justiça mais no nome que na realidade, Untitled document, beginning "Diz João Gomes de Mesquita soldado da guarnição das minas," 28 March 1753, AHU, Documentos avulsos, caixa 110.

Conclusion

On 19 May 1721, Antônia Calvagante, a free *parda* woman, made an agreement with Manoel Duarte de Crasto "to serve him as his slave in his home in every service that he might order her to perform." This agreement was to take effect immediately, and the arrangement was to last for a period of one year. Antônia Calvagante consented to these terms of her own free will and in exchange for the sum of eighty *oitavas* of gold. For whatever reasons, she contracted for her own enslavement and received payment for her services in advance of their delivery.[1]

Antônia's decision to sell herself into a temporary slavery was unusual and not likely to have been repeated by many other individuals living in the *comarca* of Sabará or elsewhere in the mining region. It, nonetheless, suggests a slave system different from the one we have learned to imagine through the evidence that many historians have presented about the oppressive nature of slave regimes. If the story of Antônia Calvagante suggests a relatively benevolent slave system, one that someone like her could consider at least temporarily acceptable, other evidence gives us a more somber picture of the slave system in eighteenth-century Sabará, one with which historians are more familiar.

In September 1756, for example, Pedro João do Valle Peixoto and his wife Dona Quiteria sold their mining lands on the Rio das Velhas as well as forty slaves. Among the pieces of equipment that went along with this sale of both land and labor was a *tronco*, the Brazilian equivalent of stocks in which disobedient slaves were held prisoner. Also listed among the

---

1. "Antonia Calvagante . . . havia ajustado com o dito Manoel Duarte de Crasto a servirlo como sua escrava de portas adentro de sua casa em todo o serviço que lhe mandasse fazer por oitenta oitavas que havia recibido para o servir na forma que tem dito por tempo de hum ano que corre de hoje em diante," Escriptura de obrigação que faz Antonia Calvagante, molher parda, a Manoel Duarte de Crasto, 19 May 1721, *Livro de notas* (13 abril 1721), MOSMG, fol. 42.

goods being sold was *hua corrente de prender negros com dous collares*, a chain with two collars used for holding recalcitrant captives.[2]

In contrast to Antônia's contract to work as a house servant, the instruments of physical constraint owned by Pedro Peixoto suggest an extreme loss of personal autonomy and a degraded social condition for slaves. The forty captives working for Peixoto knew that their master would lock them up in stocks or place their bodies in chains. Antônia's freedom to limit her period of enslavement also contrasts sharply with the ongoing and indeterminate servitude of Peixoto's slaves as they acquired a new master. Her contract provided a degree of control over her own situation, which was clearly lacking in the situation of the forty slaves continuing to labor as gold miners.

Antônia's contract also suggests that her relationship to her master was distinct from that of the slaves who, in large numbers, toiled to extract gold from mines. As a house servant, the services Antônia was to provide related more to the day-to-day life of the master than the services of those slaves who mined. Antônia therefore probably came to know and to be known by her master better than did the numerous slaves mining for Pedro Peixoto and his wife. The likelihood that her relationship with Manoel Duarte de Crasto took on a personal, intimate, and perhaps sexual nature was also much greater than the likelihood that any of Peixoto's slaves experienced such intimacy. Her enslavement might or might not have been mitigated by such personal ties, whereas the captivity of Peixoto's slaves was surely less likely to have been made less severe by a warm or more humane master-slave relationship.

Other records from colonial Sabará confirm that the master-slave relationships in this frontier, urban mining community were diverse and ranged from the extremely intimate and personal to the most distant and contractual. For example, Genobeba Lourença was a freed Black woman who died in 1752 without heirs. She decided to bequeath her impoverished estate to her former master rather than to the Church or to other friends.[3] Such a decision reveals the importance and the personal nature of her relationship to her former owner. In contrast, the slaves belonging to Thomas Pires da Ponte would not have felt the same loyalty or sympathy for him as Genobeba Lourença felt for her former owner. Luis Mina and his wife

---

2. Escriptura de venda, 23 September 1756, *Livro de notas* (3 julho 1756), MOSMG, fol. 45v.

3. Testamento de Genobeba Lourença, pretta forra, 9 December 1752, APMCMS, Códice 20, fol. 109v.

Jozepha Courana, slaves of Thomas Ponte, were both fortunate enough to secure their own manumissions, as well as the manumissions of their three *crioulo* children, Maria, Joaquim, and Manoel. Ponte, however, had driven a hard bargain for the freedom of this slave family in 1736: the parents had paid him a total of 700 *oitavas* of gold (approximately five and one-half pounds).[4] That Luis Mina and Jozepha Courana were able to negotiate the terms of their own liberation suggests, as Antônia Calvagante's contract also does, that their enslavement was a temporary condition that could be ended. The terms of liberation for Luis Mina and his family were not, however, generous, and this couple or their children most likely felt no gratitude or obligation to their former owner. They simply fulfilled the requirements of a demanding contract and were then free to go their own way.

The contractual forms of enslavement in Sabará, as the Brazilian stocks suggest, did not entirely eliminate the fundamentally coercive nature of the slave regime there but combined with that coercion better met the needs of the masters. Contractual slavery was a product, at least in part, of the organization and structural demands of a mining economy. The mostly male slave population that was actively engaged in the extraction of gold from the *comarca*'s mining fields could not always be strictly supervised as the gold ore was scattered in river beds and streams across considerable distances. Slave owners therefore demanded from slaves who worked as miners a fixed sum per day. Whatever "extra" gold was found belonged to the slaves themselves. It was possible then for slaves working a rich mining site to supplement their food supply and to acquire other goods by purchasing items from itinerant venders. It was also possible for some slaves working in rich mining sites to save the large sums necessary to purchase their manumission. The material conditions of prospecting slaves as well as their physical mobility were therefore not always rigidly defined by their masters' prerogatives.

As in other urban settings, the commercial activities that arose in the context of urban settlements in the *comarca* of Sabará lent themselves to contractual arrangements between slaves and masters, and the slaves in town enjoyed a degree of physical mobility similar to those who labored as miners. Slaves who worked as artisans and vendors in the villages and parishes could not be closely supervised and thus they were legally free to

4. Carta de liberdade, 24 January 1736, *Livro de notas* (2 August de 1735), MOSMG, fol. 107v.

wander through the streets away from their owners. Female slaves, particularly prominent among vendors, as well as male slaves, made agreements with their masters to turn over a portion of their earnings each day. The profits of the masters often depended on the access that enslaved vendors had to mining sites, where they could socialize as well as ply their wares among the prospectors. Masters in Sabará therefore tolerated and even gained by the unrestrained and sometimes illegal commercial activities of the enslaved population in the *comarca*.

The manumission of slaves in Sabará clearly reflected the contractual nature of slavery there. From the perspective of the masters, manumission most often served as an enticement for maintaining the productivity of the labor force. Most enslaved men and women purchased their own freedom with funds saved from their own labors. Because the savings of slaves in some way reflected their commitment to steady and productive work for their masters (because the slaves kept the "extra" earnings each day), masters actually reaped the greatest harvest of gold from those slaves to whom manumission was promised. In selling freedom to their adult captives, the masters in Sabará not only benefited from their captives' hard labor, but also managed to recoup their initial capital investments.

The manumission of Black children in Sabará also reflected the contractual nature of slavery in this *comarca*: masters did not free these children outright, but demanded substantial sums for their manumission. The letters of manumission for children demonstrate that few bonds of affection existed between masters and these youngsters; their mothers provided the funds demanded to pay for the freedom of these young captives. That mothers paid high prices for the liberty of infant children provides eloquent testimony that manumission in this slave society reflected the masters' greed and self-interest, rather than any underlying attitude of benevolence toward their captives.

Those personal ties that did develop out of master-slave relationships in Sabará were a product, at least in part, of the demographic features of the free population in the region, particularly the imbalance in the sex ratio in the free White community. It was mostly single Portuguese men who arrived in Minas Gerais during the boom years of gold production. These men sought and established sexual relationships with the enslaved female population, and mixed-race children were the inevitable result of these unions. For only a few of these women did these relationships bring about their own liberation; more commonly, freedom was bestowed on their children. For the lack of more suitable White heirs, Portuguese masters often chose to recognize their enslaved progeny, free them, and bequeath their estates to them. From these liberated children, the free population of color in Sabará took root and later multiplied.

Characterizing master-slave relationships in colonial Sabará as ranging from harshly coercive to simply contractual to very personal in nature is only the first step in understanding the complexity of the interactions between the free and nonfree populations in this *comarca*. Masters and slaves did not confront one another as united blocks because there were important divisions in each community. On the side of the masters, there were differences in wealth, social status, race, and sex. Masters had different economic interests in the mining region; some were engaged primarily in mining, others in commerce, and still others in agriculture. Some masters clearly developed some alliances with their slaves, through the personal ties of concubinage, through their children by slave mothers, and through their use of slaves as armed defenders of themselves and their mining lands. Inheritances from parents and widowhood increasingly brought women into the roles of slaveholders in Sabará with their own interests and strategies for controlling enslaved property. Slaves were also divided among themselves because of their ethnic origins, because of the alliances that they made with individual members of the free community, sometimes through ties of coparentage, and because of the willingness of some to become masters of slaves themselves. The lines that theoretically separated slaves from free people in this slave society were frequently blurred and could to a certain degree be completely crossed.

The free-settler conflicts characteristic of the mining region were particularly significant in allowing the divisions separating slaves from free individuals to be flexible and even surmountable at times. Free settlers competed with one another for access to, or control of, the best mining lands. Such competition led masters to defend their claims with arms and with an armed slave-labor force. Although the colonial governors paid lip service to the idea of disarming the slave population in Minas Gerais, they too were not averse to using armed slaves, either to pursue runaways or to put down rebellions of the free settlers. The participation of armed slaves in the disputes of free settlers also indicates that loyalties in the slave community in the region could be divided.

An armed slave population that was not effectively opposed by a united free-settler population led to the proliferation of runaway slave communities that were difficult to destroy and that gave haven to fugitives who regularly harassed free people traveling on the *comarca*'s roadways. Banditry, violent crimes, and a continuing trade in stolen goods resulted from the success of the runaway slaves in maintaining themselves in the hinterlands of established communities in Sabará. Their successes also encouraged and were abetted by free colonists who secretly profited from sales of goods and ammunition to the runaways.

The ineffectiveness of the efforts to reduce the disorderliness of slave life in Sabará can be seen in the continuing prohibitions against the activities of enslaved women who sold goods at mining sites and served as fences for the stolen items brought to them by runaways and other nonfugitive slaves living nearby. That such women could not be forced to curtail their illegal activities indicates the frailty of means available to local officials to enforce laws that were opposed by the local slave-owning population. Masters who sent their slaves to sell at these locations clearly did not fear retribution or punishment from law-enforcement agents.

The mercenary agents of fugitive slave control, the *capitães do mato*, were also not completely committed to eliminating runaway slaves from the *comarca* of Sabará. Mercenary agents did not always seek out slaves who were definitely runaways, but were content to capture any slave, fugitive or not, and to collect a fee for doing so. These bush captains also sometimes chose to hide runaways from both local officials and masters to profit from the labor of these captives. Although the records make clear that some bush captains did capture and kill runaway slaves in Sabará, they often did so at the risk of alienating local slaveholders, and many became reluctant to aggressively pursue fugitives for this reason.

The efforts of powerful slave owners to resist payment of taxes in the mining region of Brazil during the eighteenth century placed them in constant conflict with the governing colonial authorities of the captaincy. These efforts (hiding the slaves, sending slaves to participate in an illegal and untaxed clandestine economy, and arming slaves to defend land, gold, etc.) illustrate how the colonial relationship between free miners and crown officials shaped the master-slave relationship. All the actions that masters directed against the colonial government obviously affected the lives of their captives used in these actions. Partly because of the antagonism that characterized crown-colonist ties in Minas Gerais, slaves could be hidden with their masters' or other masters' consent. They could sell or buy food, goods, ammunition, and sex, all with their master's approval and encouragement. They could bear arms and attack free persons, sometimes even at the behest of their owners. Moreover, they turned their masters' permission into a license to pursue each of these practices for their own personal motives.

The autonomy of slaves in Sabará, Minas Gerais, was undoubtedly increased by the fact that many, or some, or perhaps just the most powerful masters in the *comarca* used slaves to defend their personal interests against those of the colonial government. Masters gave their slaves permission and encouragement to defy local law-enforcement officials because this suited their own needs. Slaves in Sabará, however, did more than simply enjoy the leeway that masters allowed to them and otherwise remain placid and loyal servants to their rather unpatriotic and tax-defrauding owners. They ran when they could; they stole money and goods when they could; they hoarded as much gold as possible to make their own lives better and, if possible, to escape from slavery through manumission. They became even more disorderly than most masters wanted them to be. Masters did not completely unite with colonial officials to effectively combat this disorderliness, because both gold and power were at risk for them in such a union.

The result of free-settler conflicts among themselves and free-settler conflicts with the Portuguese crown officials was not the complete autonomy of slaves or the elimination of slavery from the *comarca* of Sabará or from Minas Gerais as a whole. In 1805, 54 percent of the captaincy's population was still legally enslaved, but of those who were free, nearly two-thirds were non-Whites, either Black or mulatto.[5] Although it is not possible at this time to determine the proportion of Whites in the free population in plantation areas of Bahia, it seems likely that it was not so demonstrably non-White as the free population in Minas Gerais.[6] In any case, the proportion of the total population that was made up of free individuals of color in the mining region was ten times larger than that in the plantation areas in early nineteenth-century Jamaica or the U.S. South.[7]

The eventual emergence of a large free population of color in Sabará, and in Minas Gerais as a whole, does not necessarily mean that free White colonists and free White colonial officials accepted or entirely approved of this development. It certainly should not be mistaken for evidence of the willingness of free Whites to treat people of color as their equals. The slave society of Sabará had, from the very start, a highly stratified social struc-

5. "População da provincia de Minas Gerais," 294.

6. In Bahia in 1816–17, 30.8 percent of the population were enslaved. Schwartz guesses that 40 percent of this population was composed of free people of color, but he bases this guess on 1821 census data from Minas Gerais. See *Sugar Plantations in the Formation of Brazilian Society*, 462, and note 57 on that page.

7. Schwartz, *Sugar Plantations in the Formation of Brazilian Society*, 462–63. In Jamaica in 1832, 3 percent of the total population were free people of color; in the U.S. South in 1820, this figure was 3.4 percent.

ture. Although in 1805 only 19 percent of the population of the entire captaincy was White, a large proportion of these Whites made up a small but powerful economic and social elite whose status was not seriously threatened by the relatively poor free people of color. These Whites did not have to view people of color as their equals simply because they were free.

The existence of this free population of color in the *comarca* does not imply that Whites in the mining region did not express racial prejudice against darker-skinned individuals. Free males clearly preferred lighter-skinned women as concubines, and when White heirs became more of a possibility in the second half of the eighteenth century, White fathers increasingly ceased to favor their mulatto progeny as they had earlier by freeing them from slavery. The fact that masters demanded that mothers purchase the freedom of their Black children rather than freeing those Black children outright probably also reflects a basic prejudice against dark-skinned children as opposed to light-skinned ones. A free population of non-Whites in Sabará did not mean a free population unconscious of the issue of race.

In official circles at least, active opposition to upward social mobility for Blacks and mulattos did exist. In the early decades of the eighteenth century, the Count of Assumar spoke out vigorously against the phenomenon of freed Blacks and mulattos in the mining region.[8] A royal order of 1726 apparently responded to complaints about mulattos holding municipal offices in Minas Gerais by prohibiting this practice.[9] There was also, in 1723, a proposal put to the king to prohibit mulattos in Minas Gerais from being able to inherit from their White fathers. The king's counselor, João Pedro de Lanzozo, argued against this law by saying that not only would it contravene existing laws allowing illegitimate children to inherit, but it would also be impossible to enforce because the measure was to take effect only in the captaincy of Minas Gerais. The counselor did not defend the phenomenon of *mulatismo* in Minas Gerais; he simply thought that the efforts to combat it would be unsuccessful.[10]

The existence of forms of slavery that were contractual or shaped by

---

8. Bando do Governador D. Pedro de Almeida, 21 November 1719, APMSC, Códice 11, fol. 283, cited by Ramos, "A Social History of Ouro Preto," 229.

9. Royal order, 27 January 1726, APMSC, Códice 3, fol. 29v, cited by Ramos, "A Social History of Ouro Preto," 165.

10. Untitled document, beginning "Do conselheyro João Pedro de Lanzozo lhe parece q. a pretendida ley contra o mulatismo das Minas," 6 August 1723, AHU, Minas Gerais, Documentos avulsos, caixa 2, not paged, a loose document in an uncatalogued box.

very personal master-slave relationships and the concomitant development of a large slave-descendant free population in Sabará and Minas Gerais did not exclude racism as a factor that determined the lives of slaves or the exact status of a free or freed individual of color. Free persons of color in the mining region were not treated in the same manner as free Whites. The experience of Manoel da Cruz, a free *pardo* shoemaker living in the capital of the captaincy in 1723, provides a good example of this kind of racial discrimination. Cruz, who was married to a White woman, was accused by Manoel Ribeiro, presumably a free White, of stealing a mulatto slave child. The local judge, on hearing the accusation, imprisoned Cruz without condemning him for the crime. Cruz attempted to escape, and when he was recaptured, he was brought to the whipping post in the town center. He was beaten at the post with a rawhide whip "in indecent parts where masters customarily punished their slaves." Following this punishment, Cruz apparently fled the mining region, abandoning his shoemaking business.[11]

The experience of Cruz at the hands of local justice officials was undoubtedly related to his being a free man of color. At that time, no White shoemaker would have been imprisoned without a hearing and whipped *as a slave would be whipped* in the center of town. The reaction that Cruz elicited from the local justice may well have been related to the fact of his marriage to a White woman and to the objections of local White males to the rare phenomenon of a White woman married to a colored man. It is also possible, however, that non-White males who were not wealthy were regularly discriminated against in the mining region.[12]

Some slaves in colonial Sabará, perhaps even most of them, shared the deprivations and cruel treatment of slaves elsewhere in Brazil or the New World; they could be whipped at the posts erected in the squares of every urban center in the region, and they could be placed in chains or stocks by their masters. Yet, the slavery that developed in the *comarca* of Sabará in the captaincy of Minas Gerais during the eighteenth century was also specific to the evolution of the gold-mining economy located there and to the interactions of free masters with Portuguese colonial authorities and the larger colonial system. The Portuguese patterns of free male migration and

11. Petition of Manoel da Cruz to the king, 13 July 1723, AHU, Minas Gerais, Documentos Avulsos, Caixa 3, no pages, a loose document in an uncatalogued box.

12. The fact that Manoel da Cruz sought redress for his treatment at the hands of local officials may also have been related to the fact of his marriage to a White woman, which might have served as confirmation of his higher standing in the community.

importation of mostly male slaves, especially in the initial decades of the eighteenth century, were both intensified by the masculine character of a mining economy and, in turn, the resulting demographic characteristics of the comarca shaped master-slave relationships, crown-colonist relations, and the various circumstances of enslaved men and women for generations to come. Economy, demography, and free-settler conflicts (all richly informed by perceived gender norms) thus combined in this frontier colony to provide more widely available opportunities for autonomy for slaves than existed in large-scale plantation economies elsewhere in Brazil or in other parts of the New World. The slaves who came to Sabará pursued these opportunities with great vigor and helped to create the "disorderly" slave society that so many masters in this mining region objected to, and yet could not "re-order" except at the expense of their own freedom.

Appendix

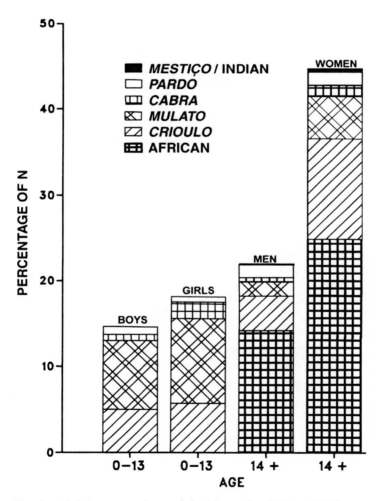

Fig. A.   Origin, age, and sex of the Manumitted (N = 1011)

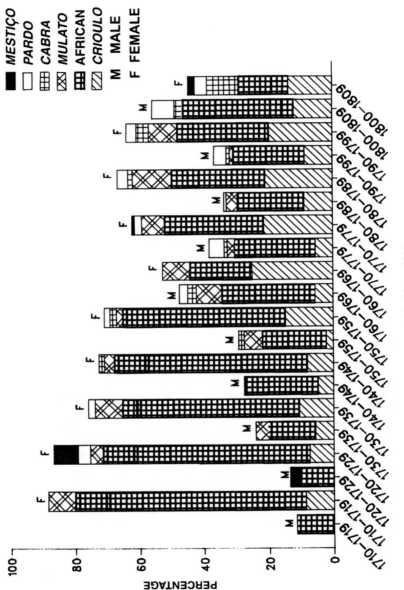

Fig. B. Origin/race of adult Manumittees, 1710–1809 (N = 681)

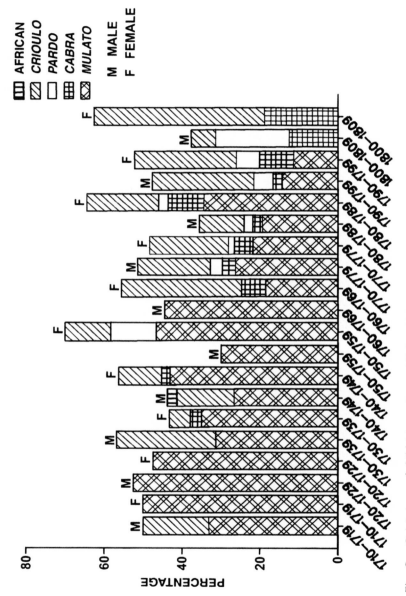

Fig. C. Origin/race of child Manumittees, 1710–1809 (N = 330)

Sources

Works frequently cited in the bibliography, notes, tables, and figures are identified by the following abbreviations:

AHU	Arquivo Histórico Ultramarino
APMCMS	Arquivo Público Mineiro, Câmara municipal de Sabará
APMSC	Arquivo Público Mineiro, Secção colonial
DI	*Documentos interessantes para a história e costumes de Sào Paulo*
HAHR	*Hispanic-American Historical Review*
LARR	*Latin American Research Review*
MOSMG	Museu do Ouro de Sabará, Minas Gerais
RAPM	*Revista do Arquivo Público Mineiro*
RIHGB	*Revista do Instituto Histórico e Geográfico Brasileiro*

In citing works in the notes, figures, and tables, short titles have generally been used after the first full citation of works listed here in full.

ARCHIVES

Lisbon

Arquivo Histórico Ultramarino:
   Minas Gerais, Documentos Avulsos—Uncatalogued loose documents that mostly represent copies of reports and correspondence sent from officials in Minas Gerais to the king of Portugal.

Minas Gerais

Arquivo Público Mineiro, Belo Horizonte:
   Secção colonial—Catalogued and uncatalogued official correspondence and reports of colonial governors to local officials and superiors in Bahia, Rio de Janeiro, and Lisbon.
   Câmara municipal de Sabará—Correspondence and records of the town council of Sabará, including sales, licenses, tax assessments, slave registrations, wills, contracts.
Cúria Municipal de Belo Horizonte: Parish records for the *comarca* of Sabará,

including baptisms, and records from the Visitor, Lourenço José de Queiroz Coimbra, about transgressions of the population.

Museu do Ouro, Sabará: Notarial records for the *comarca* of Sabará, including letters of manumissions, sales, contracts, wills, and inventories.

PRINTED SOURCES

Almeida, Lucia Machado de. *Passeio a Sabará.* São Paulo: Livraria Martins, 1956.

Antonil, André João. *Cultura e opulência do Brasil, por suas drogas e minas.* Lisbon, 1711. Rpt. São Paulo: Companhia Melhoramentos, 1976.

Bakewell, Peter. *Silver Mining and Society in Colonial Mexico: Zacatecas, 1546–1700.* Cambridge: Cambridge University Press, 1971.

Barbosa, Waldemar de Almeida. *Negros e quilombos em Minas Gerais.* Belo Horizonte, 1972.

Bazin, Germain. *L'Architecture religieuse baroque au Brésil.* 2 vols. Paris: Plon, 1956.

Bergad, Laird W. "After the Mining Boom: Demographic and Economic Aspects of Slavery in Mariana, Minas Gerais, 1750–1808." *LARR* 31:1 (1996): 67–97.

Bethel, Leslie, ed. *Colonial Spanish America.* Cambridge: Cambridge University Press, 1987.

Blank, Stephanie. "Patrons, Clients, and Kin in Seventeenth-Century Caracas: A Methodological Essay in Colonial Spanish American History." *HAHR* 54 (May 1974): 260–83.

Bloch, M., and S. Gugenheim. "Compadrazgo, Baptism, and the Symbolism of a Second Birth." *Man* 16 (Spring 1981): 376–86.

Boschi, Caio César. "As visitas diocesanos e a Inquisição na colônia." *Revista brasileira de história* 7, no. 14 (March 1987):151–79.

———. *Os leigos e o poder: Irmandades leigas e política colonizadora em Minas Gerais.* São Paulo: Editora Atica, 1986.

Bowser, Frederick P. "The Free Persons of Color in Lima and Mexico City: Manumission and Opportunity, 1580–1650." In *Race and Slavery in the Western Hemisphere: Quantitative Studies*, edited by Stanley L. Engerman and Eugene D. Genovese. Princeton: Princeton University Press, 1974.

Boxer, Charles R. *The Golden Age of Brazil, 1695–1750: Growing Pains of a Colonial Society.* Berkeley and Los Angeles: University of California Press, 1962.

Brana-Shute, Rosemary. "Approaching Freedom: The Manumission of Slaves In Suriname, 1760–1808." *Slavery and Abolition* 10 (December 1989): 40–63.

———. "The Manumission of Slaves In Suriname, 1760–1828." Ph.D. diss., University of Florida, 1985.

Cano, Wilson. "Economía do ouro em Minas Gerais (século XVIII)." *Contexto* 3 (1977): 91–109.

Cardoso, Fernando Henrique. *Capitalismo e escravidão no Brasil meridional, o negro na sociedade escravocrata.* 2d ed. São Paulo: Paz e Terra, 1977.

Cardoso, Manoel da Silveira. "The Collection of the Fifths in Brazil, 1695–1709." *HAHR* 20 (August 1940): 359–79.

————. "The History of Mining in Colonial Brazil, 1500–1750." Ph.D. diss., Stanford University, 1940.

Carneiro, Edison. *O quilombo de Palmares*. São Paulo: Nacional, 1958.

Castro, Antônio Barros de. "A economia política, o capitalismo e a escravidão." In *Os modos de produção e realidade brasileira*, edited by José Roberto Amaral Lapa. Petrópolis: Vozes, 1980, 67–107.

Chaloub, Sidney. "Slaves, Freemen, and the Politics of Freedom in Brazil: The Experience of Blacks in the City of Rio." *Slavery and Abolition* 10 (December 1989): 64–84.

Coelho, José João Teixeira. "Instrucção para o governo da capitania de Minas Gerais," 1780. Reprinted in *RAPM* 8 (1903): 399–581.

Cohen, David W., and Jack P. Greene, eds. *Neither Slave Nor Free: The Freedmen of African Descent in the Slave Societies of the New World*. Baltimore: Johns Hopkins University Press, 1972.

Conrad, Robert E., ed. *Children of God's Fire: A Documentary History of Black Slavery in Brazil*. Princeton: Princeton University Press, 1983.

Constituições primeiras do arcebispado da Bahía, feitas e ordenadas pelo ilustríssimo e reverendíssimo senhor Sebastião Monteiro da Vide bispo do dito arcebispado, e do conselho de sua magestade, propostas e aceitas em o synodo diocesano que o dito senhor celebrou em 12 de junho do anno 1707. São Paulo: Typografia 2 de dezembro, 1853.

Costa, Emília Viotti da. *Crowns of Glory, Tears of Blood: The Demarara Slave Rebellion of 1823*. New York: Oxford University Press, 1994.

————. *Da senzala á colônia*. 2d ed. São Paulo: Livraria Editora Ciências Humanas, 1982.

Costa, Iraci del Nero da. *Minas Gerais: Estruturas populacionais típicas*. São Paulo: Edec, 1982.

————. *Vila Rica: População (1719–1826)*. São Paulo: IPE/USP, 1979.

Craton, Michael. *Testing the Chains: Resistance to Slavery in the British West Indies*. Ithaca: Cornell University Press, 1982.

Cunha, Manuela Carneiro da. "'On the Amelioration of Slavery' by Henry Koster." *Slavery and Abolition* 11(December 1990): 368–76.

Curtin, Philip. *The Atlantic Slave Trade: A Census*. Madison: University of Wisconsin Press, 1969.

Davis, David Brion. *The Problem of Slavery in Western Culture*. Ithaca: Cornell University Press, 1966.

Dean, Warren. *Rio Claro, a Brazilian Plantation System*. Palo Alto, Calif.: Stanford University Press, 1974.

Dorr, John Van N. II. "Physiographic, Stratigraphic, and Structural Development of the Quadrilátero Ferrífero, Minas Gerais, Brazil." *U.S. Geological Service Professional Paper* 641–a.

Eakin, Marshall. "Nova Lima: Life, Labor, and Technology in an Anglo-Brazilian Mining Community." Ph.D. diss., University of California, 1981.

Ellis Júnior, Alfredo. *Meio século de bandeirismo (1590–1640)*. São Paulo: Revistas dos Tribunais, 1939.

————. *O bandeirismo paulista e o recuo meridiano*. São Paulo: Companhia Editora Nacional, 1936.

Ellis, Myriam. "As bandeiras na expansão geográfico do Brasil." In *História ger al da civilização brasileira*, edited by Sérgio Buarque de Holanda, tomo 1, vol. 1. São Paulo: Difel, 1981, 273–96.

Engerman, Stanley L., and Eugene D. Genovese, eds. *Race and Slavery in the Western Hemisphere: Quantitative Studies*. Princeton: Princeton University Press, 1974.

Eschwege, W. L. von. *Pluto brasiliensis*, translated by Domício de Figueiredo Murta. Berlin, 1833. Rpt. São Paulo: Livraria Itatiaia Editora, 1979.

Faoro, Raymundo. *Os donos do poder: Formação do patronato brasileiro*. 5th ed. Porto Alegre: Globo, 1979.

Fernandes, Florestan. *O negro no mundo dos brancos*. São Paulo, 1972.

Ferreyra, Luis Gomes. *Erario mineral*. Lisbon: Impressor do Senhor Patriarca, 1735.

Figueiredo, Luciano Raposo de Almeida. "Barrocas familias: Vida familiar em Minas Gerais no seculo XVIII." Master's thesis, University of São Paulo, 1989.

Foner, Laura, and Eugene D. Genovese, eds. *Slavery in the New World: A Reader in Comparative History*. Englewood Cliffs, N.J.: Prentice-Hall, Inc., 1969.

Freyre, Gilberto. *The Masters and the Slaves: A Study in the Development of Brazilian Civilization*, translated by Samuel Putnam. New York: Knopf, 1946.

Gorender, Jacob. *A escravidão reabilitada*. São Paulo: Editora Atica, 1990.

———. *O escravismo colonial*. São Paulo: Editora Atica, 1978.

Gudeman, Stephen, and Stuart Schwartz. "Cleansing Original Sin: Godparenthood and the Baptism of Slaves in Eighteenth-Century Bahia." In Raymond T. Smith, ed., *Kinship Ideology and Practice in Latin America*. Chapel Hill: University of North Carolina Press, 1984.

Guimarães, Carlos Magno. "Uma negação da ordem escravista: Quilombos em Minas Gerais no século XVIII." Master's thesis, Universidade Federal de Minas Gerais, 1983.

———. *Uma negação da ordem escravista: Quilombos em Minas Gerais no século XVIII*. São Paulo: Icone, 1988.

Handler, Jerome S., and John T. Pohlman. "Slave Manumissions and Freedmen in Seventeenth-Century Barbados." *William and Mary Quarterly* 41: 3 (1984): 390–408.

Hemming, John. *Red Gold: The Conquest of the Brazilian Indians, 1500–1760*. Cambridge, Mass.: Harvard University Press, 1978.

Higgins, Kathleen J. "The Slave Society in Eighteenth-Century Sabará: A Community Study in Colonial Brazil." Ph.D. diss., Yale University, 1987.

Hoornaert, Eduardo. "The Catholic Church in Colonial Brazil." In Leslie Bethell, ed., *The Cambridge History of Latin America*. Cambridge: Cambridge University Press, 1984.

———. *Formação do catolicismo brasileiro (1500–1800)*. 2d ed. Petrópolis: Vozes, 1978.

Ianni, Octávio. *As metamorfoses de escravo: Apogeu e crise no Brasil meridional*. São Paulo, 1962.

Johnson, Lyman L. "Manumission in Colonial Buenos Aires." *HAHR* 59 (May 1979): 258–79.

Karasch, Mary Catherine. *Slave Life in Rio de Janeiro, 1808–1850*. Princeton: Princeton University Press, 1987.

Kiemen, Mathias. *The Indian Policy of Portugal in the Amazon Region, 1614–1693*. Washington, D.C.: Catholic University Press, 1954.

Kiernan, James Patrick. "The Manumission of Slaves in Paraty, Brazil, 1789–1822." Ph.D. diss., New York University, 1976.

Klein, Herbert S. *African Slavery in Latin America and the Caribbean*. New York: Oxford University Press, 1986.

———. *The Middle Passage*. Princeton: Princeton University Press, 1978.

———. "The Portuguese Slave Trade from Angola in the Eighteenth Century." *Journal of Economic History* 32 (December 1972): 894–918.

———. *Slavery in the Americas: A Comparative Study of Virginia and Cuba*. Chicago: University of Chicago Press, 1967.

Koster, Henry. *Travels in Brazil*. 2 vols. Philadelphia, 1817.

Kuznesof, Elizabeth Anne. "Sexual Politics, Race, and Bastard-Bearing in Nineteenth-Century Brazil: A Question of Culture or Power." *Journal of Family History* 16:3 (1991): 241–60.

———. "Sexuality, Gender, and the Family in Colonial Brazil." *Luso-Brazilian Review* 30:1 (1993): 119–31.

Lange, Curt Francisco. "A música barroca." In *História geral da civilização brasileira*, edited by Sérgio Buarque de Holanda, tomo 1, vol. 2. São Paulo: Difel, 1981, 121–44.

Latif, Miran de Barros. *As Minas Gerais*. Rio de Janeiro: Agir, 1960.

Leme, Pedro Taques de Almeida Paes. "Informações das minas de São Paulo e dos sertões da sua capitania desde o ano de 1597, até o presente de 1772, com relação cronológica dos administradores delas." In *Noticias das minas de São Paulo e dos sertões da mesma capitania*, edited by Afonso d'Escragnole Taunay. Rpt. Belo Horizonte: Editora Itatiaia Limitada, 1980.

Lewin, Linda. "Natural and Spurious Children In Brazilian Inheritance Law from Colony to Nation: A Methodological Essay." *The Americas* 48 (January 1992): 351–96.

Libby, Douglas Cole. *Transformação do trabalho em uma economia escravista Minas Gerais no seculo XIX*. São Paulo: Editora Brasiliense, 1988.

Lima Júnior, Augusto de. *A capitania das Minas Gerais*. 1943. Rpt. Belo Horizonte: Livraria Itatiaia Editora, 1978.

Londoño, Francisco Torres. "Público e escándoloso: Igreja e concubinato no antigo Bispado do Rio de Janeiro." Ph.D. diss., University of São Paulo, 1992.

Lovejoy, Paul E. "The Impact of the Atlantic Slave Trade on Africa: A Review of the Literature." *Journal of African History* 30 (1989): 365–94.

Lovejoy, Paul E., ed. *Africans in Bondage: Studies in Slavery and the Slave Trade*. Madison: University of Wisconsin Press, 1986.

Luna, Francisco Vidal, and Iraci del Nero da Costa. "Devassa nas Minas Gerais: Observações sobre casos de concubinato." *Anais do museu paulista* 31 (1982): 221–33.

———. *Minas colonial: Economia e sociedade*. São Paulo: FIPE, 1982.

———. *Minas Gerais: Eescravos e senhores, analise da estrutura populacional e econômica de alguns centros mineratorios (1718–1804)*. São Paulo: IPE, 1981.

———. "A presença do elemento forro no conjunto de proprietários de escravos." *Ciência e cultura* 32 (July1980): 836–41.

Lynch, Joseph H. *Godparents and Kinship in Early Medieval Europe*. Princeton: Princeton University Press, 1986.

Machado Filho, Aires da Mata. *O negro e o garimpo em Minas Gerais*. Rio de Janeiro: José Olympio, 1943.

Marchant, Alexander. *From Barter to Slavery*. Baltimore: Johns Hopkins University Press, 1942.

Marcílio, Maria Luiza. *A cidade de São Paulo: Povoamento e população, 1750–1850*. São Paulo: Pioneira, 1974.

Mattoso, Katia M. Queirós. "A propósito de cartas da Alforria na Bahia, 1779–1850." *Anais de historia* 4 (1972): 23–25.

―――. *Ser escravo no Brasil* [To be a slave]. São Paulo: Brasiliense, 1982.

Mauro, Frederic. *Nova história e novo mundo*. São Paulo: Editôra Perspectiva, 1969.

Mawe, John. *Viagens ao interior do Brasil*, translated by Selena Benevides Vianna, 1812. Rpt. Belo Horizonte: Editora Itatiaia Limitada, 1978.

Maxwell, Kenneth R. *Conflicts and Conspiracies: Brazil and Portugal, 1750–1808*. Cambridge: Cambridge University Press, 1973.

Metcalf, Alida C. *Family and Frontier in Colonial Brazil, Santana de Parnaíba, 1580–1822*. Berkeley and Los Angeles: University of California Press, 1992.

―――. "Women and Means: Women and Family Property in Colonial Brazil." *Journal of Social History* 24 (Winter 1990): 277–98.

Miller, Joseph. *Way of Death: Merchant Capitalism and the Angolan Slave Trade, 1730–1830*. Madison: University of Wisconsin Press, 1988.

Mintz, Sidney W., and Eric R. Wolf. "An Analysis of Ritual Co-Parenthood (Compadrazgo)." *Southwestern Journal of Anthropology* 6:4 (1950): 341–65.

Monteiro, John. *Negros da terra: Indios e bandeirantes nas origens de São Paulo, Brasil*. São Paulo: Companhia das Letras, 1994.

―――. "São Paulo in the Seventeenth Century: Economy and Society." Ph.D. diss., University of Chicago, Illinois 1985.

Morgan, Edmund S. *American Slavery, American Freedom: The Ordeal of Colonial Virginia*. New York: W. W. Norton & Co., 1975.

Morse, Richard, ed. *The Bandeirantes: The Historical Role of the Brazilian Pathfinders*. New York: Alfred Knopf, 1965.

Moura, Clovis. *Rebeliões da senzala, quilombos, insurreições, guerrilhas*. 2d ed. Rio de Janeiro: Conquista, 1972.

Mulvey, Patricia. "Slave Confraternities in Brazil: Their Role in Colonial Society." *The Americas* 39 (July 1982): 39–68.

Nazzari, Muriel. "Concubinage in Colonial Brazil: The Inequalities of Race, Class, and Gender." *Journal of Family History* 21 (April 1996): 107–23.

―――. *The Disappearance of the Dowry: Women, Families, and Social Change in São Paulo, Brazil (1600–1900)*. Palo Alto, Calif.: Stanford University Press, 1991.

Nishida, Mieko. "Manumission and Ethnicity in Urban Slavery: Salvador, Brazil, 1808–1888." *HAHR* 73 (August 93): 361–91.

Novais, Fernando. *Portugal e Brasil na crise do antigo sistema colonial (1777–1808)*. 2d ed. São Paulo: Editora Hucitec, 1981.

Nutini, Hugo G., and Betty Bell. *Ritual Kinship: The Structure and Historical Development of the Compadrazgo System in Rural Tlaxcala*. 2 vols. Princeton: Princeton University Press, 1980 and 1984.

Ordenações do Senhor Rey D. Affonso V. 5 vols. Coimbra: Real Imprensa da Universidade, 1792.

Ordenações filipinas, ordenções e leis do reino de Portugal recopiladas por mandato d'el Rei D. Felipe, o primeiro, edited by Fernando H. Mendes de Almeida. 5 vols. Rpt. São Paulo: Edição Saraiva, 1960.

Passos, Zorastro Viana. *Em torno da historia de Sabará.* Vol. 1, Rio de Janeiro: Sphan, Mec, 1940; vol. 2, Belo Horizonte: Imprensa Ofcial de Minas Gerais, 1942.

Pinto, Virgílio Noya. *O ouro brasileiro e o comércio anglo-português.* 2d ed. São Paulo: Companhia Editora Nacional, 1979.

Pires, Simeão Ribeiro. *Raízes de minas.* Belo Horizonte: Minas Gráfica Editora, 1979.

Pontes, Manoel José Pires da Silva, ed. "Revisão dos regimentos das minas do imperio do Brasil, com notas e observações do guarda mor geral das minas na provincia de Minas Geraes." *RAPM* 7 (1902): 834–48.

"População da provincia de Minas Gerais." *RAPM* 4 (1899): 294–95.

Price, Richard, ed. *Maroon Societies: Rebel Slave Communities in the Americas.* Baltimore: Johns Hopkins University Press, 1979.

Prieto, Carlos. *A mineração e o Novo Mundo.* São Paulo: Cultrix, 1976.

Raboteau, Albert J. *Slave Religion: The Invisible Institution in the Antebellum South.* New York: Oxford University Press, 1978.

Ramos, Donald. "From Minho to Minas: The Portuguese Roots of the Mineiro Family." *HAHR* 73 (November 1993): 639–62.

———. "Marriage and the Family in Colonial Vila Rica." *HAHR* 55 (May 1975): 200–225.

———. "Single and Married Women in Vila Rica, Brazil, 1754–1838." *Journal of Family History* 16:3 (1991) 261–82.

———. "A Social History of Ouro Preto: Stresses of Dynamic Urbanization in Colonial Brazil, 1695–1726." Ph.D. diss., University of Florida, 1972.

"Regimento das minas do ouro de 1702." Ministerio da Educação e Saude, Biblioteca Nacional, *Documentos históricos* 80 (1948): 329–44.

"Regimento de sua majestade para as minas do sul, 7 June 1644." *RIHGB* 56 p.Ia, 110–11.

"Regimento dos capitães do matto, 17 December 1722." *RAPM* 2 (1897): 389–91.

Reis, João José. "Slave Rebellion in Brazil: The African Muslim Uprising in Bahia, 1835." Ph.D. diss., University of Minnesota, 1982.

Reis, João José, and Flávio dos Santos Gomes. *Liberdade por um fio: História dos quilombos no Brasil.* São Paulo: Companhia das Letras, 1996.

Ricards, Sherman L., Jr. "A Demographic History of the West: Butte County, California, 1850." *Papers of the Michigan Academy of Science, Arts, and Letters* 46 (1961): 469–91.

Rocha, José Joaquim. "Memória histórica da capitania de Minas Gerais." *RAPM* 2 (1897): 425–517.

Rodrigues, Raymundo Nina. *Os Africanos no Brazil.* São Paulo: Companhia Editora Nacional, 1932.

Russell-Wood, A. J. R. *The Black Man in Slavery and Freedom in Colonial Brazil.* New York: St. Martin's Press, 1982.

————. *Fidalgos and Filanthropists: The Santa Casa de Misericórdia of Bahía, 1550–1755.* Berkeley and Los Angeles: University of California Press, 1968.

————. "Prestige, Power, and Piety in Colonial Brazil: The Third Orders of Salvador." *HAHR* 69:1 (1989): 61–89.

————. "Technology and Society: The Impact of Gold-Mining on the Institution of Slavery in Portuguese America." *Journal of Economic History* 37 (March 1977): 59–82.

Scarano, Julita. "Black Brotherhoods: Integration or Contradiction?" *Luso-Brazilian Review* 16 (Summer 1979): 1–17.

————. *Devoção e escravidão: A irmandade de Nossa Senhora do Rosário dos pretos no distrito diamantino.* 2d ed. São Paulo: Companhia Editora Nacional, 1978.

Schwartz, Stuart B. "Indian Labor and New World Plantations: European Demands and Indian Responses in Northeastern Brazil." *American Historical Review* 83:1 (1978): 43–79.

————. "The Mocambo: Slave Resistance in Colonial Bahia." *Journal of Social History* 3 (Summer 1970): 313–33.

————. "The Manumission of Slaves in Colonial Brazil: Bahia, 1684–1745." *HAHR* 54 (November 1974): 603–35.

————. *Sovereignty and Society in Colonial Brazil: The High Court of Bahia and Its Judges, 1609–1751.* Berkeley and Los Angeles: University of California Press, 1973.

————. *Sugar Plantations in the Formation of Brazilian Society: Bahia, 1550–1835.* New York: Cambridge University Press, 1985.

Schwartz, Stuart B., ed. *Slaves, Peasants, and Rebels: Reconsidering Brazilian Slavery.* Champaign-Urbana: University of Illinois Press, 1992.

Silva, Antonio de Moraes. *Dicionario da lingua portugueza.* 6th ed. Edited by Agostinho de Mendonça Falcão. Lisbon: Typographia de Antonio José da Rocha, 1858.

Silva, José Justino de Andrade e. *Colleção chronológica da legislação portuguesa compilada e annotada.* 10 vols. Lisbon: Imprensa Nacional, 1859.

Silva, Maria Beatriz Nizza da. *Sistema de casamento no Brasil colonial.* São Paulo: USP, 1984.

Southey, Robert. *History of Brazil.* 3 vols. London: 1810–19.

Souza, Laura de Mello e. *Os desclassificados do ouro: A pobreza mineira no século XVIII.* Rio de Janeiro: Edições Graal, 1982.

"Special Issue: Perspectives on Manumission." *Slavery and Abolition: A Journal of Comparative Studies* 10 (December 1989).

Stein, Stanley J. *Vassouras, A Brazilian Coffee County 1850–1890: The Roles of Planter and Slave in a Changing Plantation Society.* Cambridge, Mass.: Harvard University Press, 1957.

"Táboa dos habitantes da capitania de Minas Gerais . . . no anno de 1776." *RAPM* 2 (1897): 511.

Tannenbaum, Frank. *Slave and Citizen: The Negro Citizen in the Americas.* New York: Vintage Books, 1946.

Taunay, Afonso de Escragnole. *História geral das bandeiras paulistas.* 11 vols. São Paulo: H .L. Canton, 1924–50.

Vainfas, Ronaldo. *Trópico dos pecados: Moral, sexualidade e Inquisição no Brasil.* São Paulo: Editora Campus, 1989.

Vasconcellos, Diogo de. *História antiga das Minas Gerais,* 1904. 2 vols. Rpt. 4th ed. Belo Horizonte: Itatiaia, 1974.

———. *História média de Minas Gerais.* 4th ed. Belo Horizonte: Itatiaia, 1974.

Vasconcellos, Diogo Pereira Ribeiro. "Minas e quintos do ouro." *RAPM* 6 (1901): 855–963.

Venâncio, Renato Pinto. "Nos limites da sagrada familia: Ilegitimidade e casamento no Brasil colonial." In Ronaldo Vainfas, ed., *História e sexualidade no Brasil.* Rio de Janeiro: Graal, 1986, 114–18.

Wood, Peter H. *Black Majority: Negroes in Colonial South Carolina from 1670 Through the Stono Rebellion.* New York: W. W. Norton & Co., 1974.

Index

CPSIA information can be obtained at www.ICGtesting.com
Printed in the USA
BVOW01s1801120914

366460BV00001B/43/P

9 780271 032702